DEAD RUN

DEAD
RUN

The Murder of a Lawman
and the Greatest Manhunt of
the Modern American West

DAN SCHULTZ

ST. MARTIN'S PRESS ☍ NEW YORK

St. Martin's Press books may be purchased for educational, business, or promotional use. For information on bulk purchases, please contact Macmillan Corporate and Premium Sales Department at 1-800-221-7945 extension 5442 or write specialmarkets@macmillan.com.

www.stmartins.com

Design by Steven Seighman

Library of Congress Cataloging-in-Publication Data

Schultz, Dan.
    Dead run : the murder of a lawman and the greatest manhunt of the modern American West / Dan Schultz.—1st Edition.
        pages cm
    ISBN 978-0-312-68188-3 (hardcover)
    ISBN 978-1-250-02342-1 (e-book)
    (print) 1. Murder—West (U.S.)—History.   2. Criminal investigation—West (U.S.)—History.   I. Title.
    HV6524.S338 2013
    364.152'3092—dc23

                                                                    2012038622

First Edition: March 2013

10   9   8   7   6   5   4   3   2   1

Within a tale of villains and violence is a story of heroes and hope. Communities come together. The families and friends of the victims struggle to right their lives. Wounded work to become whole. Parents love and mourn their sons, even in the face of infamy.

Above all are the men and women who every day kiss their families good-bye and go to a job with untenable risk, where with every car they pull over, with every disturbance they are called to quiet, with every report they go to investigate, and every fugitive they hunt— things could go terribly wrong; where going to work is an act of bravery.

. . . to the heroes

CONTENTS

ACKNOWLEDGMENTS

Despite the hours I spent sequestered with my laptop, *Dead Run* was far from a solitary effort. I couldn't begin to list all the people who encouraged, informed, and guided me, but as I contemplate the final manuscript, I do wish to acknowledge a few of the people who shared their stories, expertise, and talents.

First, I didn't assemble the story of *Dead Run* from scratch. I have been able to piggyback on the reporting done by news media across the country. Two accounts I found especially helpful were an article by Robert Draper in the October 2000 issue of *GQ* and a story by David Roberts in the October 2008 issue of *National Geographic Adventure*.

I also want to thank the people who took the time to speak with me, even though it was a painful subject they would rather not have revisited. Foremost among those people are Ann and Gary Mason, Jim and Debbie McVean, Corbin Claxton, and Cortez Police Detective (Ret.) Jim Shethar.

Navajo Police Chief Leonard Butler, Sheriffs Mike Lacy and Jerry Martin, Deputy Todd Martin, and SWAT Commanders Greg McCain and Ivan Middlemiss all allowed me to impose on their schedules multiple times as new questions arose in my research. I depended on several independent experts to interpret certain facts; ballistics expert Ron Scott and explosives expert John Nixon deserve special mention for their help. To all of them and everyone else who spoke with me about the events told in *Dead Run*, thank you.

My agent, Elizabeth Evans's first six words to me were, "I want to handle this project." I can never fully express how much that introduction and her vision for the story buoyed my efforts. I am indebted to her and her team at The Jean V. Naggar Literary Agency for all the hard work they do on my behalf.

I knew I was fortunate when an editor with the industry stature of Charles Spicer at St. Martins Press picked up *Dead Run*. But I didn't fully appreciate just how extraordinarily fortunate I was until I began working with him. Not only did his critique vastly improve the book, but the enthusiasm with which he has championed *Dead Run* confirms his reputation—in my book, he is the best. My thanks to Charlie, April Osborn, and everyone at St. Martin's Press.

Finally, I am most grateful for the support of my wife Lynda who makes everything I do better. Her trusted judgment is more pervasive within these pages than she realizes.

AUTHOR'S NOTE

The crime related in *Dead Run* was from the start and remains today a mystery. The people who best could have explained it died sudden, violent deaths. It is unknown if before their deaths, they told anyone else the story of what crime they plotted or why they killed Officer Dale Claxton, to where they escaped or how they lived.

It all happened not very long ago, but in those few intervening years, fact and fiction have been twisted together and reported so often that untrue elements are often recalled with certainty. Even many of the people at the heart of the story are vague in places about what really occurred. Several others had a vested interest in espousing one accounting over another. The contemporary written records, however, were manifest.

In piecing together this story, I relied on extensive police records, news accounts and numerous interviews. In instances when information from one source conflicted with another, I made a judgment based first on credible authority—which source was in the best position to know the facts or had the most reliable records. If that distinction was uncertain, I chose to believe the version most corroborated by others involved as well as which version of events fit best with other known facts.

The Colorado Bureau of Investigation provided the most extensive review of police records associated with the case, a compendium of not just their reports but also communications from and between many of the other law enforcement agencies involved. CBI allowed unrestricted access to all their records related to the case during my initial research, giving me staggering detail of both the investigation and manhunt. As my efforts to determine what happened broadened and more people became aware of my research, the files were closed to me. The CBI records were supplemented by thousands of pages received from the FBI under the Freedom of Information Act, as well as records from local police agencies.

I am grateful to the dozens of people who agreed to interviews and shared their experiences. For many, the story of *Dead Run* was painful and reliving it in the course of an interview was generous beyond my expectations. Thank you.

Some of the people portrayed and the statements attributed to them are based on interviews with the author. In other cases, statements and activities attributed to an individual are based on their statements to police as recorded in transcripts of investigation interviews or the subject's comments as reported in the media. Specifically, that was the case with Sue Claxton, and Jim and Beverly Pilon (Monte's parents). Sue Claxton very pleasantly and politely declined being interviewed, explaining she had been through it enough. She did laugh and add "a lot of hooey" had been written about her husband and the events of 1998. I have tried to avoid repeating the hooey.

Some of what happened in the desert canyons of Four Corners in 1998 will never be known with certainty. While speculation remains just that, I have attempted to fill in those gaps by suggesting events that seem most consistent with the physical evidence and expert opinion, as well as the character and habits of the people involved. In almost all cases that line of logic seemed to lead to a specific explanation rather than multiple possibilities. Readers will know by attribution within the story the source of the information. Contextual cues (such as "Based on the evidence found at the scene, it was likely . . .") will discriminate fact from speculation.

In most cases, people in the story are identified by their real names. In some cases, however, names or other identifying information have been changed.

As far as anyone knows, the following pages are the brutal truth.

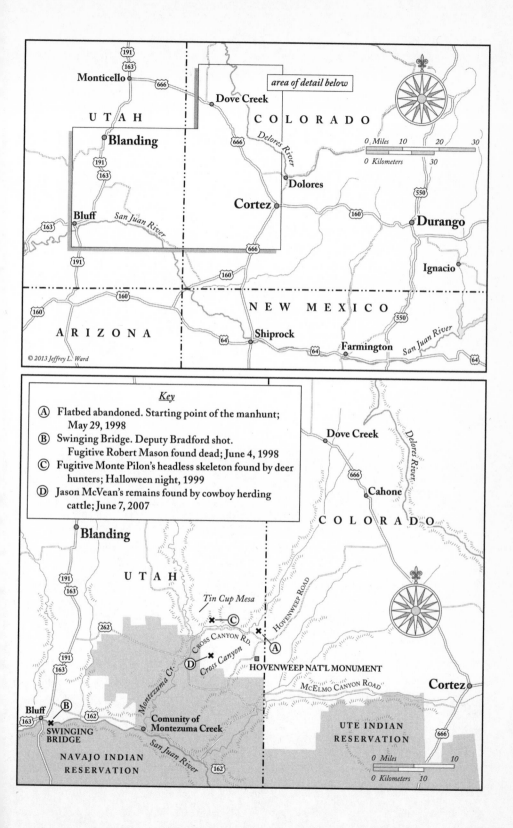

Monticello

U T A H

Blanding

Bluff

San Juan River

C O L O R A D O

Dove Creek

area of detail below

Delores River

Dolores

Cortez

Durango

Ignacio

0 Miles 10 20 30

0 Kilometers 30

A R I Z O N A

N E W   M E X I C O

Shiprock

Farmington

San Juan River

© 2013 Jeffrey L. Ward

Key

Ⓐ Flatbed abandoned. Starting point of the manhunt;
   May 29, 1998

Ⓑ Swinging Bridge. Deputy Bradford shot.
   Fugitive Robert Mason found dead; June 4, 1998

Ⓒ Fugitive Monte Pilon's headless skeleton found by deer
   hunters; Halloween night, 1999

Ⓓ Jason McVean's remains found by cowboy herding
   cattle; June 7, 2007

Dove Creek

Delores River

Cahone

C O L O R A D O

Blanding

U T A H

Tin Cup Mesa

Hovenweep Road

✕ Ⓒ

✕

Cross Canyon Rd.

Ⓓ ✕   Ⓐ

Cross Canyon

Hovenweep Nat'l Monument

Montezuma Cr.

McElmo Canyon Road

Cortez

Bluff

Ⓑ

✕

SWINGING
BRIDGE

Comunity of
Montezuma Creek

San Juan River

UTE INDIAN
RESERVATION

NAVAJO INDIAN
RESERVATION

0 Miles 10

0 Kilometers 10

DEAD RUN

PROLOGUE:
ROUNDUP

June 5, 2007: Canyonlands wilderness area, Southeastern Utah

The gnats rose in great black clouds in front of the herd and hovered over the backs of the cattle marching north along Montezuma Creek into Cross Canyon. They swarmed over Duke's head, the horse flicking his ears incessantly at the annoyance. One gnat, Eric Bayles inhaled halfway down his throat as he swung his leg over Duke's rump onto the ground, causing him to hack and spit before he dropped the reins and started up the hill through the snakeweed and bitterbrush for a closer look at what he'd just glimpsed.

Except for Bayles's periodic rides through the area to check the herd and the sporadic Navajo woodcutters who crossed over from the reservation each fall, Cross Canyon had been largely uninhabited for 30 million years—not counting the summer nine years earlier when hundreds of law officers swarmed through it on the largest manhunt in the history of the West. They never found anything.

Eric Bayles just did.

Sixty-one years old, Bayles wore a long succession of driven-snow winters and desert-sun summers on a round face framed by neatly trimmed silver-gray hair. The crinkles of a nearly perpetual smile converged with the wrinkles left by age and the elements. Dressed in worn boots, jeans, a red bandanna tied around his neck and a dusty ten-gallon hat, he looked like an aging Hopalong Cassidy. "Been a cowpuncher all my life," he explained. And except for the fact that he started his workdays by nudging Duke off a transport rack on the back of a blue 1993 Dodge pickup, there was little that separated Bayles from the cowboys who did the same job 125 years earlier.

It was a familiar job in familiar territory. The Richard Perkins Ranch of Blanding, Utah, where Bayles had worked for eighteen years had a Bureau of Land Management permit to winter cattle on a checkerboard section of deeded and federal land. It was open range and, in the course of tending the herd, Bayles had ridden the same loop hundreds of times, parking at Montezuma Creek, then going east on horseback along the Reservation fence. Past the adobe ruins known as Nancy Patterson Monument he'd angle northward into Cross Canyon until he reached the northeast edge of the cattle's range. There he'd turn west back toward the truck, picking up the creek as he rode deeper into the canyon—a round-trip of about twelve miles by Bayles's estimate.

Over the course of a winter the less sociable of the herd would scatter through the sagebrush and slip from sight among squat piñon pines on the hillsides; or sneak up a wash, around a bend. It was rugged territory; an easy place to hide, a harder place to survive. Each spring, Bayles found them, amalgamating the herd as he rode the loop and drove the cattle to summer range.

By 10:30 A.M. that morning he had been at it four hours; the temperature had risen from forty-five degrees to over ninety. But he was already at Cross Canyon, halfway around the loop, driving nearly a hundred head in front of him. Working to keep the cattle together on the east bank of the stream, the Navajo youth helping him rode on the right-hand flank, forcing back any cattle that tried to cross. Bayles kept the herd compact on the other side, riding a steady gait along a trail that paralleled the creek.

He couldn't say why he hadn't seen the object on any of his previous trips along the same path. "Maybe the last rains had washed it down or coyotes dragged it there."

He might have missed it that day too if not for a momentary change in Duke's gait, a half step over something in the horse's path. Bayles's gaze shifted from the herd trapped between him and the creek to the ground directly below his left stirrup.

A piece of fabric, brown or tan in color, lay across the trail shingled under an overlapping layer of soil. The exposed area was about the size of a bandanna folded in half and its shape implied that whatever it was, there was more of it below the surface than above. "I thought it was kind of a funny-looking saddle blanket," he recalled, "maybe one of those padded ones for an Australian saddle."

Whatever it was, it didn't appear to be anything worth stopping for. But as Bayles watched it recede under his horse's rear hoofs, he felt Duke half turn. Looking up to rein his mount back onto the path, he spotted a second curiosity, a metal bar protruding from the side of the wash behind a clump of tamarisk.

Bayles dismounted. Close up, he recognized the half-inch aluminum tube as part of a backpack frame. But most of the frame and whatever was attached to it was still buried. The soil around it was a mixture of coarse sand and small rocks. Freshly deposited by the recent rain runoff, the gravel was loosely compacted, and using his hands Bayles quickly scooped six inches of soil from around the frame, exposing its second upright bar.

Taking a bar in each hand, he yanked the frame toward him. The bars moved half an inch. Tightening his grip, Bayles jarred the frame back and forth, straining to loosen the soil around it. Sweat beaded his forehead. A few seconds later, the dirt between the bars began to shift and slide slowly down the slope between his feet, first the sand and pebbles, then the larger stones until the nylon top of the pack was free. Bayles moved closer to the frame, planted his feet firmly, and jerked outward with all his might—tearing from its grave the conclusion to a nine-year-old crime.

Setting the pack on the ground, Bayles squatted in front of it and tried opening the three side pockets first, but the buckles were rusted. Pulling a jackknife from his jeans, he slashed the strap on the first pocket. "I reached in and pulled out a whole handful of those little foil packets of ketchup, like you get in a fast-food place." Throwing them to the side, Bayles started on the second pocket. "That one held a pouch of bullets, the kind police carry on their belts." The content of the third pocket was even more ominous—two banana clips of ammunition.

Bayles went to work on the main compartment, slashing the tie-down straps in rapid succession. He lifted the cover and looked. Pipe bombs!

What from on horseback had looked like a saddle blanket turned out upon closer examination to be part of a camouflage bulletproof vest. A few feet away, among water bottles and bone fragments, an AK-47 would be found. Below his feet, in the soil heaved up with the backpack, waited a human skull shattered by a bullet.

Eric Bayles was not the first cowboy to have found the remains of a man shot at the side of the trail. Many have been killed and left in places very much like Cross Canyon—in cottonwood stands where drovers, camped for the night, were surprised by rustlers at dawn; in dry washes where fatigued horses stumbled in the loose soil and posses caught up with their quarry; in nondescript remote places where men crossed paths by chance and argued about an old poker debt.

The remains Bayles found in June 2007, however, were not a century old. They were the remains of a modern crime that in 1998 captivated the nation; a brutal murder with a guns-blazing police chase and wilderness manhunt recounted throughout that summer with headlines in every major newspaper and nightly updates on network news. Its battle lines confounded our allegiance: cops versus outlaws; freedom versus authority; individual versus the system; live-off-the-land survivalists versus a high-tech establishment; man against nature. It was a crime that was never fully resolved or understood. Its questions still haunt.

The gunshots heard on a bridge in Cortez, Colorado, that May morning in 1998 were echoes of our Wild West past, the sound of the gunshots first fired by Billy the Kid, Kid Curry, and Killer

Miller, bouncing through the decades of legend and myth. Ricocheting off attitudes and animosities as constant as the canyon walls, the bullets finally found their mark a century after they were fired.

The crime itself was disquieting. The broader social questions it raises about our relationship to government and institutionalized authority, about the militia culture that simmers below the surface of society, about the gun culture that dominates mainstream society and violence in America are even more unsettling. The answers are hog-tied to our cowboy past and the Western myth that helped forge our national character.

CHAPTER 1
OUTLAW TRAILS

Contrary to one's first mental image, Four Corners does not form a box. Life here is not constrained. Rather, the Four Corners of Colorado, New Mexico, Arizona and Utah form a cross and the lines stretch outward to an infinite western horizon. Viewed from a southwest perspective, it is an "X" on a map marking the location of a hard country, part real, part illusion.

In the blurring of that reality and illusion, glimpsed through the schlieren of superheated air shimmering above red rock canyon floors, is a heritage of guns, desperados and violence. The land and all that flows, grows or roams wild across it belongs to those who share its history, whose great-grandparents died there—whether shot, hung or simply worked into the ground. A distrust of outsiders and the government is instinctual. And lawbreakers both factual and fictional become mythical, from Butch Cassidy to Edward Abbey's George Hayduke.

Sentiments in Four Corners are conflicted. On the one hand, right and wrong are as self-evident as white hats and black hats. Legal nuance is guffawed at as horsepucky and peacekeepers, both the Colt .45 and the men who wielded it or its modern equivalent are consigned special esteem.

On the other hand, there is something romantic in the ideal of the daring, wild young outlaw thumbing his nose at the law, eluding capture at impossible odds and disappearing in the untamed expanses beyond the horizon of authority. Enough to want to overlook the wrongs and rationalize the intent, sympathize, even admire. Enough to believe that Butch Cassidy, despite Hole-in-the-Wall Gang shootouts that left bodies on the ground, never really harmed anyone. Enough to cheer for George Hayduke as a lovable vandal with a noble cause. To spur rumors, in the absence of proof otherwise, that the outlaw got away, rode into the sunset and onto the plain of legend fueled by dime novels and lurid Eastern newspaper stories—or Web sites.

The duality is not surprising. It is, after all, the American Wild West, a synthesis of geography and history; supernal red sunsets and bloodstained boardwalks; the ethereal silence of a desert night and the jarring crack of gunfire; truth, exaggeration and outright fabrication. Unlike those myths borrowed and burrowed into our psyche from foreign cultures, it is one of our own making, and for better or worse, a fundamental determinant of who we are as Americans.

Like the land and legends that created it, the spirit of the American West is too expansive to capture in cohesive thought, yet we know it by its landmarks: individualism, excess, self-reliance, resourcefulness, impatience and, above all, freedom.

More than the institutionalized freedoms assured by our Constitution and body of law, it was the freedom of hidden canyons, impregnable mountains and unassailable desert. You are free not because a court says so, but because you've got a fast horse and a faster gun. It is the freedom of wide-open spaces; of unregulated rivers, unturned earth, unmolested cliffs and unencumbered spirit. It is the freedom of defiance; the right to spare the other cheek and answer any provocation with escalated force.

It is an ethic of contradictions, as a parched desert canyon channels the occasional flash flood. Where self-reliance and independence can flow over to extreme rebuke of all law and authority. Where resolve and courage to stand your ground can become a sudden torrent of violence. It is an ethic suited to making outlaws into outlaw heroes.

Multimillion-dollar ski homes line Butch Cassidy Drive in the town of Telluride, Colorado, on the northeastern edge of Four Corners territory. The gentrified resort community of East Coast second-home owners is uncharacteristic of the real West that rolls endlessly across successive horizons beyond it, where the vehicle of choice is a pickup truck rather than a Prius. Where ranches aren't hobbies but the livelihood of fourth-generation families, and everyday life still has a raw edge to it. But Telluride was not always distinct from the West. It began as a hardscrabble mining town and it is ironic that today there is a street named after Butch Cassidy. His connection to the community is not as a founder or honorable former mayor, a civic-minded resident or leading businessman. On June 24, 1889, he robbed its bank. He stole twenty thousand dollars of the town's money, threatened extreme violence against any citizens who might be tempted to interfere with his theft by firing warning shots in the air and, with two accomplices from nearby Cortez, Colorado, rode as fast as he could into the wild canyons over the Utah border. It was, in fact, his first bank robbery and as the plaque on the building that now sits on the bank site proudly reminds, it was on that spot that the Butch Cassidy legend began. It is even more odd that his legacy is summoned in that particular upscale subdivision. Rich Easterners taking control of the choicest Western land were exactly the people Butch Cassidy claimed to be waging his populist war of crime against. Still, even the economic descendants of his victims find Cassidy's outlaw hero appeal irresistible.

Throughout the decade that police searched for the outlaws whose story is told in the following pages, they scolded the public time and again, "These killers are not heroes." Privately they were deeply frustrated by the public's fascination with the fugitives. But such perverse interest was inevitable; especially considering the Wild West nature of the crime.

The tradition of the outlaw hero is universal but it flowered most profusely in the American West. There, the distinction between an outlaw hero and an outlaw hung was not always apparent, but the trail from repugnant criminal to popular desperado was well ridden. Something about life out-of-bounds fascinated the public and even in the face of atrocious crimes, law-abiding citizens seemed more than willing to view bad guys with nervous admiration. In moments of musing as they bent to the task of ordinary life, it was as Eugene Man-love Rhodes, the "cowboy chronicler" who lived in and wrote about the Old West, suggested, "Outlaws are just more interesting than in-laws."

Part of what made the celebrated outlaws of the American West interesting was their daring crimes and reckless confrontations—in-your-face close and brazenly public. Stripped of one-hundred-plus years of fanciful pop-culture embellishment and decades of Holly-wood gilding, Western gunfights were usually less knightly than legend portrays. Many were ambushes, back shootings or long-range shootouts with adversaries crouched behind cover. But others were eye-to-eye with mortal danger so imminent that a reasonable man would slip away and find someplace safe to puke. To engage in them required courage and public opinion turned on such displays of brav-ery, regardless of what color hat the gunman was wearing.

The one other standard of behavior consistently expected of our outlaw heroes was adherence to an outlaw code of honor. It was an unspoken, ill-defined standard of morality above the law that could overlook unwarranted violence, but required a measure of personal integrity: loyalty to friends and gang members, discrimination be-tween adversaries and bystanders, and straightforward actions. If they were going to steal from you, they robbed you right up front, not by a Ponzi scheme. If they were going to kill you, they rode up and shot you. They were, in most respects, true to their word, transparent in their motivations and intentions.

Although not cheered as revolutionaries or vanguards of a partic-ular political cause, Western outlaw heroes were associated with a populist philosophy. They cultivated the same "true citizen and pa-triot" image claimed by today's militia movement. In writings attrib-uted to Butch Cassidy, he describes himself as "a citizen of the United States against cattle barons." And in another reference, "an outlaw fighting for settlers' rights against large cattle companies." In a West where settlers sought the American Dream but where few found riches, on land they worked but of which the largest, most profitable pieces were owned by British and Eastern cattle conglomerates, railroad magnates and mining companies, it was a popular image. Even if the outlaws didn't redistribute their loot Robin Hood style, they were heroes just for sticking it to the establishment.

There is one more element common to leading Western outlaw heroes—they got away, at least according to legend. Their ability to remain at large for years despite significant efforts to capture them bewitched the public. Better yet, some outlaws were, by legend, never captured at all. They simply eluded the law and disappeared. Jesse James lived on by the wishful thinking of his public, despite the fact that his body was positively identified by the scars of former wounds, put on ice and photographed. Billy the Kid and Butch Cassidy's final escapes are also based on popular rumors, but the historical record leaves room to believe that for each man, the rumor could be true. The truth, however, is not the point. We want them to have escaped. Their wild, unbounded outlaw freedom and wholehearted disregard for authority captures the public imagination and has us in some small manner rooting for the bad guy.

But the main reason the ideal of an outlaw hero resonates so broadly in our society, why we have created a peculiarly American variety within our broader national myth of the American West is that the Western outlaw hero is a twisted extension of core American values.

The desperate outlaw on the run not only had the freedom of the free-roaming cowboy disengaged with society; he pushed back at subjugating social forces—the relentless press of civilization and regulation. For however long he could stay at large, the systematic oppression of government, bureaucracy, corporations, technology—of ordinary do-the-right-thing life—was overthrown. Like standing on the rim of a mesa staring westward across miles of jagged, wild country and feeling not small, but distinct and vital, the outlaw speaks to our elemental ache for individualism. The voice may not have sufficient force to drown out our social conscience or sway our better judgment that an uncaptured outlaw is a menace, but it's a whisper loud enough to intrigue, to rationalize and romanticize, and in the right circumstances transform a villain into a hero.

It is the myth of the West as much as the reality that forges our national identity. One of the great propagators of the myth, Western moviemaker John Ford, put it best in the 1962 classic, *The Man Who Shot Liberty Valance*. "This is the West. When the legend becomes fact, print the legend."

Hardwired by a Western narrative of guns and frontier justice, we revel in the positive attributes of strength, courage and daring action even as they open the door for acts of violence. In cheering for the outlaw hero, we are making a psychological stand for freedom, standing up to authoritarianism and dehumanizing social forces, but we are also sanctioning brutal, inhuman antisocial behavior. Historian Frederick Jackson Turner, whose preeminent Frontier Thesis first asserted that the American character was formed by the Western experience, warned of the danger of "pressing individual liberty beyond its proper bounds." The proper balance is as elusive as Butch Cassidy.

Dynamite Dan Clifton was known as "the most killed outlaw in America." A cattle rustler and train robber in Oklahoma Indian Territory, he lost three fingers in an 1893 gunfight while riding with the Doolin Gang. He was a relatively minor criminal for the times, not destined for the outlaw hall of fame. Nevertheless Clifton accumulated a sizable bounty on his head—thirty-five hundred dollars. It was enough that posses would constantly turn in a shot-up corpse claiming the reward, but the ten-fingered bodies were quickly identified as someone other than Dynamite Dan. In those cases where the bounty hunters had the foresight to cut fingers off the unfortunate soul they had shot to pieces, they invariably chose the wrong three fingers.

Like Dynamite Dan, the Old West is forever vanishing, but never vanished. It is a way of life successively pronounced dead, allowing each generation in its lament to appreciate it more poignantly. The West most Americans hold in their minds, the unfenced foundational West of open-range grazing and long cattle drives, was barely of drinking age when it was reportedly strangled to death by the barbwire.

It died again a few years later when the 1890 census found the nation no longer had a contiguous line of settlement. American civilization stretched from Plymouth Rock to San Francisco Bay and the frontier was closed. But in case those who lived in the West hadn't noticed, the Census Bureau published another obituary after the 1900 census: with an average population of two people per square mile, the West was officially "settled."

Some believed it. Western artist Frederic Remington wrote wistfully, "I knew the wild riders and vacant land were about to vanish forever . . . the end of three centuries of smoke and dust and sweat."

Still, like many of its legendary outlaws and lawmen, the West refused to go down easily. Train and bank robberies, horseback posse chases and six-gun shootouts continued well into the twentieth century. Historians pushed the time of death for the Old West forward to 1920, coinciding with the end of the Mexican Revolution. But as a way of life, despite the eventual sparse web of paved roads, gasoline-powered vehicles and electrification, the West persisted. In every decade, social observers continued to note its dying flickers. Writers Zane Grey and Will James found it still taking shallow breaths in the 1920s and 1930s. Cormac McCarthy found a vanishing West set in the 1930s and 1940s. And Larry McMurtry, through his character Duane Moore, traces the slow death (or lingering life) of the West through the entire second half of the twentieth century, into the twenty-first.

The West lives. Despite the Walmarts and tourist information centers, the satellite dishes and Social Security, there remains a vital intrinsic West that is as it always was. Many of the attitudes, loyalties and animosities rooted in the Old West have only been fanned by the ensuing decades. In vast parts of the territory that was the historical West, there are no more residents today than there were in 1900; in many counties there are fewer. Across its vast horizon, between the larger communities that dot it, even the pockmarks of mining, timber-cutting, energy and water projects are diminished by scale. In many locations, the land features are immutable. Within the millions of acres of wilderness areas and yet unfenced country there are timeless places. You can still stand on a mountaintop and gaze across broad vistas to distant ridges. Or stare up at the same immense milky night sky that trail riders did a century ago. Or bear witness to a sunset indistinguishable from those that inspired Frederic Remington and Charles Russell.

Beyond the real West is the mythical West; the West of movies, books, song and video games; the West of enduring legend. It is the West that leads thousands of people every year to pull off the road and stand at the graves of Billy the Kid, Wyatt Earp or Wild Bill Hickok. The West that draws millions of East Coasters and Midwesterners to vacations in the Mountain States, where they stay in accommodations with cowhide-upholstered sofas and elk-antler chandeliers. The West where the receding vibrations of a wild, audacious America still tickle the hair on the back of your neck.

It is real and it is mythical. And one sunny morning in May 1998, near the epicenter of Old West outlaw violence, it happened all over again: the guns; the killing; the posse chase and shootout; the escape into a vast wild country of sagebrush, box canyons and the occasional cowboy on horseback; Native American trackers; a grueling manhunt; and a populist outlaw disappearing into legend.

Such is Four Corners. As it was in 1898. As it remained a hundred years later.

CHAPTER 2
McELMO BRIDGE

By mid-May of 1998, the Animas River, swollen by snowmelt from the San Juan Mountains at the northeastern edge of the Four Corners region, was flowing near its annual peak. It cascaded alongside US Highway 550 and the 1880-era narrow-gauge railroad where tourists were treated to a reenactment of an "Old West" train robbery. Entering Durango from the north, the last free-flowing river in the Western United States rushes under the North Main Avenue bridge, sweeps around the west edge of the historic district, pours past the city's southern boundary, and crashes untamed and unrestrained, indifferent and unrepentant along outlaw trails once used by Butch Cassidy, Ezra Lay and Kid Curry.

Officially, its name is El Rio de las Animas Perdidas—The River of Lost Souls. It was the name first whispered around the campfires of early Spanish explorers who sent successive scouting parties down the river to oblivion. No contact. No bodies. No ascension to heaven.

Alan "Monte" Pilon, Robert Mason and Jason McVean had lived and conspired on a steep bluff overlooking the river. In the early morning hours of May 28, they crossed it as they sped along Camino del Rio toward Ignacio, Colorado, to steal a water truck—on their way to becoming lost souls.

Forty-five miles west of Durango, May 29, 1998, began with mixed emotions for Carrie Evans. The exuberance of graduating from Cortez High School the previous evening along with 201 other students still flickered. But at the moment, a little after 9:00 A.M., she sat distracted in the rear seat of a black Camaro convertible turning south onto Montezuma County Road 27 toward McElmo Bridge, on the way to have her wisdom teeth pulled.

Not far away, on the opposite side of McElmo Creek, sixteen-year-old Matt Weston's day was already well under way. He'd already driven to school where he was officially dismissed for the summer and now was leaving again to pick up a computer desk at Kmart. Driving a silver Ford Explorer, he too would turn onto CR 27, converging on the bridge from the opposite direction as Carrie.

Elsewhere in Cortez, others also gravitated toward McElmo Bridge. Michelle Dorn would reach it a few seconds ahead of Matt; Evelyn Pearson a few seconds after him. A garbage truck heading for the county landfill rumbled toward it. A mechanic working in the school district's bus barn two hundred yards south of the structure paused, screwdriver in hand, and tipped his ear toward it. A deejay in the radio station up the road glanced out the window toward it. And at houses within earshot of McElmo Bridge, residents tending their gardens or half listening to the police scanner as they cleaned up breakfast dishes looked up at the distinct sound coming from it.

Cortez city policeman Dale Claxton's trajectory that morning also led him to McElmo Bridge. At the eastern edge of the city where Main Street begins to reclaim its identity as Colorado State Highway 160, the ramp onto North Dolores plunges the motorist off the plateau of community and into the sagebrush fringes of civilization. In less than two hundred yards, the road gives up fifty feet in elevation, crosses over the city limits and merges onto County Road 27, a half mile north of McElmo Bridge. The city doesn't peter out; it ends. A short distance behind but erased from sight by the plateau ridge, tree-lined boulevards front tidy yards and well-kept homes. Far ahead the pine-covered hills guarding Mesa Verde National Park frame the horizon. Between lay miles of low scrub and barren gravel wasteland.

A dilapidated trailer house ringed with rusted appliances and vehicle parts sat a hundred yards to the left of CR 27. Another dwelling occupied a dirt yard on the right side of the road, just beyond the bridge. Between them flows McElmo creek. Even in the parched Southwest, where men fight over water, it is a no-account stream; under the bridge a muddy meandering trench crossable with a single wide step.

The bridge itself is even less remarkable; a bridge only by the technicality that it spans the creek and a few feet of gully. From the perspective of an approaching driver, there is no visible structure of steel girders, creosote beams or concrete buttresses. The roadbed neither narrows, nor rises. Low guardrails and the falling away of the land to each side of the road are the only clues that ahead there is a bridge at all.

Filling in on his day off for a colleague who was attending a training seminar that morning, Claxton went on duty at 6:30 A.M. He typically arrived at the station about ten minutes ahead of his shift, and as far as his coworkers recall, that day was no different. Pouring himself a cup of coffee, Claxton likely sat down at one of the empty desks shared by patrol officers, took a sip from his mug, opened his notebook and bent to complete his reports. The station was, by and large, vacant at that time of day, with only a handful of other department employees present who may have remembered Claxton's exact motions and comments that morning. And their memories of the mundane were overprinted by the events about to take place. After completing his paperwork, Claxton dropped it into the file basket near the dispatch desk. Then, as a last step before going out on patrol, checked the briefing board hanging on a nail in the wall above the shelf.

The briefing board was a clipboard logging all the police calls and activities for the past twenty-four hours. "All in all, there was nothing out of the ordinary, mainly things like a fender-bender or a complaint about a neighbor's dog running loose," according to Roy Lane, Cortez chief of police.

In 1998, Cortez, Colorado, was a relatively safe town; less than ten violent crimes of any kind per year according to federal statistics. So the eleven-line printout from neighboring LaPlata County didn't raise much alarm.

```
*********ATL  STOLEN  WATER  TANKER  TRUCK*********
MKE/STOLEN VEHICLE
ORI/COO34OOOO  LIC/ IRF2783  LIS/NM  LIY/99  LIT/AP
VIN/ 1M2P267COWMO35159  VYR/98 VMA/MACK
VMO/TK  VCO/WHI/WHI
DOT/052898  OCA/ 9820959
MIS/80  BARREL  TANK  OVERRIGHT  TRUCKING  ON  DOORS
NIC/V418783994
ORI IS LA PLATA CO SO DURANGO CO
IMMED CONFIRM RECORD WITH ORI

AUTH LA PLATA COUNTY SO    06:09:14 MT DJS
Message sent  5/29/98  6:09 (A.M.)
```

If the stolen water truck passed through Cortez, it would be hard to miss—a white Mack truck with a four-thousand-gallon tank, New Mexico license plates and the name OVERRIGHT TRUCKING on the doors.

It might have been kids joyriding. At worst, it was another low-level incident of ecoterrorism. Sabotaging work sites and stealing construction equipment had become common practice among radical environmentalists in Four Corners ever since Edward Abbey's 1975 novel, *The Monkey Wrench Gang* became the Magna Carta of the movement's extremists.

The book's main characters—ex–Green Beret Vietnam vet George Hayduke, Jack Mormon river-rafting guide Seldom Seen Smith, billboard-burning surgeon Dr. Sarvis and his girlfriend, Bonnie Abzug—escalated their crimes against the "spoilers" of the Southwest from pulling out survey stakes and filling bulldozer fuel tanks with Karo syrup to dynamiting coal plants and transmission lines, ultimately engaging in a full-blown shoot-out with authorities. Even though the story was set in the Four Corners area, the most virulent, destructive Monkey Wrench disciples had struck elsewhere in the West. Stealing a water tanker truck from a work site would be more in line with the local MO.

Sometime between 7 and 7:30 A.M., Claxton left the station and buckled into a white '96 Chevrolet Impala with CITY OF CORTEZ PO-LICE DEPARTMENT emblems on the front doors, waited for the parking lot electric gate to lift and pulled onto Empire Street. His patrol that morning took him to his home on the north edge of the city where he picked up his son Corbin. Dropping Corbin at school for his last day of sixth grade, Claxton then zigzagged across town to Cortez Middle School where his wife Sue taught seventh grade. Poking his head around the door of her classroom, he made a last-day-of-school lunch date with his wife, gave her a kiss as they stood in the hallway outside her room and left to resume his patrol. Other than two cell phone calls, one from a citizen with information about a property damage complaint that Dale had responded to a few days earlier and one from a fellow officer wondering what Dale knew about a car that had been towed the previous evening, nothing more was heard from him until 9:24 A.M. when he radioed Cortez police dispatcher Connie Johnson: "Behind Mack truck reported stolen; south on County Road 27, approximately one-half mile from McElmo Bridge."

Robert Carpenter watched a white tanker truck roll slowly down Highway 160 past his auto repair shop. A police car followed a few feet behind. "The truck was going ten or fifteen miles per hour, like it was having engine trouble or running out of gas and the patrol car was escorting it," he told police. In his witness statement, Carpenter described watching the two vehicles for about half a mile until they turned south at County Road 27 and headed down the hill toward McElmo Bridge. It would have been about then that Claxton made his first radio call reporting that he had spotted the stolen vehicle.

It was also at that time that Michelle Dorn crossed the bridge driving north into town to meet her mother. Normally she wouldn't remember a white truck coming toward her. But as she watched, the corner of a police car showed itself from behind the truck, the red and blue lights on its front bumper flashing. Her foot tapped the brakes. "I slowed because I thought he was pulling the truck over for a ticket and I didn't want to get one."

As Michelle continued up the hill on the north side of McElmo Bridge she glanced in her rearview mirror. The tanker and police car crossed the bridge and rolled to a stop. Matt Weston's silver SUV, was approaching the bridge behind her.

From a hundred feet away Matt Weston could see three men in the tanker's cab, in itself nothing out of the ordinary. But as the distance closed between his Explorer and the tanker stopped on the side of the road, he suddenly felt uneasy. Each occupant was wearing camouflage and holding what appeared to be rifles, barrels pointed toward the cab ceiling. Tightening his grip on the wheel, Matt kept his eyes focused on the tanker cab, searching for any flicker of movement. He couldn't explain what was wrong, but a Klaxon alarm powered by instinct vibrated a warning through his whole body: "Something bad was about to happen."

Matt was nearly even with the tanker when the man in its passenger seat suddenly swung open the door, jumped from the cab and ran toward the rear. A moment later, automatic gunfire crackled from behind the truck.

Matt gasped. It was happening at that very moment behind the tanker and he dared not drive past it. Twisting the steering wheel violently to the right, Matt plowed the pickup into the ditch and drove the brake pedal to the floor. As his body snapped forward from the sudden stop, he looked out his side window. Directly across the road, the men in the tanker cab stared down at him from twenty feet away.

"They watched me the whole time," Weston told police. In a motion that in retrospect was absurdly futile, he slowly slunk lower. With his butt overhanging the seat's front edge, his legs contorted between the pedals and the underside of the dash, and his torso in an awkward backward lean between the steering wheel and seat back, he peered over the edge of the door and witnessed murder from the knees down.

Looking under the tanker, Matt could see only the lower legs and boots of the man who had jumped from its cab as he moved about at the rear of the truck. Another vehicle was stopped just a few feet behind the tanker and although he could see little more than the front bumper, Matt knew it was a police car. Even in midmorning sunlight, the reflected glow of the red and blue flashing lights strobed the space immediately in front of it, subtly illuminating the camouflage pant legs of the man standing between the vehicles.

A second burst of shots sounded. The legs moved quickly to the left and disappeared from Matt's view. A third burst of shots. Matt later guessed he'd heard about thirty shots in all, but at the moment he wasn't counting. The legs reappeared. The man was running, moving swiftly back along the far side of the tanker, his boots kicking up little puffs of dust with each step. Matt shifted higher in the seat to maintain his view under the truck as the legs came closer. The legs stopped directly across from him, then disappeared as the man climbed into the cab.

Weston knew he was going to die. "I was really scared," he recalled. "They killed that cop and now they were going to kill me because I saw them do it." From near point-blank range, he stared up at them, focused on the tip of the rifle barrel held by the tanker's driver, waiting for it to tilt downward at his head.

In the deadly silence it was the sudden scuffing sound of gravel moving that startled him from vacant resignation. Matt's eyes darted to the tanker's wheels. Rock and dust arced behind them. The tires bit and the tanker shot forward, accelerating past him.

Matt didn't move for several seconds, not until he fully comprehended the menace was quickly moving away from him. Pulling onto the road, he slowly drove past the police car. "I didn't see anyone inside but the car was full of bullet holes," Weston reported. In his rearview mirror, he watched the water truck speed up the hill as he sped to the Circle S station and called 911.

Evelyn Pearson, a sixty-eight-year-old grandmother, knew the driver of the silver SUV ahead of her was her neighbor Matt Weston. Matt had been backing out of his driveway as she got in her car and she'd been a short distance behind him since turning onto County Road 27. Knowing Matt was just sixteen, she didn't think there was too much he could do behind the wheel that would surprise her. But he did.

"I couldn't figure out what Matt was doing, slowing way down like that, then driving into the ditch," Evelyn said. But as she approached the vehicles, she too slowed and then stopped, right in the middle of the traffic lane, a few feet before the tanker. She locked eyes with the man climbing back into the cab of the truck. "He knew I got a good look at him. We made eye contact and held it," Pearson told police as she described the suspect.

As the tanker pulled onto the road and passed alongside her, Evelyn saw the police car that had been behind it. What she did next would leave her traumatized.

Memory of the morning's events would fragment and slip deep into her subconscious mind, to resurface as small pieces of terror in nightmares and flashbacks triggered by seeing a tanker truck on the highway or a police car on the side of the road. It would be several weeks of such episodes before she could assemble a cohesive recollection of that morning, up to the last thing she did that day on McElmo Bridge—"I pulled alongside the police car; got out; walked up and looked in."

CHAPTER 3
DALE

Four days after Officer Dale Claxton drove onto McElmo Bridge, nine-year-old Alex Valdez scooted apprehensively below the police sniper's nest on the school roof before being ushered along the football field sideline, past rows of tan metal folding chairs to a seat up front near the coffin. Hundreds of police officers from across Colorado stood rank and file on grass. Filling in the bleacher seats around him were over a thousand people from the community Dale Claxton had patrolled and called home. Alex had talked to his uncle about this day five months earlier, he told a reporter after the funeral.

Afflicted with an incurable blood disorder, Alex thought about death with a sense of inevitability unnatural for a child. During a last family visit to Marshfield, Missouri, Uncle Dale took him aside, found a quiet corner and talked. They talked about death, their deaths, for over an hour. About how they were alike—both facing death. Alex because of his disease; Dale because of his job. "I have a job where I know something could happen to me at any time," Dale told his nephew. Alex told his uncle he wanted the song "Lament" from *Riverdance* played at his funeral. Dale said he would like "Amazing Grace" played on bagpipes.

After an hour of eulogies by Cortez Police Chief Roy Lane, Colorado Governor Roy Romer and others, Dale's wish was honored.

Although aware of his profession's inherent dangers, Dale was anything but fatalistic or morbid, according to family and friends. If anything, he was just the opposite, a larger-than-life personality.

For Dale as with most police officers, acknowledging that something could happen and believing it really might happen were two different things. The likelihood of a police officer dying in the line of duty in a small, friendly community like Cortez was statistically remote. The Cortez Police Department had never lost a member to gunfire, and the last peace officers to meet such a fate in that corner of Colorado were killed in the 1930s. Before that it was La Plata County Sheriff William (Big Bill) Thompson who despite his reputation as a "fast gun" lost a saloon argument-turned-gunfight on the streets of Durango in 1906.

"We knew it was possible, but none of us truly believed it would happen, not randomly without warning like happened to Dale," fellow officer Todd Martin said. Add to that the fact that Dale was not a reckless cop. Forty-five years old, he had been on the force just three years. Nevertheless, in the estimation of his colleagues and other law enforcement professionals, Dale was "a smart cop." While midlife was an inauspicious time for a sudden and radical career change, especially when the new profession was highly physical, Dale seemed to have a knack for the job.

"It was like putting a fish in water," Chief Lane said. "Police work came natural for Dale. He was serious about his work, streetwise and made good decisions in whatever situation he found himself in." In situations that seemed by training or instinct to pose elevated risk, he took the proper extra precautions. Even on warm days, he wore a bulletproof vest while on patrol.

Dale's six-foot-three, 225-pound stature and no-nonsense professional demeanor belied a shy nature, according to his widow and high-school sweetheart Sue Claxton. Even as a star tackle on the suburban Denver Wheat Ridge High School football team, he didn't display the swagger his size and athleticism would have allowed him. But drawn to fun and fast cars, he wasn't the quiet, studious type either. Their high school romance was more than youthful passion, Sue insisted, but she was determined to have an independent career as a teacher. Easygoing and ambivalent about the future, Dale wasn't ready for more school. After graduation he drifted and his life unfolded, unplanned and undirected.

As Sue headed off to college and out of his life, Dale, whose most obvious assets were his size and strength, found work as a laborer on construction crews. He also discovered an innate talent for building. By the time he was twenty, he'd begun a nomadic life as a carpenter, following the work from one new subdivision to another across Colorado, Kansas and north Texas. Along the way he got married, and with the birth of Colton and Judy, Claxton settled briefly near kin in the rural hamlet of Marshfield, Missouri.

The bruises from that failed first marriage and acrimonious divorce were still tender when Dale, by then twenty-eight, crossed Sue's path once again. They agreed to get together over coffee just to catch up on each other's lives. "Considering our past relationship and breakup after high school, I hoped that the meeting would at least be civil," Sue said. By the time they'd poured second cups, it was clear the spark was still there. Four months later they were married.

Together they traveled back and forth across the Southwest; Dale hoisting walls and setting rafters, Sue giving birth to Caitlin and Corbin. As Caitlin reached school age, however, Sue insisted it was time to settle down. Cortez seemed like the right place to raise their family and call home—*Our Town* community values, good schools and lots of opportunity for wholesome outdoor family activities. Plus, after Dale had graduated from high school and left home, his parents had relocated there. His father, Dairl, managed the Redburn Tire Co. store in Cortez and Dale had a job waiting for him. Selling tires wasn't a career he'd ever pictured for himself, but then again, Dale was never intent on any specific career. It was steady work and paid well enough that he could provide for his family.

It was—life. Work. A mortgage. Remodeling the kitchen and fixing the broken toilet. Teacher conferences and school plays. Little League and church. Weekends camping with the family and evening horse rides with Sue. Holidays and birthdays, one year blending seamlessly with the next. It was unremarkably ordinary. It was remarkably good.

Then, dressed in sweatpants and an old T-shirt, his face pressed against a gymnasium floor mat as he and a buddy practiced escaping from each other's headlocks, Dale Claxton had a shot-out-of-the-blue revelation, a calling as powerful and urgent as a religious conversion.

Earlier that year Dale had joined the Montezuma County Sheriff's Posse. Officially a citizen's group charged with assisting the sheriff's department when they needed extra manpower, informally it was kind of a fraternity, a civic rationale for male camaraderie. In fact, the original posse was a "ropin' club," said Bruce Tolzer, a former old guard member and leader of the group. Today, posse members might help with crowd and traffic control during parades, provide rear guard support for enforcement actions or provide backup administrative and tactical assistance. "Back when the sheriff's department was small, the posse were the men that folks turned to when they needed help," Tolzer explained. "The posse was cowboys and territory tough guys who could jump on a horse and ride up onto the mesa in a snowstorm to rescue stranded travelers, drive trapped livestock out of a flooding canyon, hunt and kill a marauding mountain lion or track a fugitive across the desert."

As the sheriff's department got larger with more specialized functions, the posse's role changed. Training in law enforcement methods and procedures became requisite. Dale joined in that transitional period and it was during a Saturday morning posse training exercise in basic hand-to-hand combat that Dale realized what he was meant to do with his life.

"He came home for lunch all excited and said 'I gotta do this,'" Sue Claxton remembered. Normally an easygoing, low-key personality, his sudden enthusiasm and sense of purpose were striking. "It was the first time in twenty-five years I'd ever heard him utter those words," she said.

At the age of forty, he quit his job as a tire salesman and enrolled at the police academy. Upon graduating he was nervous competing for one of just two openings on the Cortez Police Department against men twenty years younger, but he did exceptionally well on the tests. In the weeks between being awarded the job and his first day of work, Sue would tell friends, "He was like a kid waiting for Christmas."

Like his father was, Corbin Claxton is a big man, gridiron line-man big. He has a young man's face, but a boyish expression that suggests he will still be carded every time he orders a beer well into his thirties. His features are less chiseled than were Dale's, more se-rene. His countenance and physical stature are comforting, reassur-ing rather than intimidating. His voice is soft, but forcefully steady.

Almost twelve years old when his dad was killed, Corbin Claxton saw his father for the last time on the morning of his last day of sixth grade when Dale drove him to school. As Corbin jumped out of the patrol car, his dad was smiling; not a big grin, just a contented, amused kind of smile. Dale Claxton smiled a lot like that, Corbin said.

The Claxton family lived on the edge of the city in a hundred-year-old house that Dale was always remodeling. They had a few acres of property and a couple of horses. They went to church on Sundays unless they were camping. "If the choice was going to church or going fishing, we'd go fishing." Corbin grinned.

While fishing and camping with his family may have trumped go-ing to church on Sundays, Dale was a live-what-you-preach Christian in his daily life. More than a decade after his death, the community of Cortez remembers him warmly. "Dale was a real good guy; a straight shooter who always tried to do right by people," recalled Eddie Fosnot, who worked for Claxton at the Redburn Tire store. For Dale, that was demonstrated by the day-to-day little things—showing up with his tools to help a friend with a building project or volunteering for community service. "He was always a friendly, decent man, in or out of uniform," said Bruce Tolzer, who from time to time shod Claxton's horses and had known Dale for years.

For Sue, Caitlin and Corbin, Dale was a joyful man who loved his family and made life fun for the people around him. He loved

Irish music. He liked to cook Cajun food and would add so much extra spice to his portion he'd get hiccups eating it, sending his family into fits of dinner-table giggles. And when they would least expect it, he'd jump out from around a corner and startle them *Pink Panther* Cato style.

A wife and family he loved, a community he belonged to and finally the career he was born for; what Dale may have been thinking as the tanker slowed to a stop in front of him will never be known but you can be sure that in the back of his mind he drove onto that bridge a happy man, his sister Carolyn Valdez still contends. "Dale loved being a policeman and he said as much to his family and friends many times. He had found the perfect job for him. He felt his days had real purpose."

Whatever game the men in the stolen white tanker truck were playing with their slow rumble across the southeast corner of Cortez while he trailed them, Patrolman Claxton had had enough. As the tanker crawled toward McElmo Bridge, moving farther beyond the Cortez city limits and his patrol area, Claxton flipped on the flashing red and blue wigwag lights on his patrol car's front bumper. To his relief, rather than bolting, the stolen truck slowed further and edged onto the road shoulder.

Trailing thirteen feet from the back bumper of the truck, Dale's squad car was in the truck's blind spot when it pulled over. Crime scene investigators suggested that because of the hill beyond the bridge, Dale likely decided that pulling around the truck to stop in front of it would have created a traffic hazard. Instead he swerved slightly to the left as he stopped. There was no siren, no flashing-light bar on the roof of the squad car, no loudspeaker command to "pull over." This was a low-key contact. And the truck, apparently responding to the flashing wigwag lights, edged farther off the pavement onto the shoulder and stopped; properly, cooperatively, deceptively. Sixty-six feet beyond the bridge, Dale stopped too, maintaining the gap between his car and the truck.

His position relative to the vehicle he'd pulled over was textbook proper. Tucked in tight to the truck and left of center Dale had an uninterrupted view of the suspect's driver's side door, but the position left him blind to the tanker's right side. He could not see a man jump out of the passenger side of the truck the second it stopped. He could not see the man's boots and camo-clad legs running along the gravel shoulder toward him.

Based on his last radio call, Claxton didn't suspect he was in lethal danger. His voice betrayed no alarm, tension or heightened concern. It was anticlimatic, routine: "He's pulling over. I'm going to contact him."

As Claxton put the car in park, his mind likely jumped ahead to the pending encounter. He took a final, careful look down the left side of the tanker, making sure the driver remained behind the wheel waiting for his approach, then diverted his gaze downward as he began the rote sequence of hanging up the radio mic, retrieving his hat from where it rested on the passenger seat and unbuckling his seat belt. Movement at the edge of his vision may have drawn his attention back to the windshield. The man stepped from around the truck and stood a few feet in front of the patrol car's right front fender. Bright light flashed from the AK-47 he held in his hands.

Sold legally as a semiautomatic weapon that requires the trigger be pulled for each shot, the rifle is easily converted with instructions available over the Internet to the illegal full-automatic operation for which it was designed. Just pull and hold the trigger back and the gun keeps firing until the trigger is released. In effect, a machine gun. An AK-47 converted to full automatic status, as was the weapon that killed Officer Claxton, carries a thirty-cartridge magazine and fires ten rounds a second, according to Ken Banks, a gun expert and owner of Shooter's World in Cortez where Claxton's killers purchased several of their weapons and munitions.

Witnesses report three distinct bursts of approximately eight to twelve rapid shots—a firing pattern trained combat soldiers use to correct aim forced off target by the weapon's successive recoil motion. Based on bullet holes, the location of ejected shell casings and blood splatter patterns, forensic investigators with the Colorado Bureau of Investigation (CBI) suggested that the first round hit the right front headlight. Leaving the weapon's muzzle at twice the speed of sound—one bullet every tenth of a second—the shots ripped up across the hood at an angle, spiderwebbed the windshield directly in front of the patrol car's steering wheel.

Found slain in the driver's seat of his patrol car, his service revolver snapped in its holster and the radio mic lying next to his hat on the passenger seat where it had fallen from his outstretched right hand, Dale had been caught by surprise.

It happened too fast to react defensively. The flash from the gun's muzzle froze in place. The windshield blurred with sunbursts of crack lines and a half dozen bullets slammed into Claxton's chest. His head jerked forward as the shots violently pounded his torso against the seat back, penetrated his armor and plowed into his body. Reflex ceased midsynapse. In an eternity too short for cohesive thought but long enough to know it instinctively, Dale Claxton understood he was about to die.

With his weight already oriented to his right as he reached to re-place the radio mic in its cradle, Dale slumped across the center-console organizer. At the same time, the shooter released a second salvo. Swinging the gun back toward the passenger-side of the patrol car, he drew a horizontal line of bullet holes across the windshield, this time hitting Dale in the shoulder.

In less than four seconds from the moment the shooter stepped out from around the tanker, Patrolman Dale Claxton had been hit multiple times and lay across the center console of his police car. His head, turned facedown, was suspended a few inches above the passenger seat. "At that moment, there was a possibility Officer Claxton, who was wearing body armor, was still alive," according to CBI agent Kevin Humphreys, the first forensic expert at the scene of the shooting.

If Dale was still breathing, it was only long enough for the assassin to sprint from the position he held for his first two fusillades to the patrol car's front passenger door. "This wasn't somebody shooting a cop because he was cornered, scared and desperate or to facilitate an escape," Humphrey said. "This was an execution."

Holding the AK-47 inches from the passenger door window, the assailant unleashed a final barrage at a sharp downward angle into the car. Witnesses within earshot of the assault said it sounded like a string of firecrackers, one pop blending into the next too fast to count, but everyone agreed it was eight to ten shots in duration.

Most hit their target.

CHAPTER 4
CHASE

While the expanse of scrubland surrounding McElmo Bridge gave the location an aura of isolation, it was far from the ideal spot to commit murder undetected and slip away unchallenged. Beyond the couple of low-slung dwellings visible from the bridge, out of sight but within hearing distance of a gunshot were several more homes. Tucked in the hills a mile or so southeast of the bridge the rooftops of a small neighborhood were discernable. County Road 27 not only connected that cluster of residents and outlying ranchers with Cortez but was also the route for travelers turning off U.S. Highway 666, the main north-south highway through the region. In 1998, traffic over the bridge averaged thirty to forty vehicles per hour on any given weekday morning.

At the time Dale Claxton was shot, there were, according to estimates of standard patrol schedules in 1998, at least four other Cortez Police cruisers, five Montezuma County Sheriff vehicles, and a Colorado State Patrol car cruising within five miles (three to eight minutes) of the bridge. A short mile and a half away at the Cortez police station on North Park Street and in County Sheriff headquarters on Driscoll Street, eight to ten more officers were on duty, poised to respond to an emergency within seconds.

And on that particular day, at the National Guard Armory a little over a mile north on the same road as McElmo Bridge, "Desert Snow," an in-service training class on drug intervention, had gathered forty more officers from police agencies throughout the region.

In the course of investigating the crime, police interviewed more than a dozen people who were close enough to hear the shots: residents of area homes, workers in the school district bus barn a short distance up the road from the bridge and nearby motorists.

Matt Weston drove up to the bridge in time to witness the shooting and raced to report it as soon as the assailants peeled away. Seconds behind Weston, Evelyn Pearson came upon the crime scene and, in the hysteria of the moment unable to dial 911 on her cell phone, also sped away to report the crime. Within minutes of the shooting, several other motorists came upon the shot-up police car and attempted in one way or another to alert authorities.

Paula Evans, dialing 911 on a cell phone as she stood looking at the carnage, was the first to report the shooting—just two minutes after Claxton transmitted his last radio message. Within minutes of that call, Cortez Police Dispatcher Connie Johnson recalls receiving at least half a dozen other citizen reports.

Johnson's call, "Officer down on 27. Officer shot by bridge," went out on a universal channel shared by all police agencies in the area. Virtually every law enforcement office and officer in Montezuma County heard it. The dispatcher at the Montezuma County Sheriff's Office heard it and alerted the deputies working in the building. Deputy Jason Bishop, just about to leave for work, heard it on his portable radio and sped from his driveway. Sixty-five-year-old District Attorney Investigator James Davenport heard it on a police scanner as he worked at his desk and jumped up to join the chase. Deputy Lendol Lawrence, patrolling westbound on County Road G, heard it, executed a fast three-point turn and accelerated back toward the bridge. A "Desert Snow" instructor relayed the call to Deputy Terry Steele. He and several other police officers in the class scrambled for their cars to assist in the pursuit. Cortez police officers Jim Bob Wynes and Sue

Betts, along with Assistant Chief Russell Johnson, heard it from across the room as Dispatcher Johnson struggled to control her emotions and speak the call clearly into the microphone.

By 9:29, less than five minutes after Claxton's last radio message, at least eighteen patrol cars from six different agencies, along with EMT rescue units from the Cortez Fire Department, were converging on McElmo Bridge.

The first to reach Claxton was the Cortez Police Department's D.A.R.E. car. Coming off of early patrol, Officer Vern Rucker had no more than walked through the station door when he heard the fragment of static that precedes the tone-flattened voice of the dispatch radio. "Ssss—Behind Mack truck reported stolen—sss." Turning on his heels, Rucker ran back to his patrol car, distinguishable by the decals that identified him to Cortez school kids as the city's Drug Abuse Resistance Education officer.

His dash through the office caught the attention of Assistant Chief Johnson. "What's going on?" he shouted at Rucker's back.

"Dale's behind a stolen truck," came the reply.

Rucker was barely out of the parking lot when he heard Dale's last call and less than a minute from Claxton's location when he heard Dispatcher Johnson's page for an ambulance conclude with the words, "Officer down by bridge."

People had already gathered on the shoulder opposite Claxton's car when Rucker drove up. Their demeanor sent a shudder of dread through him. They stood silently, respectfully, staring across the road at the bullet-riddled vehicle, subdued by the gravity of what they'd seen. Rucker knew there was no one to save.

Still, he couldn't help asking the women closest to the vehicle as he rushed toward it, "Is Dale okay?" He was alongside of the car, seeing for himself before they could answer.

Rucker's stomach lurched. Blood splattered the windshield, dotted the ceiling, ran in thick streaks down the instrument panel and puddled in the passenger seat. Chunks of flesh and brain littered the dashboard. Smashing through the passenger-side window at point-blank range, multiple shots had exploded the back of his friend's skull into a bloody, grayish mash on entry, cleaving his face as they exited on their path through the seat cushion before embedding in the car's undercarriage.

Tearing the latex gloves from his hands, he threw them violently to the ground. Then, tipping his head toward the radio mic clipped to his shirt, Rucker quietly reported, "It's a Frank."

"Frank" was a code word used by police departments throughout the region to soften radio reports citizens might overhear on police scanners and to dissuade morbid spectators from showing up at accident scenes. It meant "fatality."

As Rucker returned to his own patrol car for a roll of yellow crime scene tape, other responders showed up en mass; firefighters, followed by an ambulance and EMTs, followed by a steady stream of police. The first of those who stepped from their vehicles and looked south noted a large white tanker truck in the distance, still visible as it turned from CR 27 onto County Road H.

Upon learning that Dale was behind a stolen truck, Assistant Chief Russell Johnson had gone to the dispatch desk to monitor radio reports and help handle phone calls. When he overheard the dispatcher say, "Officer down," he abruptly hung up on a citizen seeking information and headed to the bridge.

By the time Johnson arrived, hardly more than a minute after Rucker, the initial steps for securing the scene were already under way. The suspects were no longer in sight but, according to reports, they were only a short distance ahead. A firefighter had parked crossways on the road to block traffic. Ordering the man to let him pass, Johnson wove his green Ford Taurus through the slalom course of onlookers, witnesses and emergency personnel, then sped south in pursuit of the white tanker.

A gun battle was not on the agenda when Johnson came in to work that morning. It was supposed to be a day of administrative duties and he was unarmed. But he did keep a pistol under his front seat. Steering with one hand, he reached with his free hand under the edge of the seat where he thought the pistol would be. Not there.

Hunching down so he was peering at the road through the steering wheel, he probed farther under the seat. Nothing.

Now, as he sped down the road hunting for the men who shot one of his officers, desperate to arm himself, he took one last glance through the windshield and dove so his head was below the dashboard. Reaching deep under the seat, he frantically swept his hand side to side, fingers stretched toward the gun he knew was there—someplace. He felt the Taurus swerve sharply into the oncoming lane, popped up long enough to execute an abrupt course correction before disappearing again below the dash. This time the car veered toward the shoulder. Another course correction and down again. Still the gun stayed beyond his grasp. When he rose to look at the road a third time, the rearview mirror revealed a black Jeep, emergency lights flashing, closing quickly on his rear bumper. At the same time, the radio reported patrol cars heading south on CR 25, two miles west of his location in the direction the tanker had turned.

The county sheriff's deputy driving the Jeep recognized the weaving Taurus in front of him as belonging to Assistant Chief Johnson. On a day when unthinkable things were happening, Johnson's erratic driving and hunched posture behind the wheel, at times doubling over so his entire head disappeared below the seat back, suggested an alarming conclusion. "Russell was hurt, maybe shot like the officer back at the bridge."

With the Jeep tight on his rear bumper and radio reports of other patrols in the area, undoubtedly armed, Johnson abruptly pulled over and waved the Jeep around him. "With this many officers in the area, they'll get those guys," he concluded, then swung into a U-turn and headed back to assist at the bridge.

One of the patrol cars Johnson heard report its location as southbound on CR 25 was driven by Montezuma County Sheriff's Deputy Jason Bishop. Doubling the road's 35 mph speed limit, Bishop screeched past the County Road H intersection where a second police car driven by Colorado State Trooper Steve Keller swung in behind him and held tight to his tail. A mile behind Keller, cars driven by Cortez police officers Jim Wynes and Sue Betts, also southbound on 25, pushed to close the gap. At County Road G, the last remaining intersection where the suspects may have turned, Bishop and Keller held straight on 25. They carved through a set of curves where the road dove over a small hill past a cluster of houses and a squat, plain building with a painted plywood sign identifying it as the Church of the First Born. Beyond the hollow of homes, CR 25 arced up a gradual slope, leveled and forked in two directions. Keller heard the sound of his tires change from hum to crunch as he left the blacktop and churned a wake of dust along the gravel continuation of CR 25.

Bishop followed the sweeping curve of asphalt to the left where the road morphed into County Road F. Both branches would hit a dead end within a half mile: Keller's at a pasture; Bishop's at the county landfill. At those points, both would turn around and double back into a trap.

From the moment Dale Claxton spotted it, the stolen white tanker truck was never out of sight of police or civilian witnesses for more than a minute or two. Witnesses at the bridge observed it during the shooting and watched it pull away. The first emergency personnel at the murder scene spotted it in flight as it turned west along the horizon line. Ninety seconds later, Sheriff's Deputy Lendol Lawrence, en route to help Officer Claxton, saw it coming toward him southbound on CR 25. He started to turn on it but at the last second, uncertain of Claxton's condition and unaware that rescue units had already reached the scene, he decided his first duty was to get to the bridge. A short mile later where the pavement branched left toward the landfill, the tanker nearly struck a car pulling onto the road from a stop sign. Seconds after that Thelma Fletcher, listening to the chase on her police scanner, watched through her front room window as the tanker made a sudden high-speed right turn off CR F. Then Paul Ibarra saw it parked and idling fifty feet down the long driveway leading to his employer's house.

Ibarra drove the shovel into the ground deep enough to hold the tool upright, then moved to take a closer look. Crossing in front of the yellow and black Ford flatbed he'd been loading for an upcoming concrete job, he suddenly drew up short. From the other side of the flatbed a masked man with a gun stepped into his path.

Even with an AK-47 pointed at his chest, Ibarra took detailed note of the man. He was six feet tall with a slim build. An olive-green balaclava masked his lower face. But his eyes were blue and sticking out from under the hood were strands of long blond hair. Otherwise the man was dressed head to toe in military drab: floppy brimmed boonie hat, camo pants and shirt—no breast or sleeve insignias or markings—olive-green gloves and black boots. His voice was soft, calm, almost friendly. "We don't want to hurt anyone, but we're taking this truck," he stated firmly, indicating the Ford. "You better get in the house."

Ibarra put his hands up and began taking large steps backward.

"Up here. Come on," the man shouted to two similarly dressed comrades who appeared to be hiding near the tanker. Despite the command, it was clear the men were not going to expose themselves.

The gunman opened the flatbed's driver's side door, tossed his rifle onto the front seat and climbed in after it. The keys were in the ignition. The sound of it starting brought Debbie Williams to the door of her home in time to see Ibarra turn and dash the last few feet toward her. "He's got a gun. Stay inside. Keep the kids in," he shouted at Williams.

As he swung open the door and bounded inside, he shouted again, "Call the cops!"

Upstairs Bob Williams dialed 911 as he raced to the window overlooking the driveway. The truck he had bought two days earlier for his construction business was backing fast down the drive. As Ibarra and Debbie Williams watched from the doorway and Bob Williams from an upstairs window, the gunman drove the flatbed past the tanker to a wide spot in the drive, in two steps spun the truck around 180 degrees and backed up alongside the tanker. One of the men who had been waiting by the tanker, rifle in hand, took over the driver position in the flatbed. The other, also armed, threw a duffle onto the truck bed and climbed up after it. As the flatbed accelerated down the drive, the man standing in the back braced himself against the back of the cab, his rifle in shooting position over its roof.

The truck rumbled the last few yards down the incline of the driveway, but just before it reached the road, Ibarra and the Williamses saw a police car pass in front of it heading west on County Road F. The flatbed pounced onto the road a few feet behind the patrol car and the vehicles passed out of sight. A split second later, the firing recommenced.

Shortly after splitting away from Trooper Steve Keller, Deputy Jason Bishop reached the end of County Road F. A large gate stood open allowing him to continue up a small gravel incline to the dumping area for the county landfill but the only vehicles visible were refuse trucks and a bulldozer busy rearranging piles of garbage. It was as far as any vehicle could go in that direction and there had been no sign of the white tanker truck. As he swung in a wide semicircle to head back west on CR F, the radio reported, "Armed robbery at 25-257 Road F. Suspects taking vehicle."

County Road F between CR 25 and the landfill was only a half-mile long. Bishop wasn't sure which house and driveway it was, but he knew he was within blocks of the hijacking. Driving slower on his way back over the same road he had just followed to the dump, he studied each mailbox for the reported address and every driveway for signs of the suspects. The home on his left just before F ended with a curve onto CR 25, however, was set far back from the road. Other than the wide gravel apron tying it to the road, its driveway was hidden from a westbound driver. Bishop glanced at his rearview mirror as he passed. A yellow truck suddenly filled the reflection. A man with a green mask over his face and a rifle at port-of-arms across his chest leaned out the open passenger window. Then Bishop's back window exploded.

"Shots fired! Shots fired!" Trooper Keller hollered over the radio. Keller had reached the end of CR 25 about the same time Bishop had entered the dump. He too heard the report of suspects commandeering a vehicle at a County Road F residence and had doubled back to where 25 and F split. He turned his patrol car in the direction he'd last seen Bishop heading. Only a couple hundred yards and a curve that blinded one from the other separated them when he heard the barrage.

A stream of bullets punched holes in the Plexiglas divider separating the front seat from the rear behind Bishop's head. A staccato of hollow popping sounds ended with a ring as one slug glanced off the divider's metal support bar at nearly a 90-degree angle. Bishop slumped forward, the ricochet bullet lodged in the back of his head. His patrol car careened off the road churning a trough across the adjacent front lawn before crashing to a stop against the home's carport.

Keller didn't hear the crash. At the sound of the shots, he stopped in the center of the road, listening to determine which direction the gunfire was coming from. The shooting was incessant and the answer came quickly—east, from around the curve in front of him. But one other aspect of the rifle reports caught his attention. They were getting progressively louder. The flatbed flew around the curve. By the time Keller could see it, it was twenty yards away centrifuging into his lane. The shots he was hearing now were slamming his car. The back driver's side window shattered as he flattened his body across the front seat. Still the sound of bullets hitting his car continued; a metallic thud as they punctured the body, a short mid-tone crack when they smashed through glass and a soft drawn-out puff from those that buried themselves in the upholstery. At the last second, the flatbed veered sharply to the right, narrowly avoiding a head-on collision as it slid within inches past Keller's vehicle.

Keller guessed that it had all happened in a span of five seconds. He waited a few more seconds to be sure he was no longer a target then sat up, backed his wounded but still running patrol car around and thumped on flat tires in futile pursuit.

Even as Keller sensed that his car was no longer being shot at, the shooting continued. Police cars charged into the fray like a moving line of metal duck cutouts at a shooting gallery, each officer caught by surprise at the sudden appearance and overwhelming firepower of the bullet-spurting flatbed speeding toward them.

Less than a hundred yards behind Keller, closing fast on a garbage truck that had somehow turned into the middle of the pursuit, Cortez patrolman Jim Bob Wynes sped into the onslaught. Keller's and Bishop's radio calls of shots fired coincided with the crack of gunfire directly in front of him. Suddenly a spray of bullets chewed across his patrol car as the flatbed flashed past. A short distance behind him, Deputy Todd Martin slid his Jeep to a stop in the oncoming lane. As Wynes came about to pursue his assailants, he witnessed the gunmen open up on Martin.

Forty-five seconds beyond Martin, the flatbed ran a stop sign and turned left onto County Road G just as Deputy Terry Steele approached the intersection. He was still looking for a white tanker, when he noticed the men in the flatbed rounding the corner in front of him were dressed in camouflage and wearing masks. At the last instant, he leaned right across the front seat as bullets ripped down the length of his patrol car and the windows disintegrated into a microburst of glass shards.

Thirty seconds behind Steele, Montezuma County Undersheriff Joey Chavez was also uncertain about what kind of vehicle the fugitives were in. He figured it out as the oncoming yellow flatbed truck with no warning veered into his lane, sideswiped him into the ditch, then punctuated the effort with rifle fire into his vehicle.

Behind Chavez came Deputy Lendol Lawrence. Less than thirty seconds separated their vehicles. Also looking for a white tanker truck, he thought the gunfire he was hearing must be coming from someone hiding in the adjacent truck-stop parking lot. Then he saw the asphalt directly in front of him chipping into puffs of dust and realized they came from the yellow flatbed coming at him. Two seconds later, the flatbed was past him. His car had been shot nine times.

CHAPTER 5
MARTIN

The Jeep Cherokee had slid to a stop broadside across Highway 25. Crouching on the pavement alongside of it, Montezuma County Sheriff Deputy Todd Martin pressed his forehead against the sun-warmed metal of the vehicle's left front fender, closed his eyes and exhaled slowly. He knew he'd made a fatal mistake.

Surviving the next two minutes would take all the presence of mind he could muster; yet one thought kept intruding on his focus, "Damn, this was my last day. I'd quit this job."

It should have been like everyone else's last day who had left the sheriff's department during the ten years Martin had worked there: cleaning out his desk, a supermarket bakery cake with GOOD LUCK TODD squiggled across the top, handshakes and good-byes; culminated by turning in equipment he'd been assigned—like the 12-gauge pump shotgun he now held tight across his chest. The sound of the truck bearing down on him grew louder. He thumbed the safety to off as his index finger tightened around the trigger.

Just shy of six feet tall, Martin was every inch a professional. His sandy-colored hair was neatly trimmed, his uniform tidy and, at thirty-four years old, he maintained an athletic build consistent with his disciplined, purposeful approach to life. His presence conveyed an uncommon degree of alertness, cool competence and self-confidence.

His aptitude and capabilities would have been valued by any law enforcement agency, but in a department as small as the Montezuma County Sheriff's Office, advancement opportunities and earning potential were limited. For that reason, Martin had applied to join the Colorado State Troopers and been accepted into its next training class. He'd turned in his resignation to the sheriff's office thirty days before.

The day had started out as Martin expected. A couple of good-natured "short-timer" jibes from coworkers as he arrived at the station; a short hunt for an empty cardboard box, which he found in the janitor's closet; and a few minutes to start clearing personal items from his desk. Martin placed the picture his wife Carolyn had taken of him and his dog relaxing on a camping trip upright along one side of the box, padded it with the workout clothes he kept at the office, and then fit his running shoes and an insulated coffee mug so it was all wedged securely in place.

By 9:05, he sat on one side of a small conference room table. Sheriff Sherman Kennell sat on his right. Undersheriff Joey Chavez and Deputy Colin Boggs, the officer assigned his detective duties, sat across from him. One by one Martin pulled a file from the stack on the table in front of him, slid it across to Boggs, then explained nuances of the investigation that eluded the paperwork. They were four cases into the task when Sheriff Kennell's administrative assistant burst through the doorway, eyes wide with alarm. "Officer down on 27 at the bridge," she announced.

Martin didn't hear how she completed the sentence. As he jumped to his feet, she backed cautiously against the door frame, clearing a path from the room. Brushing past her into the office, he broke into a full run, cutting close around the first desk in his path. His holster snagged a tray full of paperwork. He didn't look back as it crashed to the floor.

Others responded with equal urgency. A clamor of footsteps closed on Martin's heels. He was now leading a small charge toward the exit to the parking lot. Reaching the security door, he jammed down the latch bar and flung it open. A half-dozen officers burst into the cloudless May morning sunlight like a covey of flushed quail, fanning in sprints to their patrol cars.

Martin fastened his seat belt as he turned from the lot onto Mildred Street, accelerating toward McElmo Bridge; then calmly he reached over to flip on his strobe lights and siren before settling unworried into his seat. Conditioned by the peaceful routine of small-town Cortez, Colorado, Martin's rapid response to the words "officer down" was a consequence of training rather than true dread. He replayed Denise's words in his mind—"Officer down on 27 at bridge." She hadn't added anything about gunshots and the idea didn't enter his thoughts.

Three minutes later, he cruised slowly past Claxton's patrol car. Its broken windows shattered his illusions. He had expected to see a colleague who, in an altercation with a belligerent motorist, had been punched in the face. Instead, he didn't see the officer at all, but blood splattered on the car's windshield drove the point home with ice-pick ferocity. Martin's stomach tightened with the realization, "This was a shooting."

The squawk of his radio short-circuited further emotional response. "Suspect in 1998 Mack white tanker truck." Martin made his decision fast. Glancing in the rearview mirror he confirmed another unit from the Cortez Police Department had arrived at the scene ahead of him and was parked in a protective position behind the damaged patrol car. The EMTs were slipping in right behind him. The down officer was in good hands and other police would secure the scene, he reasoned. "There's nothing more I can do here; I'm going to find that truck."

Martin sped south from the bridge, braking enough to glance left or right up each turnoff he crossed, then accelerating between them, the speedometer needle dancing between 40 and 70 mph. Most were short driveways or accesses into farm fields. He needed just a fraction of a second to scan each as he passed. Some streets, however, reached behind the hills that rose alongside the main road, offering curves, dips or sufficient vegetation to hide a tanker truck. At these, Martin slowed further; stared longer; finally moving on with the uneasy feeling he might be missing his prey. His attention shifted from the last driveway back to the road ahead. A yellow sign warning the road was about to end at a T-intersection triggered an idea. He knew every road and intersection in that area by heart and quickly formed a map in his mind. Swerving abruptly around a green Taurus that had slowed in front of him, Martin waited for the last second to brake, before the Jeep dove right onto CR H. He now knew how to catch the shooter.

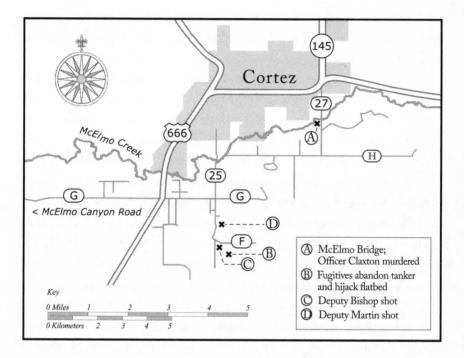

As a rule, Montezuma County roads diced the territory into mile-square township sections. In most rural areas of the county that created a grid of continuous north-south and east-west roads, and an almost infinite number of ways to zigzag to any point on the compass. But immediately south of Cortez, the roads didn't form complete squares. Due to a combination of topography and a lack of population

requiring access, every section had at least one side where the bordering road dead-ended. Even the few side roads that branched off the
main county roads were no more than short spurs and two block loops.
The grid was broken and, like a maze puzzle, if you wanted to escape
the area there was only one path out. Martin was on it.

Abandoning his search of side streets, he pressed harder on the gas
pedal. Still close to the City of Cortez, the area was semirural with
pockets of homes and businesses. The county roads were zoned for
35 mph. At 80 mph, Martin's focus shifted from searching for the
suspect to watching for innocents. He strained to see movement at
every driveway and mailbox. His leg, steady on the gas, tensed ready to
slam on the brakes. But if the shooter was ahead of him, he had to
catch up quickly.

The CR 25 intersection was in flat, open country, peppered with
knee-high clumps of grass and sage. A curved corner eased the
90-degree turn onto south 25. From seventy-five yards away Martin
scanned the intersecting road in both directions for traffic, judged
his opening and banked around the radial corner. Accelerating out of
the curve, he blew through the stop sign and slid in behind two other
patrol cars speeding south. At County Road G, the two lead cars
shot through the intersection and screamed straight ahead. Like the
other roads in this area, theirs would soon end. Martin turned right,
gripping the steering wheel tighter as the Jeep tilted around the corner. As the vehicle's suspension rebounded, he pressed the pedal to
the floor and leaned forward, desperately searching the road ahead
for a glimpse of a white tanker truck. It was the last turn; G was the
only way out. Seeing nothing but empty pavement through his windshield, Martin felt his plan slipping away.

From McElmo Bridge there was only one possible route to his
current position, the route he had just taken with no sign of a white
tanker—south on 27, west on H, south on 25, then west on G. There
were other roads the suspect could have turned down, but sooner or
later he would have to turn around and backtrack to that singular
path. In half a mile, that advantage ended. A couple of hundred
yards beyond Fosnot's junkyard, G crossed the Devil's Highway, US

666.[1] From there the possible routes a fugitive might take expanded exponentially.

Even from two hundred yards away, Martin recognized the figure on the roadside frantically waving both arms above his head as Eddie Fosnot. Six feet, heavy-set, with a ZZ Top–length beard and light brown hair that looked like it had been hacked off at shoulder length with a pruner, Eddie had a comic quality about him. He wore the same uniform he'd had on the other times Martin had met him: a black Harley-Davidson T-shirt, jeans with pant legs tucked into the tops of beat-up motorcycle boots and an orange Denver Broncos cap.

Resigned that the chase was over, Martin turned off his siren and lowered the passenger-side window as he slowed to a stop at the entrance to Fast Eddie's All Auto Parts salvage yard. Eddie leaned in through the window before the car came to a full stop, hopping sideways to keep up with the vehicle.

"Didn't come past here. Been watchin' the whole time," he blurted.

Martin raised his eyebrows, his mind leaping ahead to what Eddie's message meant.

"That white tanker truck from the bridge." Eddie's words spilled out with excited urgency. "Heard it on the scanner. Been out here the whole time watchin' for it and it didn't come by." Eddie understood what Martin did, if the tanker hadn't come past his driveway, then it was behind them—trapped.

"Got it," Martin shouted, pulling the shift lever to drive—Eddie's cue to back away. Slapping the side of the vehicle as he stepped clear, Eddie watched the Jeep's U-turn loop onto the opposite shoulder, the tires spraying gravel until they bit into the asphalt, rocketing Martin back the direction he came.

Martin summoned his mental roadmap once again and saw the endgame: by now the bridge would be plugged full of police and he had the other end blocked. Still in the early stages, the police response was chaotic but soon it would settle into a coordinated systematic search. With dozens of police units involved and only a few miles of roads to check, every foot of roadway, driveway, parking lot and easement that could accommodate a tanker truck would be cleared within an hour. The shooter would be flushed out and every mile Martin backtracked, the noose tightened. An encounter was inevitable.

The hair rose on the back of Martin's neck. As a detective, he seldom wore a bulletproof vest on duty and in the rush this morning hadn't even thought of it. Now, traveling 70 mph toward a man with a gun, he wanted it. Reaching back he pulled the vest from where he'd left it on the rear seat. It took the rest of County Road G, alternating his hands on the steering wheel, to wriggle it on. That done, he pulled his shotgun from the ceiling rack and laid it across his lap.

At the same moment Martin reached for his shotgun, a voice screamed over the police radio, "Shots fired. Shots fired, Road F." Martin clenched the steering wheel tighter. His encounter wouldn't have to wait for a systematic search to begin. He'd watched patrol cars go south on 25 toward County Road F when he turned right onto G. Now he was at that same intersection. The shooter was fleeing his way. Martin turned south on 25 to meet him.

Like the confusion of reports suddenly screaming "shots fired," radio chatter since the incident at McElmo Bridge fifteen minutes earlier had been frantic and sketchy. There had been a barely discernable report that the suspect had switched vehicles, but no confirmation. All Martin knew for certain was that an officer had been shot. In a peaceful community like Cortez, that in itself was almost unthinkable. The true nature of the assailants was unimaginable. Martin formed his own, more probable picture of who he was after— a solitary man, drunk or flipped out and wild-eyed over some personal problem, steering with his right hand while leaning out the window taking potshots with a pistol.

It was with that assumption in mind that Martin slammed on the brakes of his patrol car and cranked the wheel as hard as he could, steering left into the Church of the First Born driveway. A yellow flatbed truck had rounded the curve a quarter mile ahead doing 70 in a 35 zone. A voice in his mind spoke with certainty, "This is it!"

Before the Jeep's back end skidded to a complete stop sideways across the oncoming lane, he was in motion. Ramming the shift lever into park, he gripped his shotgun, opened the door and bailed out, slamming it behind him; the entire sequence of actions collapsing into a single perfectly coordinated split-second motion.

Martin's plan had the solitary lunatic shooter come to a screeching halt right in front of his car. At that moment, he would jump up and have an across-the-hood shootout with a guy with a pistol. But as he ducked below the Jeep's fender he glimpsed the gunmen. His plan disintegrated. He saw not one but two gunmen, plus a third man driving. One shooter stood braced in the bed of truck. A second leaned out the passenger-side window. Except for that man's shoulder-length hair streaming wildly in the wind, neither shooter conformed to Martin's image of a crazed local. In the quick second he had to assess his adversaries, Martin saw instead trained soldiers. Wearing fatigues and body armor, they wielded their weapons with apparent ease and expertise. Their movements were calm, intent. They were men on a mission. Even more shocking, the shots from the flatbed truck bearing down on him weren't from a pistol. The staccato of automatic weapons fire was deafening as the large caliber guns tore his vehicle apart. Jagged shards of metal and glass from the Jeep rained down on him. The intensity of the barrage was startling and Martin had a fleeting thought that he'd been ambushed; that hidden in surrounding hills were more gunmen aiding the assault. Pinned in place and armed with only a shotgun, a wave of fear washed through him as he sunk lower behind the Jeep. "Damn. This was my last day," he murmured.

Outgunned, Martin had one last hope. As the flatbed slowed to slip around his one-car roadblock he'd take out the gunman positioned on the truck's bed. As for the other shooter leaning out the truck cab's passenger-side window, maybe having to shift from shooting forward out ahead of the truck to shooting behind it as the truck passed would be an awkward enough move that Martin would have time for a second shot. From a tactical standpoint, it was a bad plan.

Martin judged the closing distance from when he had last seen the oncoming truck as he jumped from his own vehicle. At about twenty feet of separation, he sprang to a standing position, at the same time sliding the shotgun's fore end toward the trigger, one half of the motion that pumps a shell into the chamber. The complete move takes about a second. But the flatbed didn't slow.

Swinging sharply onto the left-hand shoulder, the truck flew past the Jeep at 70 mph, exposing Martin unprepared to shoot. He watched the truck over his right shoulder. Nothing but ten feet of air separated him from the gunman standing in the bed. Martin turned to run to the front of the Jeep but the instant transpired in crisis-time. His feet seemed welded to the pavement. He didn't move.

A sudden burst of heat pressed over Martin's face as the muzzle blast from the first shot pounded him. In the same instant, he watched with detached curiosity as his left arm exploded in a cloud of red mist. The shot ripped away a fistful of flesh and bone above the elbow. His shotgun clattered to the pavement.

The second shooter, his entire body from the waist up leaning out the passenger-side window, was still swinging around to shoot in his direction. Martin's brain reengaged with a scream, "Cover! Cover! Cover!"

He dove for the ground. As his upper body slammed against the road he felt a sharp hammer blow behind his right knee, coinciding with the sound of a second shot. With the instincts of a wounded animal scrambling from the jaws of a predator, Martin clawed desperately at the asphalt with his one good hand, trying to drag himself under the vehicle. Alternately moving his upper body a few inches, then swinging his hips and legs forward, he wiggled his body under the Jeep. As he pivoted his head fully under the car, the sound of bullets slamming the side of it grew louder, the vehicle quivering with each impact.

Squirming deeper under the vehicle, Martin stopped in what seemed to be the most protected position; he lay breathless, angled between the left rear tire and right front tire. In a final act of survival, he tucked his chin to his chest and drew his legs into a fetal position, making himself a smaller target. He was far from safe.

The stream of gunfire was constant. As the distance between the flatbed and Jeep lengthened, the angle of sight between the shooters and the space under the Jeep flattened providing a straighter shot at him. Already bullets were chipping white streaks in the blacktop beneath the Jeep's doors before glancing up into the undercarriage, hitting inches above Martin's body. The shots came too fast to even flinch with each near miss. Instead Martin closed his eyes in one prolonged cringe driven by one overwhelming thought, "The next one is going to kill me."

A final volley from the receding flatbed bounced sharply off the pavement directly behind his head, slamming into the engine. Then, twenty seconds after the shooting had started, it was deadly quiet. A warm stream of green radiator fluid flowed down over his face onto the road, mixing into a dark puddle with the blood that gushed in spurts from his wounded arm.

His cheek pressed heavily against the rough pavement. He felt the puddle spread around his head, under his chin and down his once tidy uniform shirt and thought, "Dogs die from drinking this stuff."

CHAPTER 6
ESCAPE

Deputy Jason Bishop stumbled from his crashed patrol car. "I've been hit," he radioed. "I'm okay," he added, and then collapsed. Residents of nearby houses streamed from their homes and gathered around the fallen officer, facedown on the lawn with an obvious bullet wound in the back of his head. One ran back and forth between the wounded man and her home reporting his condition to the 911 operator. Another ran and got a pillow they slid under Bishop's head. Others began scouting the immediate area, wondering what else might be amiss.

Many had seen what happened, both to Bishop and a half mile down the road to Martin. They could describe the truck (a yellow and black Ford flatbed pickup), its path and speed, what it appeared to have loaded on the bed (boards for concrete forms). They could describe the sound of the gunfire, when it commenced, the rapidity of the shots, the intervals between bursts, the approximate number of shots. They could describe the men in the truck even though they wore masks over their faces: which had shoulder-length sandy-blond hair (the passenger in the cab), which had shorter brown hair (the driver), which wore glasses (the man in the back), which was slim and which had a heavier build.

In the two minutes that elapsed from the time the fugitives opened fire on Deputy Bishop until they sailed with guns blazing past Deputy Lendol Lawrence, the outlaws gunned down two Montezuma County sheriff deputies and shot up seven police cars, disabling five of them. Slipping in between the parade of police cars taking fire were several more police vehicles that were spared the assault. Some arrived on the scene seconds after the gun battle had moved farther down the road, missing an encounter. Others rushed head-on toward the fleeing flatbed truck, but with the multitude of targets approaching the suspects, were passed over in favor of easier shots. Some of the officers stayed at the scenes of the shootings to aid the wounded, secure evidence and take witness statements. Others turned their cars around and joined the pursuit.

Sue Betts of the Cortez Police Department was among those in the thick of the shooting. Having raced into the action between Officer Wynes and Deputy Martin, she watched both men take fire as she pulled right into a driveway and turned her car around for the chase. By the time she pulled back onto the road headed north, she saw in her rearview mirror that Wynes, and behind him Keller, had completed the same maneuver and were heading in her direction. The flatbed meanwhile was a hundred yards out front, swinging left around Martin's Jeep. She stepped hard on the gas and felt the car surge ahead.

Accelerating for the chase behind Betts, Wynes also saw the flatbed fly past the black Jeep. For a moment Martin had been standing behind it. The next second he was lying on the road. Rocketing around the Jeep just as the flatbed had done, Betts pressed ahead. Wynes braked to a jarring stop near the wounded deputy. Even from across the road, he could see the arc of blood spurting from Martin's arm. Dragging Martin from under the Jeep, Wynes pressed the heel of his hand hard against the torn artery and spoke into his portable radio. As the call, "Officer down; request ambulance as soon as possible," crackled across the emergency radio channel, other officers arrived from both directions. From the direction the suspects had fled, a deputy raced to help Wynes save Martin's life. From the trail of shell casings and havoc behind them, Keller's patrol car emerged.

The metronomic *thwop* of his flat tire slowed to silence as he stopped in front of the Jeep. Determined to catch the outlaws, he bolted for Wynes's vehicle. "I need your car," he shouted.

"Take it," came the answer, as Keller leapt behind the wheel.

Despite the fugitives' success disabling several cars and the overwhelming firepower to keep police at bay, the concentration of patrol cars in the area kept the gap between pursued and pursuers small. Like tag-team wrestlers, as one police car fell back, others jumped into the chase. Sue Betts, accelerating from a standstill in an effort to catch a truck already moving at 70 mph, lost ground right from the start. By the time the fugitives turned west on County Road G, the hundred yards separating them when Betts began the chase had stretched to nearly a half mile. Keller, who had to abandon his disabled car and jump into another to continue the chase, was even farther behind. But at the turn onto G, Deputy Terry Steele was in position to close tight on the fugitives' tails.

The flatbed turned onto G crossing in front of him, its driver and a man lying in the truck bed shooting down at him as it sped alongside his vehicle. Bullets from the receding truck were still hitting the trunk of his patrol car when Steele screeched its rear end around in a 180-degree power turn and tore after the flatbed.

The firing continued as Steele shortened the distance between them. At less than a hundred straight, unobstructed yards—no dips or bumps in the road that made him an erratic target, no hills or curves that momentarily hid him—he was an easy shot. Only the street vibration that added a slight wobble to the gunman's aim assured that not every pull of the trigger would find its mark. In the rush of the chase, neither that fact nor the sight of pavement chipping around him from near misses, nor the thuds of direct hits to his patrol car took root in his mind and grew to reasonable fear. He drove steadily closer to the flatbed, into the stream of gunfire.

Thump! The energy of the hit traveled up the steering column. Steele felt the blow to his vehicle as much as heard it. Like a deer running full speed that suddenly has the air knocked out of it by a hunter's shot, the car seemed to buckle. The hit was more than a sheet metal wound, Steele sensed. It was something vital. Even so, he was startled by the sudden pop and loud hiss of escaping gases from underneath his car. The tachometer needle flung itself counterclockwise. While the gas pedal remained jammed to the floor, the engine lost power.

In disbelief, Steele glanced from the falling speedometer to the widening gap between him and the fugitives. Then, as if reacting to his despair, the car gasped back to life and in a last desperate attempt to catch the truck, hurtled full-speed after it.

The race blitzed past the oncoming vehicles of Undersheriff Chavez and Deputy Lawrence. Steele held close to the truck, his patrol car billowing a comet tail of dense gray smoke. The intersection with US Highway 666 loomed ahead. Unlike the previous intersections the suspects had blown through, it was no country crossroads. The stop sign the fugitives and Steele were approaching at over 80 mph checked motorists from cruising headlong into the cross traffic of a major four-lane highway.

Still the sound of gunfire from the flatbed never let up. Chavez and Lawrence took some of the heat but Steele had also remained a target. Now as the outlaws raced through the stop sign into the intersection, he didn't know who they were shooting at, but it was no longer him.

As the flatbed crossed the first lane of the highway, the gunmen commenced a new battery of firing, aiming at no particular target. Some wild shots narrowly missed observers watching from outside an adjacent business, but the intent was clearly not to hurt anyone. Most often, according to multiple witnesses, the weapons were pointed skyward. Like cowboy bank robbers who rode through town firing six-guns in the air, making citizens cower against the buildings and clearing a path for their escape, the gunfire accomplished what the trailing police sirens didn't. Traffic slowed. Vehicles dodged to the shoulders or stopped short where they happened to be. The flatbed slowed only slightly as it wove through the path that had opened between the panicked motorists. As it passed, confusion filled in behind it.

By the time Steele entered the intersection, the way across had all but disappeared. Drivers frightened by the gunfire were now flustered in their rush to make way for police. Efforts to get out of the way clogged the passage even further.

It took Steele nearly twice as long to cross the highway as it did the fugitives, but west of the highway County Road G remained flat and laser-beam straight for several miles. The flatbed was still in sight. Even closer, however, was a pickup truck stopped sideways in the road.

Shaun Murphy was one of those guys whose pursuit of a good tale to tell buddies over a couple of beers outweighed common sense. "It's like me to put my nose where it doesn't belong," he told police. As the sound of gunfire drew nearer, that's exactly what he did.

Murphy had been listening to the gunfire for nearly a minute as he stood outside Rick's Towing just west of the Highway 666 and County Road G intersection. His curiosity as to what could be going on was piqued as several police cars flew past heading south on 666. "I'm gonna go see where those shots are coming from," he told the coworker he'd been chatting with and ran for his truck. He planned to follow the police cars south on 666 but as he turned east on G he saw the yellow flatbed barreling across the highway toward him. "It was flying," Murphy recalled. "Flying straight at me . . . shooting!"

He slid the truck sideways and as it swayed to a stop in the middle of the road, ducked low behind the wheel. Then, misjudging the timing and thinking the flatbed had passed him or turned onto the highway, he popped back up. The end of the barrel was right in his face. The flatbed passed alongside of him, inches from his truck. Had they chosen to, they could have killed him easily, Murphy thought. They were shooting as they approached and after they passed, but as they swept alongside, they didn't pull the trigger.

As ruthless as the fugitives had already proven themselves to be in confrontations with law enforcement, they weren't on a mindless rampage. Just as they spared Matt Weston and Evelyn Pearson, point-blank witnesses to Claxton's murder that morning, as well as the many other residents and motorists they passed in the ensuing high-speed chase, they let Murphy live.

There seemed to be a code they adhered to, something they had agreed upon before that morning—this was a war with the police and government authority; civilians were not their enemies. In their minds, in fact, they likely believed they were waging a battle on behalf of the ordinary citizens of Four Corners. As they told Paul Ibarra when they stole the flatbed, "We don't want to hurt anyone."

Murphy sat stunned by his close call as the flatbed moved on into the distance. "The next thing I knew, all hell broke loose," he recounted. "People came running to see if I'd been shot, and then there was more cops than I ever seen in the city."

The first to race past Murphy was Terry Steele, but whatever mechanical phenomenon had granted his bullet-riddled patrol car its final burst of speed, the chase through the intersection undid it. Once again, Steele felt his car lose power. The suspect vehicle lengthened its lead until it was no longer in sight. Two miles later, Steele's engine quit completely. He coasted to the side of the road and got his M-16 from the trunk. Minutes later, when Captain Chavez came by, he hopped in with him.

District Attorney Investigator James Davenport was next in line after Steele in the pursuit. After driving south on Highway 666 in search of the suspects, he had turned around and was a hundred and fifty yards back in the traffic when the fugitives snarled the intersection. By the time Davenport turned onto G, he could only see the flatbed on long straightaways. For a little while longer, as the road began to wind, he would capture a fleeting glimpse of the truck as it disappeared around a bend ahead of him. Shortly he was too far behind to do even that.

Davenport did keep the outlaws in sight long enough, however, to report that they had not turned off at the last viable option to do so and had instead continued on into McElmo Canyon. Like much of the police radio communication that morning, the message was not relayed by dispatch or received by other patrol cars. Heavy skid marks right before CR 21 led several pursuers to deduce the fugitives had turned there. Multiple patrol units headed that direction before realizing they were off track, losing even more time in the pursuit.

Deputy Lawrence had to change a tire that had been shot flat before he rejoined the pursuit. Captain Chavez had to extricate his car from the ditch after being forced off the road before he could take up the chase. Officer Sue Betts and Trooper Keller continued west on G but fell miles behind the outlaws. As the road wound down into McElmo Canyon, other patrol cars joined them. While the gap between the outlaws and the police widened, the separation between the various patrol vehicles entering the pursuit shrunk to July Fourth parade spacing. The chase vehicles coalesced into a long peloton of police cars, lights flashing, moving cautiously westward toward the Utah desert.

For the fugitives, the chase ended when they crossed Highway 666. The county sheriff deputies and Colorado State Patrol troopers who routinely would have been patrolling west of the highway had been drawn into Cortez by reports of Claxton's shooting and were now behind them. The path ahead was unchallenged and within three miles, the last threat of serious pursuit slid from their rearview mirrors.

Beyond the Cortez airport on the southwestern edge of the city, CR G suddenly tips downward and twists toward the McElmo Canyon bottomlands. It is a niggardly two lanes wide with narrow gravel shoulders. The canyon wall rises on the left and drops off fifty feet to the canyon floor on the right. Even along the bottom, it is not a road that should be driven fast. Most of the next thirty miles to the Colorado-Utah state line is posted for 35 to 50 mph, with several curves rated at 25 mph.

The flatbed cruised through the canyon much faster. Various witnesses estimated its speed past them at 70 mph. At one point, swinging wide into the left lane around a blind curve rather than reducing speed, they forced two oncoming cars into a ditch. But the fugitives' haste was more of a prudent lope than a desperate gallop.

In any place but the rural West, where police forces are small and the areas they have to patrol are vast, entering the canyon would have been tantamount to capture. A stretch of land twenty-five miles long but less than a mile wide and bound by high sandstone walls, it had been for centuries a refuge from the inhospitable arid mesa that stretched for miles at the top of the walls. Before the ranchers that occupied it for the last hundred years, Ute Indians lived there. Before them, the Anasazi built stone and adobe structures there and then mysteriously disappeared. And before the Anasazi, another ancient people left scraps of their civilization behind.

But it was not Eden. In a landscape that otherwise resisted life, it was livable. In some parts, rounding a bend in the road revealed a sylvan setting: groves of cottonwood trees along the creek, rail and barbwire fences shaping patches of pasture where cattle or sheep grazed and small hayfields abetted in their yield by irrigation. In other locations along the canyon, the harsh reality of Western life was more apparent. For every acre cultivated or thick with natural vegetation, two were barren; brown eroded exposed bedrock edged by red rock-strewn soil. There in late May, between the intermittent scrub juniper tree and sage, an occasional clump of spring-green grass forced its way among three-foot-tall dead brown stalks from last season. One generation succeeding the next, one civilization following another; none really prospering, but making it.

Unlike the rugged land the outlaws were heading for, where hundreds of canyons formed a giant web of escape routes, McElmo Canyon was a single, contained slash in the earth. It had neither numerous side canyons that would complicate a search nor the opportunity to move surreptitiously beyond its walls. Rather than thousands of square miles of relative wilderness stretching into four states, it was small: less than twenty-five square miles in length and populated by self-reliant families who had their own guns and kept a sharp eye on their surroundings. A single road wound the length of the canyon.

In a more densely populated and patrolled part of the country, police may have used the twenty-five minutes or so it takes to travel the length of the canyon to amass a resolute roadblock at the other end, trapping the suspects. Police communications, however, were poor. Despite reports that the suspects had entered the canyon, confusion and uncertainty as to where they were prevailed. Radios within the canyon stopped working and what messages did get through remained garbled with adrenaline. Even if clear alerts had reached authorities west of the canyon, there was little they could have done. Beyond its cities, patrol cars in Four Corners were typically spread thin, often thirty minutes or more from each other and any given location. Getting a single patrol car out in front of the fugitives before the road exited the canyon and branched off into multiple possible routes proved impossible.

On the other hand, word of the chase spread quickly down the canyon, even outpacing the flatbed truck. Some canyon dwellers had been listening to events in Cortez unfold on their police scanners. Others received phone calls from friends in town.

They peered out windows, stood on porches, idled in front yards and watched. They sent someone from the household trotting down to warn family members working near the road that desperados were on the way. As the flatbed passed, they relayed the news to neighbors living farther down the canyon.

By the time the police caravan slipped into the canyon, the route was marked by residents who stood on the shoulder of the road waving and pointing the direction the fugitives had preceded. Police in the lead cars, who upon entering the canyon slowed to ask, were told they were four minutes behind. Within a few miles, that gap would more than triple.

The fugitives moved at speeds well above the posted limit most of the way into Utah but evidently relaxed with the realization they were beyond imminent capture. They removed their face masks, smoked cigarettes and drank beer.[1]

Bruce Tolzer is one those canyon residents who was working near the road that morning. The head of the sheriff's posse back in the day when the posse was the action arm of the Montezuma County Sheriff's Office, Tolzer was an area old-timer with *High Noon* bravado and Wyatt Earp confidence in his abilities to take care of himself and watch over his neighbors too. Rancher, cowpoke, farrier, Tolzer had grown up with guns, horses and open space.

The Tolzer ranch was fifteen miles into the canyon. On that May 29, Tolzer was driving cattle from pastureland on the south side of McElmo Canyon Road to a corral on the north side where they would be coaxed into a semitrailer and transported to summer range. It was a job he did on horseback with a pistol snugged into a makeshift holster sewn from an old boot top tucked in the back of his jeans. "I've packed a six-shooter since I've been eight or nine years old," he explained.

He moved the herd out of the field onto the path that ran along the edge of the road for seventy-five yards. Then, directly across from where the semitrailer was parked against a loading chute, he turned the herd toward the corral. The stream of cattle crossing the road blocked traffic for several minutes but the only vehicle halted by the bovine barrier that morning was a yellow flatbed truck.

He heard the truck rumble over the cattle guard before looking up from the herd and seeing it. As he crossed the road himself, riding between the cattle and the flatbed, Tolzer gave a slight nod toward the truck's occupants. A barely perceptible gesture that meant "Hello. Sorry for the inconvenience. Appreciate you stopping," and "Tough shit. This is the West; this is the way we live," all at once. He received a polite, no-worries nod back.

Among his herd were several calves and those on the outside wanted to break. Tolzer put his attention back to his work and was only vaguely aware of the truck driving on as the last of the cattle cleared the road. There was no honking or revving the engine impatiently, he recounted. The boys in the truck didn't gesture or act up as if they minded the delay. They didn't pull away excessively fast when the road cleared. "I got the impression they were in no hurry."

The outlaws had already passed when Tolzer's cousin rushed down the path with news of the shooting in Cortez and fugitives in a yellow Ford flatbed. Figuring immediately where those boys were heading, Tolzer directed his cousin to get back to his house and call another relation who lived on the road to Cross Canyon. He would be waiting.

Tolzer continued to sort cattle in the corral, keeping the calves with their mothers. He'd been at it thirty minutes, maybe more, when he heard it coming. Sirens whining, lights flashing, it was the longest line of police cars he'd ever seen. "It looked like a funeral procession," he said. "And they were in no hurry," he added, estimating the speed of the cavalcade through the canyon at something under 25 mph.

"Those boys had already seen all the action they wanted to see that morning," he speculated. "They didn't want to catch up with the fugitives." None did.

As it had done intermittently since entering the canyon and encountering residents on the side of the road, the line stopped long enough for police to confirm the suspects were still out ahead of them and hadn't turned off at one the ranches they'd passed. "Yep, they'd come through here," Tolzer told them. Down the road, some of the police would set up a roadblock long after the horse had left the barn. Others would soon concede that the outlaws had outdistanced them and return to Cortez. A few would follow reports of the killers, trailing too far behind to ever catch a glimpse of them, a circumstance that would haunt law enforcement for the next nine years.

Past Tolzer's cattle, the flatbed regained its reckless speed. The road, while still paved, was cracked and broken. The truck bounced wildly and the occupants shook with it. The lumber stacked in the back began to shift. The added side-to-side sway around the curves unsettled the stacks completely and boards slid loose across the bed.

Crossing into Utah, the road did not so much exit the canyon as the canyon disappeared from around it. The tall vertical bluffs that had formed the canyon walls gradually shrunk, reclined back into rounded low hills and then vanished completely, as if someone had stretched a wrinkle out of a bedspread. From the windshield of a car, what was left was an arid, flat, featureless hardpan mesa salted with sagebrush. From the perspective of the buzzards that stripped the bones of those who ventured there, it was neither flat nor featureless. The mesa was etched like aged flesh as far as the eye could see with lines and creases—a crisscross of canyons, many of which were hundreds of feet deep and miles long.

Roads through this area of Four Corners were sparse but just over the Colorado-Utah border a small, narrow strip of alternating pavement and gravel branched north toward Hovenweep National Monument and the nearest of the great canyons that open into the labyrinth. Along the way, the relation that Bruce Tolzer had warned leaned against the car parked in his front yard. As the flatbed approached he centered the scope crosshairs of his .233 rifle on the truck's driver. A civilian version of the standard military issue M-16, the .233 is one of the smaller "big game" rifles but it is also used by some police departments as a sniper rifle. Effective for over a half mile, the shot of a couple hundred feet would have been relatively easy, but it was never taken. "He couldn't kill someone based on a phone call," Tolzer explained. The fugitives continued on, unaware that at least one of them had just escaped death.

The name Hovenweep means "deserted valley" in the language of the Ute Indians who hunted there long after an earlier agrarian culture had abandoned it. Comparatively speaking, the name was still appropriate. Remote from cities or even any major byways, the monument was one of the smaller attractions in the national park system, drawing a tiny fraction of the annual visitors that its larger, better known neighbor, Mesa Verde National Park, attracted. On that morning, its parking lot up a short hill from the country road that curved around the monument held just two visitor cars. A couple of those tourists were poking about the small, one-room visitor center. The rest were starting toward the 1.5-mile walking trail that loops past seven-hundred-year-old Pueblo ruins perched on the rim of a small slot canyon.

US National Park Service Ranger and Hovenweep Monument Superintendent Art Hutchinson was winding down his usual tourist talk about the site when his counterpart at Mesa Verde called with news of the Cortez shooting and fugitives heading in his general direction. It was about 10:15 A.M., almost an hour after Claxton was shot.

Hutchinson's mind fumbled for a plan. It was not a situation he'd been trained for or one anticipated in operations memorandums.

There was nothing here for the fugitives, he thought. No weapons. No good place to hide. Nothing to aid in an escape. Except people. It was the only place for forty miles where desperate fugitives could expect to take hostages. "Get the people from the trail. Don't let anyone leave," he barked to his assistant. "If I call, get out of the building, fast. Hide in the canyon," he instructed, then darted for his car, an official Park Service vehicle recognizable by the emblems on the doors.

At the end of the driveway he stopped and, in a gesture to false security, pulled the swinging gate shut behind him. The plan was to reach a Y-intersection a few miles down the road before the fugitives did and divert the outlaws by parking across the branch leading past the monument. Unaware of what had happened to others who tried to block the flatbed, Hutchinson thought it might work.

Two miles from the monument it got more complicated. Two vehicles approached. Hutchinson knew immediately they weren't dangerous, just tourists on their way to Hovenweep. Waving out his window he flagged them to the side of the road and pulled alongside. "There are armed fugitives in the area," he told them. "Get to Hovenweep; let yourselves in the gate, close it behind you and stay there."

The huddle of cars broke, the two cars of tourists heading north, Hutchinson south. At the next bend, long before the intersection he hoped to reach, he saw it. The flatbed came at him at 70 mph. The truck bounced violently but the shots hit close to his car. Hutchinson slouched low in the seat and drove for the ditch. He peeled the ranger hat from his head and covered his badge with his hand, but if the outlaws were still discriminating between law enforcement and civilians, they knew him for the former. The shooting continued, even after the truck swept past.

Hearing a "popping noise" behind them, the two vehicles of tourists pulled to the side of the road to check their tires. As they leaned out their open doors and confirmed they didn't have flats, the truck roared past. "The man on the passenger side had his elbow out the window as if they were just out for a drive. The man in the back of the truck looked to be enjoying himself," the excited visitors told authorities.

Hutchinson pulled from the ditch into a U-turn as he punched the number for the visitor center on his cell phone. "Get out now! Get everyone to the canyon and hide," he commanded. By the time he reached the tourists, still parked where they had pulled off to check their tires, San Juan County (Utah) Sheriff Deputy Hank Lee was right behind him. Entering the chase from the west rather than Cortez, he was, at that point, the only officer besides Hutchinson close to the fugitives but he was not pressing the pursuit. "Leave the area immediately. Go back the way you came," he told the visitors.

Hutchinson's assistant, Gina, hung up the phone and tried to speak calmly, but couldn't disguise the fact that she was shaken. "We need to go down into the canyon right away," she told the alarmed tourists. From the gravel path leading to the first ruin and the canyon rim, she saw a yellow flatbed speed past the monument driveway on the road below. She guessed it was the fugitives. They didn't stop but they were close, she thought. At any moment, they could turn around and come up the drive looking for hostages.

The switchback path to the bottom of the canyon, eighty feet below, was a well-maintained park trail free of rocks or roots that might cause a stumble, but the pitch in areas was such that hurried hikers could slip and fall. The outside edge of the trail was not steep but stepping off the edge would mean an uncontrolled rough tumble over sharp rocks and brush, and certain injury. Threading her way along the canyon wall with the half-dozen visitors following single file, Gina replayed Hutchinson's order in her head, "Get out NOW!" Then, in five words it was over. "Gina," Hutchinson's shout echoed down the canyon. "It's clear. Come up."

Park Ranger Don Whyte arrived at Hovenweep at the same time as Hutchinson and Lee. Hutchinson set about securing the monument. After calling Gina out of the canyon, he summoned an archeology crew from Kansas State University to come in from a site they were working a few miles away and, over the course of the afternoon, had everyone at the monument escorted from the area. Lee, with Whyte driving behind him as backup, headed out after the suspects. In a few miles, they would each slow down and look down a dirt road that branched off to their left across a hundred yards of whitish-brown, dusty-dry mesa, then dropped steeply into Cross Canyon. By that point several minutes behind the suspects, they would see nothing and continue on without turning.

The fugitives gave no indication of wanting hostages and their flatbed continued on past the monument visitor center. The road, known by several names—Hovenweep Road, Pleasant View Road, Trail of the Ancients Scenic Byway—angled northeast back into Colorado as it skirted along the edge of Cross Canyon. Rounding a near 90-degree curve, two pieces of lumber that had jarred loose from the stack slid from the flatbed and landed at the edge of the pavement. A few yards beyond that the truck braked hard and turned left on a dirt track leading toward the canyon and stopped.

There are no witnesses to what happened next. Facts ascertained over the course of a long investigation suggest that one of the three fugitives, most likely the thin man who had ridden in the passenger seat, hopped from the truck.[2] The details can only be surmised.

The man slung his AK-47 over his shoulder, took a sip from his water bottle and confirmed the plan with his companions. Then, nodding good-bye, turned and stepped into an easy trot that even in the one-hundred-degree desert heat, he knew he could maintain for miles.

The flatbed followed the dirt road down over the edge of the canyon wall where it wound back and forth along the face to the floor. Rolling from one hairpin turn to another the driver braked to check speed on the steep descent, staring anxiously at the rearview mirror to ensure he wasn't raising a smoke-signal plume of dust. Near the bottom, where the road flattened into a long chalky strip, the driver spotted a gravel wash and stepped down on the gas pedal. A vestige of flowing water that had since changed its course, the wash was lined with belly rolls of deposited gravel. If they could get the truck to the other side of the nearest mound, it would be hidden from the road. It could take days for the authorities to find it.

The speedometer swept past 40. The driver hoped the momentum would carry the flatbed across the dry streambed, up and over the mound to its far side. Instead, it left the road airborne. Then as the front bumper cleared the top of the berm, forward motion ceased. The truck crashed to earth hard. Lumber in the truck bed launched twenty-five feet through the air. The chassis buried itself in gravel past the door bottoms. It was likely at this point that the impact of the floorboard hitting the top of the mound surged upward against the feet of the occupants, forcefully jamming the left ankle bones of the heavyset man in the passenger seat. A sharp pain spiked up his leg.

Shifting gears, the driver urged the truck forward but the flatbed straddled the mound, denying traction to tires suspended in loose gravel. Attempting to get out, they pushed against the doors but the bottoms were burrowed too deep in the earth to open. Pressing their feet against the windshield, they popped it out; shimmied through the opening and stepped across the hood.

Left where it was, the truck compromised their hope to vanish without a trace. But the flatbed had been outfitted for construction work and in its toolbox they found a winch. Stretching it between the front bumper and a tree on the backside of the mound, they cranked the winch handle back and forth until the webbing yielded all the elasticity it had, but the truck didn't move. Their headstart was rapidly eroding.

Rifle in hand, the passenger scrambled to a narrow rock shelf overlooking the wash. There he slid on his belly into a crevice under overhanging rock, spread his legs for stability, set a spare clip of ammo on the rock near his right shoulder and swung his SKS rifle from right to left and back again, making sure he had clear shots covering the entire area.

With his friend on lookout, the second man began tearing branches from greasewood bushes and clumps of sage from the hillside. In five minutes the truck was covered. It wasn't invisible from up close, but it would be hard to spot by someone glassing the area from a distant rim, or flying over in an airplane.

The two men, dressed in camouflage clothing and bulletproof vests, left their assault rifles near the truck, took .308 FN FAL combat rifles from the duffle bags they had transferred from the tanker to the flatbed and walked into the desert.

It had been two hours since the flatbed and fugitives were last seen speeding past Hovenweep Monument. At the speeds they had been reported traveling, that expanded the search area by a hundred and fifty miles. Still, patrols from the San Juan County Sheriff's Office cruised the area where the flatbed was last seen. Sheriff Mike Lacy, following the same path the fugitives had taken past the monument, slowed when he spotted lumber at the edge of the road. Figuring it fell from the flatbed, he reported it but had no hint that a few feet beyond the lumber was the dirt road the outlaws had turned down.

At the same time that Lacy drove past the dirt road leading into the depths of Cross Canyon, his deputy, Alan Freestone, was on it. Cross Canyon Road (Utah Road 214) snaked down one wall of the canyon, cut diagonally across the bottom and climbed back out the other side. Having entered the canyon from the west, Freestone was traveling in the opposite direction that the fugitives had driven. He traversed the canyon floor and was just beginning the twisting climb to the east rim when he spotted tire tracks leaving the road. He didn't see the truck on his first scan of the area but when he looked again, there it was, peeking out from behind a pile of brush. It was 12:47 P.M., more than three hours since Claxton was killed and the search for the murderers began.

Three other officers in the vicinity responded to his call for backup. One was only three or four minutes away, the others less than ten. Freestone didn't wait. In a move that, if the suspects were still in the area would have meant his certain death, he drew his gun and approached the flatbed's driver's side door.

As the other officers arrived, they cleared the immediate area and secured the scene. Empty casings from the truck bed were on the ground. Bullet holes across the hood attested to the difficulty of shooting an automatic weapon from a bouncing vehicle. The first of two duffle bags found in the rear of the truck was empty. The second held a loaded SKS rifle.

The officers spiraled outward from around the abandoned truck, systematically widening the search area. "Gun," one yelled and they dropped low. The deputy who shouted pointed to a rifle barrel protruding from a crevice under a rock ledge. Crouching they moved toward the weapon until they were each within fifteen feet and stood surrounding it. "Don't move," they ordered. No response. The only things left in the crevice were an SKS rifle with a white plastic stock and bayonet knife attached, and an extra clip of ammunition.

Freestone and a Utah state trooper followed two sets of footprints a few yards into a gully, then deciding not to venture too far on their own, rejoined the others and waited for help to arrive.

Police estimate that more than six hundred rounds were fired in the course of the chase. None by police. In fact, the only officer to have even managed to get his weapon out with the suspects in sight was Deputy Todd Martin, and he was shot down before he could get a shell in the chamber. It was a full two hours, 3 P.M., before the first four-man SWAT team arrived at the site of the abandoned flatbed to begin the search. By 6 P.M. that number had swelled to more than two hundred officers. What would rapidly expand into the largest manhunt in the history of the West, a grueling, embarrassing search that would last nine years, had begun.

CHAPTER 7
NAMES

Sergeant Detective Jim Shethar sat up in the same instant he woke up. With his receding hair cropped too short to be mussed by restless sleep and a lean strong-jawed face that at age forty-seven still resisted the sags of fatigue, only the crumple of his clothes betrayed the long hours he'd been putting in. It took a moment to collect his thoughts, to recollect why he was not home in bed. The ache in his shoulders reminded him just where he was. He rolled them forward, then backward to stretch out the cramp pressed into his body by the hard sleeping surface; then stood from the exercise mat in his stocking feet. Carrying his shoes, he made his way in the dark to the door, careful not to step on any of the other officers still sleeping around him.

It was the second night in a row he'd worked well past midnight at the command center, then slept a few hours on the floor of the Cortez Police Department exercise room before resuming the investigation of Dale's murder. It was one of many such nights in the first couple of weeks after the incident and what sleep he got was inadequate respite from the eighteen-hour workdays they were putting in, hoping to get a step ahead of the killers.

Agents from the FBI resident agency in Durango as well as the Denver field office had shown up the afternoon of the murder. For the uniform officers of the Cortez Police Department in shock from the brutal murder of their colleague hours before, there should have been some comfort in the agents' presence. There wasn't. "They walked around in their suits telling everyone what a good job they'd done and to buck up," one Cortez policeman recalled. It would be too strong to use the words "arrogant" for the feds or "resentful" for the locals, but a culture gap was evident right from the start and it quickly became clear Cortez PD wasn't going to get help on the terms they wanted.

"We needed someone to take over, take command," Shethar said. The case had escalated far beyond a local department's scope or capability in its first twenty minutes, he explained. In addition, the Cortez department and the county sheriff's office had just taken severe blows to their staff and morale. "The departments were devastated, the officers were numb, frozen," a CBI agent noted. For reasons no one understood, the FBI offered assistance but refused to take over the case.

There were multiple grounds on which the FBI could have assumed control as the lead agency: during their escape the killers had shot at a federal officer, National Park Service Ranger Art Hutchinson. The killers had crossed state lines. Finally, much of the search would take place on Indian reservation land, thus in the FBI's jurisdiction.

Cortez Police Chief Roy Lane knew taking the lead on the investigation of Dale's murder was the straw that could break his grief-stricken department's back but someone had to take responsibility for finding out who those boys were, what they were up to, who else might be involved and, most important, how they could be caught. So the twenty-two officers and staff of the Cortez Police Department buried their pain. They didn't talk about their anxious sleepless nights, their blood-splattered nightmares, or the moments when they were alone and suddenly, without warning, found themselves sobbing. They went to work.

"Chief Lane explained the situation, that it was something we had to do. I was a detective. It was my job; so I stepped forward," Shethar said. At first, Shethar and his Cortez PD colleagues moved cautiously among the celebrated crime-fighting agencies. In time, however, Shethar's desk would become the repository for every lead, theory and piece of evidence uncovered. Shethar would become the point man for the investigation and his fellow officers would drive the case forward long after it had lost its priority and momentum within the other agencies.

The official flow chart listed Cortez PD along with the Colorado Bureau of Investigation as overseeing the investigative side of the case, the county sheriff departments responsible for pursuit based on leads and the FBI managing the manhunt. The lines of responsibility blurred, however, even before Officer Claxton's body was removed from his car. San Juan County, Utah, Sheriff Mike Lacy and Dolores County, Colorado, Sheriff Jerry Martin had assumed joint control of the manhunt as tactical teams poured into Cross Canyon at the site of the abandoned flatbed truck. As the FBI asserted its authority, command of the manhunt was vague and fluid.

CBI set up a command post in the training room of the new Cortez police station the afternoon of the murder and confidently took control of the crime scene investigation, but with a forty-mile path of mayhem and the identification of eight separate crime scenes plus ten impounded vehicles within the first three hours, the staff from the regional office in Montrose was quickly overwhelmed. As a result, one of the first and most important of the thirty locations eventually identified as significant to the case, the site of the abandoned flatbed in Cross Canyon, received only tertiary attention from the case's lead investigators.

Complicating the situation further, while officially not in command, the FBI asserted its control through its expertise and superior resources. "They were not in command . . . but they were in charge," Shethar said. "They were the ones who assigned priority to leads and directed people each morning." The ambiguity weakened the police response in the first critical weeks after Claxton's murder. "It was a problem all along, no one was in clear command, no single agency had control and coordination of the entire operation," he added.

By the second day, the FBI moved into the command post and onto the case full force. Shethar watched a steady stream of trucks pull up to the station and workmen wheel office equipment into the training room. Large marker boards on rolling stands covered one wall. A setup crew placed three long tables parallel across the width of the room, each divided into multiple workstations for the twenty-five or so people usually occupying the command post at a time, but there were additional equipment and supplies for the frequent times when the number of people bustling about the room swelled to fifty. Used to the budgets and operations of a small city police force, Shethar stared drop-jawed at the feds' resources but CBI agent Earl Christenson was equally impressed. "The amount of resources the feds pulled into a rural area overnight was powerful, truly amazing," he exclaimed. "Copy machines, secretaries, surveillance equipment, every technology, tool and skill that may have been helpful."

Except one: the new facility had been wired to accommodate a large phone bank and one was quickly established, but it hadn't been wired for cable TV. The major news organizations had mobile units covering the manhunt forty miles from Cortez in the Utah canyons. "Without a TV and the ability to tune in to CNN, we really didn't know what was going on out there," Shethar said. The Cortez command post was essentially blind to the manhunt for the first days of the operation, until it finally got a TV hooked up, he said.

Among the resources the FBI brought to the investigation was its Rapid Start Information Control System. Unknown to the local police agencies, it was a technology for recording, connecting and tracking leads. It was an imperfect system, dependent on the officers and agents who received the tips or investigated a lead to record it properly. Over the course of the investigation leads were lost or missed, statements from witnesses misplaced, and efforts duplicated. But without the Rapid Start System, the investigation would have been quickly paralyzed. News of Claxton's murder and the guns-blazing escape spread quickly across the region. By evening, it was national news. Among the residents of Four Corners, there was no shortage of opinions as to who was involved, what the fugitives were planning and where they might be. The phones in the command post began ringing almost immediately and tips flowed in by the hundreds.

Claxton's body remained in the bullet-riddled vehicle. Blood, pooled on the passenger seat, began to skim over. Brain and tissue on the dashboard dried and shriveled. Even to a veteran policeman, hardened to violent death encountered at car accidents or other tragedies, being on McElmo Bridge that Friday morning was hard duty. The dead man didn't look peaceful. It wasn't a body with a tidy small-caliber bullet wound in the chest or a stab wound in the back. It was a body mutilated by repeated, concentrated gunfire. And it wasn't the body of a stranger.

Duty forced Cortez police officers Vern Rucker, Russell Johnson and Chief Roy Lane to be there. In the performance of that duty they found activities to shield them from the full, brutal, devastating force of Dale's death. Robotically, they unrolled yellow crime scene tape, drew chalk circles around shell casings scattered across the pavement, shot photos, made measurements, drew diagrams and jotted down the names of citizens who may have seen or heard what happened. Sometime around 10 A.M., a little more than half an hour after Dale's murder, Chief Lane requested help from the Colorado Bureau of Investigation.

It took CBI agents Kevin Humphreys and Wayne Bryant five hours to pack and prepare for the assignment, then drive the 145 miles of mostly winding mountain roads separating their agency's western region office in Montrose, Colorado, and McElmo Bridge. Both veteran criminologists, Humphreys was the "blood and guts" specialist; Bryant was the weapons and fingerprint guy. They were first of several CBI agents who would arrive in Cortez that day and spend most of the next several weeks in the area.

Humphreys showed his credentials to the police blocking traffic onto CR 27, then wove the CBI evidence van slowly through the tangle of police cars parked in front of the bridge. He stopped a few feet short of the crime scene tape. It was 3:00 P.M. The few officers inside the corral of yellow tape and police vehicles moved about slowly, going through the motions of purposeful activity. They had long ago completed what tasks they could to protect the crime scene. Now, they were just waiting for his and Bryant's arrival.

At every crime scene but Cross Canyon that day, the local officers had done an exemplary job of protecting the scene and preserving the evidence, Humphreys said. The search of crime scene number one took two hours. The location of several empty shell casings on the pavement and road shoulder had already been marked. A search with a metal detector on the far side of the guardrail turned up a few more. In the end they found twenty-five casings of the presumably thirty shells in a full clip emptied at Claxton. Other than tire tracks from the tanker, nothing else was discovered at the scene significant to understanding the incident.

At Bryant's request, officers placed numbered placards next to each shell and photographed them while a sheriff office investigator from a neighboring county made plaster casts of the tanker's tire tracks left in the gravel shoulder. Bryant meanwhile examined bullet holes in Claxton's car to approximate the slugs' trajectories.

At 5:45 P.M., more than eight hours after the murder at McElmo Bridge, a sheriff deputy from La Plata County helped Assistant County Coroner Will Porter and mortician Keenan Ertel remove Claxton's body from his vehicle and place it in a body bag. The vehicle, itself, remained at the bridge until it was dark enough for Bryant to resume trajectory studies. As Bryant aimed a laser beam along bullet paths in the vehicle, another officer sighted a rifle along the beam back toward the car.

By 10:15, Bryant knew exactly where the killer stood for each fusillade, but for him and Humphreys the long hours had just begun. Following the tow truck pulling Claxton's car to the Cortez City Garage, the two investigators embarked on a three-day, around-the-clock forensic marathon processing the evidence routed to the site from various crime scenes. Eating food delivered to them and napping in chairs while one waited for his partner to complete his part of a sequential task, the two never left the garage except for white-knuckle dashes "over the hill" to evaluate evidence at the CBI crime lab in Montrose.

The first of those occurred before sunrise on Saturday, one day after Claxton was killed. Humphreys sat stiffly behind the wheel of the CBI evidence van, his brow furrowed in an effort to keep his eyes wide open. Beside him Bryant had in his possession a small case in which he'd placed slides of latent fingerprints found on the tanker, flatbed and recovered weapons. As the van raced along the guardrail that separated it from thin air, climbing toward the ten-thousand-foot summit of Lizard Head Pass, Humphreys' eyes snapped open with a jerk of his head and refocused on the road ahead. It was his third turn driving already and it had only been fifteen minutes since they last traded off, but he knew the next time exhaustion pulled his lids shut it would be for more than a nanosecond. He nudged Bryant awake and watched for a wide spot in the road to pull over. Twenty minutes later it would be his turn again. The frequent switching turned the difficult three-hour trip into an impossible four-hour journey but it was either that or stop for a few hours of sleep. Even at that moment, police were amassing on the Colorado-Utah border and still they had no idea who it was they were seeking. Rest was not an option.

The Automated Fingerprint Identification System at the CBI crime lab sorted scans of the fingerprints Bryant brought from Cortez according to general characteristics, the existence of loops, whorls or arches. Then, within which of those general categories the latent prints belonged, it searched for a match from its statewide database of criminal fingerprint records. The statewide database for the young technology, however, was still limited. While there were ten-print ink cards on file at local police jurisdictions for two of the men ultimately linked to the crime, they hadn't yet been added to the AFIS system and the search came up blank. By 4:30 P.M. Humphreys and Bryant were back at the Cortez City Garage without a forensic identification of Claxton's killers.

As Humphreys and Bryant processed the crime scene at McElmo Bridge and searched the many vehicles involved in the spree for evidence, other CBI agents worked the multiple other crime scenes created by the day's events: the site where the tanker was left and the flatbed pickup truck was stolen, the scenes where Deputies Bishop and Martin were shot plus the locations of six other vehicles hit by gunfire.

CBI agents wouldn't make it to Cross Canyon where the flatbed was abandoned, however, for over a week. Instead they relayed instructions for preserving evidence at the scene. Weapons, ammunition, shell casings and duffle bags found at the site, as well as the vehicle itself were delivered to them in Cortez.

It was in Cross Canyon on the day of Claxton's murder that police response to the incident unexpectedly swelled and the search for the fugitives veered out of control. Virtually every law officer in a lead position with either the manhunt or investigation concurs that the first serious setback in bringing the killers to justice was the failure of officers first on that scene to protect it and investigators to properly process it. By the time forensic specialists did attempt to process the site, hundreds of police had descended into the canyon and crossed the crime scene. Where there had been two sets of footprints leading away from the truck, by the time of CBI's arrival there were dozens. Much of what evidence or clues the site might have yielded was trampled and destroyed.

On the tenth day of the manhunt, after having been summoned to document footprints in another location that turned out to have been made by San Juan County deputies, Humphreys and Bryant hiked into Cross Canyon to find what was left of the fugitives' tracks. The hope was to find some distinguishing characteristics of their boot prints that would allow manhunt officers, many of whom were not expert trackers, to readily distinguish them from footprints made by the hundreds of police walking the area in similar military-style boots. Based on footprints found at the disposal site where the tanker was stolen and then on the truck's dashboard, searchers already knew one of the fugitives left a somewhat distinctive footprint: parallel tread lines across the fore-sole, interrupted by an oval imprint under the ball of the foot, and round lug impressions on the heel.

Enough of the fugitive's trail remained that Humphreys and Bryant, like other officers before them, managed to follow it into the ravine, but as they moved out of sight of the spot where the flatbed was abandoned into the area where an outlaw sniper could be settling crosshairs on them, FBI agents in charge of the manhunt ordered them back. The faded footprints provided Bryant with enough information to classify the footwear into a narrower category of sole characteristics, but left little to document.

Losing the opportunity to photograph the tracks and make plaster casts was a mistake that would haunt the investigation for years to come as law enforcement agencies debated which two fugitives began their flight on foot together.

Also overlooked in the rush to chase after the killers was the windshield the fugitives had kicked from the flatbed to exit the vehicle. Lying on the ground a few yards from the truck, it too would have shown boot prints as well as possibly palm and fingerprints. Unfortunately, it lay in the desert for a month before a police officer touring the scene with a reporter discovered it. The windshield was sent to the FBI crime lab as vital evidence, but whatever clues it may have provided had been erased by the elements.

Shethar and FBI agent Dot Graham compared statements from the few witnesses who had gotten a close look at the suspects either at McElmo Bridge or during their flight. Their descriptions were encouragingly uniform and disappointingly vague. It was a small community, yet no one recognized the assailants. Not by name or even recollection of having seen them around. Most witness sightings were fleeting glimpses of masked men in a truck flying by at 70 mph, or glances stolen under the duress of gunfire.

Estimates of the individuals' height and weight varied but there was general agreement that there were three men in the trucks: a thin man with shoulder-length sandy-colored hair; a heavy-set man with a full fat face, glasses and long brown hair; and a man with shorter, brown hair. All were Caucasian and appeared to be in their mid-twenties. At McElmo Bridge the tanker driver was reportedly wearing a yellow slicker and headgear with a clear face shield. Sightings after that, including a long careful look when the trio stole the flatbed truck, reported all three men in commando-style clothing. They wielded assault rifles.

Even that much of a description was enough to start the flow of tips. Callers inundated police dispatchers with general leads and specific accusations, none of which named or provided information directly pointing to the three men that in time became the focus of the investigation. Many reported activities of paramilitary militia groups. Others turned in acquaintances, "My ex-boyfriend is an escaped convict from prison in Ohio. He could have done this." Or, "A guy I work with hates cops and has automatic weapons in his basement."

The fugitives hoped to remain anonymous. They had been secretive about their plans, made up cover stories for their whereabouts, and even as their grand scheme came apart at the seams after killing Claxton, the most visible of them wore a mask. Their hope was short-lived.

Although the forensic teams were frustrated in their efforts to identify the killers based on physical evidence, investigators were well on the path to putting names to the suspects within twenty-four hours of the murder. Canvassing homes near the disposal site where the tanker was stolen, police quickly located a homeowner who not only noticed a suspicious vehicle in the area within the last couple of days—a blue and gray Nissan pickup truck—but also wrote down its license plate number. At the same time, the Bureau of Alcohol, Tobacco and Firearms traced one of the SKS rifles recovered near the abandoned flatbed through its serial number to the gun store that sold it. With a little more footwork, those breaks would lead police to the trailer home of the twenty-six-year-old construction worker who owned the Nissan pickup truck and the name of a thirty-year-old mechanic linked to the SKS rifle found near the abandoned flatbed. As it turned out, an anonymous tip and frantic family members led to the suspects' identities even faster than that line of inquiry.

The complaint clerk at the FBI's Denver regional office checked the caller ID as soon as she hung up the phone. The woman on the other end wouldn't give her name but the information was all there on the electronic display, the phone number she'd called from and a name associated with that number. The woman's message was passed on to Special Agent Pete Klismet in Cortez. "Alan L. Pilon from Dove Creek is a person who might have been involved in the Cortez shootings. He is a known militia affiliate and recently told someone he was going to do something drastic."

It was one more of many cryptic leads and seemingly groundless tips police had received since Claxton was killed just ten hours earlier. A quick records check, however, kept the lead near the top of the pile. Alan Pilon, police determined, was in fact a real person who had close relatives living near the spot where the flatbed was ditched. In addition to parents in Dove Creek, police erroneously concluded Pilon had a brother, Shawn, living in Dolores.[1]

The anonymous call originated in the Denver metro area. Klismet reached FBI Agent Jeff Snow there at home. It was past 9 P.M., but Snow needed to interview the woman as soon as possible. At 4 A.M., the day after Claxton's murder, Snow called back. The news was discouraging. After a fifty-minute phone interview with the woman in which she claimed to have consorted with notorious crime figures from Denver's past and to have supplied the gun that killed Martin Luther King, Snow concluded she was of "questionable mental stability."

"I seriously questioned the credibility of anything she had to say," he added.

What she did have to say was that she knew people in Dove Creek who were close friends of Alan Pilon. Through them she learned that Pilon had that same week confided to friends that he was going to commit a crime, "something drastic." And Pilon's friends, some of whom supposedly knew more of his plans, were certain he was one of the shooters.

Later that morning, despite the informant's patently false claims and odd self-aggrandizement, her tip gained considerable weight. The purchase registration linked the SKS assault rifle with the white composite folding stock found near the ditched flatbed to a Francis Pilon of Dove Creek. The gun store clerk recalled that the gun was purchased by Francis for his son, Alan Pilon, who didn't have proper ID to purchase it himself. It was the same name supplied by the anonymous informant.

At the same time, Colorado vehicle registration records provided a second name. A Jason McVean owned the suspicious vehicle spotted by a homeowner near the disposal site where the water tanker was stolen. The connection between McVean and the crime was tenuous, but as had been the case with Pilon at first, it was a straw worth grasping in light of what little else had been discovered. Bryant flew to Montrose with fingerprint cards for the two men obtained from local police agencies but a comparison to the latent prints found on the tanker, flatbed and recovered weapons proved inconclusive. In addition, investigators still did not have a name for the third suspect nor a connection between the two individuals who had emerged as persons of interest. That came later that evening when Chuck Mason walked into the Durango police station.

Chuck Mason had been stewing about it all day: the news reports of the incident and descriptions of the assailants, the timing and location of his brother's camping trip, his brother's antigovernment attitude and militia posturing. In his mind he knew the painful truth, Bobby was part of it.

He had driven from Denver to Durango to visit his parents, Ann and Gary Mason, the day before—the day of the shooting. Radio newscasters described the drama incessantly during the six-hour drive. Then, before going to his parents' home, he stopped to visit a friend at a local police agency and together they speculated on what it was all about. Now, late in the afternoon the day after the shooting he had to do the hardest thing he had ever done. He had to tell his parents that he was all but certain their youngest child was a murderer.

Earlier that afternoon Ann had called the Cortez command post to let police know her son was camping in the same area as the manhunt. Now as Chuck suggested that the camping trip was a ruse, Ann Mason reeled at the implications. Rebelling at Chuck's logic, her mind scrambled for another explanation. Other than improbable coincidence there was none, but with a mother's faith she clung to the one sustaining conviction her psyche would allow, "No, that could not be true! He would not do such a thing."

Chuck's reasoning tore at Gary Mason's soul as deeply, but with growing horror as Chuck talked, he found himself thinking the unthinkable: "Bobby was one of the three men at McElmo Bridge yesterday. He was being hunted by police at that moment."

Hoping to find some shred of evidence that contradicted reason, Chuck and Gary sped across town to the industrial park where Bobby's best friend and camping buddy Jason lived in a trailer and where Bobby often hung out. What they hoped to find was uncertain. If neither Bobby nor his truck were there, that would be consistent with his story of going camping but not diminish the possibility that he was one of the fugitives. Even if his truck was there, it would only imply they took Jason's vehicle this trip.

What they found, however, further confirmed their suspicions. Bobby, it appeared, was not camping. No one was home at the trailers. Bobby's truck was there. In the bed were four fully packed backpacks along with extra clothing and water containers. One of the packs was Bobby's. It was gear Bobby would have had with him if he were camping. On the way back home to deliver the bad news to Ann, Gary dropped Chuck off at the Durango police station.

"I suspect that my brother, Robert Matthew Mason, might be involved with the shooting in Cortez," Chuck told the police sergeant. His statement continued with a description of Bobby's antigovernment, anti-cop attitude; survivalist paramilitary self-identity; possession of commando gear and guns, including AK-47s; the suspicious circumstances of his supposed camping trip; and his friendship with Jason McVean.

The questioning had gone on for hours; first a statement to Durango police and then telling everything all over again to a Detective Shethar from Cortez PD. It was past midnight by the time Chuck Mason left the station and the close of day two after Claxton's murder. The evidence was circumstantial and even by those standards awfully thin. It wasn't enough to release names to the media. But police knew who they were looking for. Pilon was linked most directly to the crime through a gun found with the abandoned flatbed truck. McVean's name had surfaced through two separate inquiries. Mason fit the profile of the suspects and was linked to McVean. From the moment Jim Shethar shook hands with Chuck Mason and thanked him for coming in, the investigation focused on those three men. It would remain so for the next nine years.

The next day, Robert Mason's driver's license photo was among the photos of eighteen different men spread on the table in front of the McElmo Canyon motorist who had been run off the road by the speeding flatbed truck. The motorist didn't get a good look at the other two men in the truck but he did notice the driver. He pointed immediately to Mason's picture, "That's the man who was driving." Police at last had positive eyewitness identification of one of the fugitives.

Sunday, May 31, the third day after Claxton's murder, police put Jason McVean's trailer in Durango's Animas Air Industrial Park and Mason's truck under surveillance. The effort was rewarded shortly after noon. A couple of miles from the stakeout, Detective Shethar sat in the Masons' living room talking to Gary and Ann Mason about their son. In the course of the interview, he learned that a woman named Linda Wallace, whom neither Gary nor Ann knew, had called their home worried about Bobby and Jason. At about the same time, police watching McVean's trailer watched a dark-haired woman pull up, take a shotgun from her car and head for an adjacent shed.

Wallace told police she was McVean's girlfriend. Jason had given her the shotgun and she was moving it and her other possessions into the shed which Jason had built for her to live in temporarily. She had left a message on the Masons' answering machine because she too had noticed the camping gear in Bobby's truck, recognized one of the packs as McVean's and leapt to the same frightening conclusion—Jason and Bobby were at McElmo Bridge.

She talked cautiously about McVean but off-handedly mentioned he had recently purchased shooting glasses with rectangular amber lenses. The description matched glasses found above the tanker's passenger-side sun visor and tied McVean tighter to the crime. Then she provided the information that pulled it all together. Jason and his best friend Bobby Mason had a friend named Alan who lived in Dove Creek right across the street from the high school (Pilon's family residence). Plates on a second camping trailer on the opposite edge of the McVean Construction Company property showed it was registered to Alan Pilon. Together on the same property within a hundred feet of each other stood two camping trailers and a pickup truck. All three suspects whose names had surfaced through independent threads of the investigation were tied together.

Before the afternoon ended, Wallace led police to a nearby gravel pit where she and Jason had shot his AK-47. Jason picked up most of the empty casings, she explained, but he'd missed some. The next morning CBI matched one of those casings with a casing found on McElmo Bridge, concluding both had been fired in the same gun.

At the press conference Monday, police made public that the investigation had identified three men as persons of interest in the case. Contrary to rumor, the men were not from Cortez, they confirmed. Police refused, however, to identify the men by name, claiming they were not yet suspects. In truth the men were more than suspected. Police were certain they did it. Leads unrelated to McVean, Mason and Pilon were no longer relevant. The investigation focused on a new set of questions: What were the three planning? Who else was involved? Where would they turn for help? Who might aid and abet them? Where were their caches of guns and supplies buried? Underlying all those questions was the one police wanted the answer to most of all—where are they now?

Police believed the answer to that question hinged on another mystery; where was McVean's truck? It was not parked near his trailer in Animas Air Park or any other locations connected to the suspects. Despite the BOLO (Be On the LookOut for) broadcast to surrounding police agencies, it had not been spotted since it sped from the Ignacio disposal facility on the day the tanker was stolen.

That evening, luck again moved the investigation forward when a telephone company technician doing line work along a rural road reported its location—thirty miles from Cortez and even farther from the search area. The technician didn't know the truck was sought in connection with the Cortez shooting everyone was talking about, only that it appeared suspicious. He first spotted the vehicle alongside the road Saturday and at noon two days later it was still there. Towed to the city garage in Cortez along with Mason's truck, the vehicles provided clues about the killers but no further hints where they might be or where they were headed.

As police searched for McVean's truck, investigators began questioning people on their growing list of McVean associates and Pilon confidants. The answers they heard further convinced police the men they were seeking could indeed have committed such a crime. The fugitives' closest friends were not shocked to learn the three were suspects in the brutal murder of a police officer. Amongst themselves they had already reached that conclusion. But none admitted to knowing of their buddies' criminal plans, the location of desert caches and hideouts, or to having heard from them since McElmo Bridge.

The chain of evidence identifying McVean, Mason and Pilon as the men who killed Claxton and wounded Deputies Bishop and Martin was more than sufficient for Colorado District Court Judge Sharon Hansen. At noon on Tuesday, June 2, four days after McElmo Bridge, she signed arrest warrants for the three men charging them with first-degree murder of a police officer, assault in the first degree and aggravated motor vehicle theft. At the same time, the FBI secured federal arrest warrants in US District Courts charging each of the subjects with carjacking, interstate flight to avoid prosecution and attempted murder of a federal officer. The killers had a public face.

CHAPTER 8
TANKER

The evening of Wednesday, May 27, two days before McElmo Bridge, had found the almost inseparable trio of McVean, Mason and Pilon without each other's company. McVean was with his girlfriend, promising upon leaving that he would return from his camping trip by Saturday night to help her move. Mason stopped by his parents where he told them he was going camping until Sunday and left his German shepherd, Dirk, in their care. Pilon, without a driver's license or transportation, was probably waiting at his trailer. He had told friends earlier he had a job out of the area and would be gone several weeks. Sometime after 9 P.M., however, they were together once again at Animas Air Park, an industrial park on the southwest edge of Durango, where McVean and Pilon both lived in trailers parked next to the shop for a metal building construction company owned by McVean's father.

Some of the men's movements between then and the time they crossed McElmo Bridge were affirmed by witnesses and other evidence. Some of what transpired between those known moments can be reasonably inferred. The rest is blank.

The dozens of other people who worked at the industrial park and drove past the McVean property between seven and eight o'clock the morning of May 28, 1998, didn't notice if McVean's Nissan pickup truck with a pinto pattern of original blue and spray-can gray primer was still there. Sometime around then it left. McVean drove. Mason and Pilon crowded into the passenger seat alongside of him. The drive to the oil field brine disposal facility near Ignacio, Colorado, took a little over thirty minutes.'

On the short road that flanked the eastern edge of the facility, McVean stopped twice, allowing first one passenger to bail out, then a hundred yards farther on, the second man. A gas wellhead and dirt berm between the facility and the road provided sufficient cover that anyone at the facility glancing that direction would not have seen either deployment. McVean waited behind, ready to drive his friends to safety if they came dashing back.

The facility was a complex of two metal buildings and several large steel storage tanks with gantry ladders welded to their sides, all linked by oversize plumbing and surrounded by a graded dirt driveway and parking area. There was no perimeter fencing or security equipment. It was normally unmanned except for the tanker truck drivers who transported water pumped up with the crude at area oil wells. Separated at the surface, the saline wastewater was hauled to disposal sites like the one Mason and Pilon were sneaking onto. Only two drivers had been working at the facility in recent weeks. Most of the time they were away siphoning up brine and hauling it. In addition, two welders were doing some repair work on the far western edge of the complex.

The temperature was still in the low forties when tanker driver Caroline Clark arrived at the facility a few minutes after sunrise. By 8 A.M. Caroline had dumped her second load. The thermometer was climbing rapidly toward a high of eighty-one, ten degrees hotter than normal. She took her first soda break of the day, pulling a can of Wild Cherry Pepsi from the cooler she kept in the back of her pickup. The cooler was exactly where it always was, tucked tightly against the cab directly behind the driver. At 10 A.M. she went for a second soda. The cooler was still there, but now it sat a foot out from the cab on the passenger side of the truck.

Based on their footprints leading from the berm and wellhead,

Mason and Pilon entered the disposal site a hundred yards apart and converged at the parked pickup trucks where they milled about the vehicles. Sometime between Clark's soda breaks, one of them apparently reached across the bed of Clark's truck, dragged the cooler by its handle toward him and helped himself to a soda while they bided their time.

Overright tanker No. 3 was parked on the south side of the complex. It had been idle since company owner Mike Overright downsized his Ignacio operation from three to two trucks. Clark drove unit No. 2 and Robert DeHerrera was out with unit 4. All three tankers were about the same except for model year—white with OVERRIGHT TRUCKING painted on the doors. They were big brutes of trucks; thirty-two feet in length, tandem rear axles with dual wheels, waist-high tires and an imposing eighteen-foot cylindrical tank on the back.

Clark and DeHerrera were servicing nearby wells that day. The runs were short and they hauled the wastewater to the site faster than the injection pumps could force it back into the earth. By 11:30 the storage tanks were full and their workday was over. They parked their tankers next to unit 3, looked about the facility double-checking that this valve was open and that valve was shut, bid each other good-bye and left. DeHerrera headed home. Clark headed to Ignacio to get a cold soda since those remaining in her cooler were warm.

Shortly after Clark and DeHerrera ended their workday and headed home, Mason and Pilon headed for what looked to be the newest of the three tanker trucks, unit No. 4. It was, in fact, the current year model, only a few months out of the factory. The truck was locked but from having worked on such vehicles, Pilon would have known it was a common practice to hide the key in the battery box. Within minutes they gained entry to the cab, started the vehicle and drove it away.

McVean, meanwhile, waiting in his truck parked adjacent to the site, was being viewed suspiciously by a nearby resident. When she stepped from her home and began walking toward him to ask what he wanted, McVean sped away. She took down his license plate number.

On her way back a few minutes later, Clark saw DeHerrera's unit churning a cloud of dust as it turned from the facility and headed down the road in front of her. "Damn. How come DeHerrera gets to go work at another site and I have to go home?" she muttered to herself. By midafternoon it was still eating at her. She decided to call her boss. "Did you come and get a truck?" she asked, planning to work up to demanding why DeHerrera got extra hours.

"Don't know what you're talking about," Mike Overright answered.

"Unit four is gone. I saw it heading down County Road 311 about noon."

Overright was not overly alarmed. Friends and former drivers often borrowed his trucks to haul stock-water. They almost always asked first but he always said yes and the most likely explanation was that one of them just presumed it was okay. If the friend had used one of Overright's tankers before, he would know that the vehicle's keys were left in the battery box on the side of the truck. Nevertheless, Overright loaded his two small children into his car and drove the hour and a half from his home in Farmington, New Mexico, to Ignacio. He cruised the back roads around the facility hoping to catch sight of the tanker. At sunset, he reported it stolen.

Based on the mileage recorded in the tanker's logbook, the stolen truck had been driven 157 miles after DeHerrera parked it. About a third of those cannot be accounted for, but it appears that from the disposal site, Mason and Pilon drove the tanker thirty-three miles to McVean's trailer in Durango where they stripped it of equipment. Found at McVean's trailer were the tanker's logbook as well as a propane tank and air hose that had been secured to the back of the cab. Also found at McVean's were a five-gallon bucket, a gallon of antifreeze, oil and a grease gun that had been taken from the truck. Among standard Overright tanker equipment apparently left in the truck was a hard hat and a yellow raincoat, articles that eyewitnesses claim the tanker driver wore on McElmo Bridge but which police never found. Added to the truck were an eight-foot stepladder and a coil of rope that belonged to the McVean Construction Company. With black spray paint, they covered over the name OVERRIGHT TRUCKING and the DOT registration number on the doors.

No one who worked at the air park or made deliveries to the businesses there recalled seeing the tanker, but its presence would not have been particularly noteworthy. Part of McVean's shop was leased to a company that serviced hydraulic systems and did mechanical work on oil field vehicles. A water tanker parked on the property was common.

By 3 P.M. Mason and McVean lounged at a friend's home where they often hung out. They acted perfectly normal according to one of the people present. They played video games, talked, did nothing in particular. Toward evening, they showed up at the home of yet another friend, this time with Pilon in tow. In all, a half dozen people whom the trio routinely hung around with showed at the impromptu party. Among them was a man who had been friends with Mason and McVean since eighth grade and felt he knew them best of anyone. He also recalled them behaving as if nothing was wrong that evening. In fact, Mason gregariously ordered pizza for everyone. They were in good moods, he said, except for one uncharacteristically aggressive incident. Everyone was drinking beer and playing horseshoes when Mason and McVean were bothered by a neighbor trimming grass. When the man's Weed Wacker started kicking small pieces of nylon cord over the fence, Mason and McVean got in the guy's face, threatening to "kick his ass."

After the party, sometime in the small hours of the night, the three conspirators embarked on the next stage of their criminal plan. Before leaving Animas Air Park, each man placed a backpack in the bed of Mason's truck parked alongside McVean's trailer. The packs were recognizable as ones the men usually took on their frequent trips to the desert but in addition to camping gear they held winter clothing that wouldn't be needed for months.

Upon the discovery of Mason's truck, the mystery deepened: Who was the fourth pack found in the vehicle intended for? Was a fourth conspirator handed Mason's keys and instructed to rendezvous with the others as their plan unfolded? Police would ultimately catalog everything Mason had with him in the desert, right down to his fingernail clippers. The keys to his truck were not among the items listed, nor were they found among the personal affects the suspects left behind.[1]

Into McVean's truck, the men placed green canvas cargo bags loaded with an assortment of assault rifles, explosives and thousands of rounds of ammunition. One of them got behind the wheel of the tanker, probably Mason since he demonstrated the next morning his proficiency at driving the big multi-geared rig. McVean got into his Nissan pickup and Pilon rode with one of them. Around 4:30 on the morning of May 29, both vehicles turned off Highway 160 running between Durango and Cortez, traveled 3.5 miles south on La Plata County Road 105 and stopped. McVean parked his truck several feet off the roadway. Working by flashlight, the three men piled brush around McVean's vehicle, then climed into the tanker and took off.

Based on the tanker's tire tracks, it backed up to a nearby driveway where it turned around and headed back toward Highway 160. Although the area was remote, CR 105 was traveled during early morning hours by the farmers and ranchers who lived along it. They were able to narrow the time when the distinctive blue and gray-primer Nissan pickup with a homemade wooden flatbed first appeared to within an hour. A telephone company employee servicing the area spotted it the next day and when it was still there at noon two days later (Monday, June 1), he reported it to police. Driven directly, it was twenty-seven miles from McVean's trailer in Durango to the spot where his Nissan was abandoned.

The next positive location for the tanker and three outlaws was across from a campground at Joe Moore Reservoir, nineteen miles from McVean's truck and on the edge of the San Juan National Forest. Campers at the area reported it arrived before 6 A.M., about the same time that the La Plata County Sheriff's Office broadcast an Attempt-To-Locate bulletin for the tanker to surrounding police agencies and entered the theft into the national and state crime information centers. Witnesses said the tanker stayed about an hour but what they did during that time is unknown. Left at the site were cigarette butts, AA batteries (presumably from the flashlights used while concealing McVean's truck and replaced with fresh batteries) and a handheld CB radio (the mate to a unit discovered in the yellow pickup abandoned later that afternoon in Cross Canyon).

The tanker left Joe Moore Reservoir before 7 A.M. Just twenty-six miles from that location, but nearly two and a half hours later, Officer Dale Claxton followed it onto McElmo Bridge. From the parking of McVean's truck alongside CR 105 until the tanker pulled out from Joe Moore Reservoir, the time lapse was consistent with the mileage between the points and the activity or reported length of stay at each location. Between Joe Moore Reservoir and Cortez, however, there was close to two hours when the tanker's whereabouts was beyond conjecture. Assuming that was when the unaccounted-for miles were added to the odometer and not prior to ditching McVean's truck, it appears the fugitives took a forty-five-mile detour and stayed someplace for about an hour. Where or with whom may never be known.

Even more puzzling for police was, Why a water tanker? What criminal plans involving the large truck would be significant enough that the thieves would kill to preserve them? The answer to that question remains speculative but one explanation emerges above all other theories. The intent most in keeping with evidence, reason and the psychological makeup of the suspects was so shocking that authorities hesitated to publicly acknowledge it. What is known is that minutes after reaching Cortez, those plans were interrupted by Officer Claxton. Fifteen minutes after that, the tanker would be in police control, having played its role in the sudden transformation of three young men with virtually no criminal backgrounds into the most-wanted outlaws in the nation.

CHAPTER 9
JASON

. . . Probably going to end up moving to Utah, to the desert. I've got to go live in solitaire . . .

If they attempt to take everyone's firearms away it will be the 1984 everyone once feared. (The 1994 Crime Bill included a Federal Assault Weapons Ban.) If they come busting into my house, I will shoot them. Terrible thing, but the truth is the truth.

I hope Jesus comes quick, or the revolution or whatever is going to happen. Maybe some people can go through life blind and vertically dead, but I can't. I've got to do something rather than nothing. . . . War is necessary in this world and I'm willing to give my life for what is right. I've been burying food over by Lake Powell. So if anything happens like war over the New World Order, I'll be prepared. . . .

—Unmailed letter McVean wrote in February 1995, three years before killing Officer Dale Claxton and fleeing into the Utah desert.

Jason McVean was committed, fanatical; considerate, callous; loving, ruthless; friendly, lonely; informed, credulous; self-reliant, self-indulgent; honorable, treacherous; cooperative, dictatorial; protective of life, a cold killer. He was complex.

In the opening days of the manhunt, police presumed Jason McVean was the group's leader. He was the one who acted the boldest on McElmo Bridge. It was his finger on the trigger of the gun that killed Dale Claxton. It was his vehicle that had been driven to steal the water tanker. It was his trailer that seemed to be the trio's meeting place, where supplies were kept, maps were drawn and bombs were made. After McElmo Bridge, the mystery of McVean's whereabouts long after the other men were accounted for seemed to underscore that impression and in the public's mind fit his growing legend.

The presumption was, in fact, true. Police interviews with people who knew the suspects confirmed McVean was the planner and the decision maker; the other two went along with no evident resistance. Broadly speaking, Mason followed McVean's lead out of intense loyalty; Pilon perhaps out of fear. But in truth, McVean's command over others was subtler than that. He was a natural leader: intelligent, competent and decisive.

He was, first of all, a likeable person. Jason always had a certain charisma, according to people who knew him at different stages of his life. He smiled easily and didn't hesitate to greet people as he passed them on the street. Even the various pictures used on his WANTED posters all show him smiling, from tight-lipped amusement to a wide-open grin. In junior high, parents of classmates found him outgoing, pleasant and polite. In high school and at San Juan Basin Vocational Technical School, which McVean attended after receiving his GED, teachers described him as "quiet and courteous." An instructor at the school emphasized, "This person was not a problem at all." As an adult, people who knew him, from associates at work to casual acquaintances and close friends, remembered him as a nice guy; an extremely courteous, low-key man. His words and actions demonstrated sensitivity to people's feelings, consideration of others, concern for the world around him and a conscious effort to conduct his life according to an idealized moral standard. "Jason was the kind of guy who if he saw someone walking along the side of the road with a gas can, would pick him up, drive him to a gas station, drive him back and even help him put the gas in his car. He was real laid-back and always ready to help people," said Keith Dahl, who owned the business next door to where Jason worked.

It was undoubtedly that nature that earned Pilon's friendship—helping the isolated man with a suspended driver's license and no car to get groceries, make appointments and socialize.

"He brought me firewood all winter long from the free wood pile at the sawmill because he said he didn't want me to be cold," McVean's girlfriend Linda Wallace recalled. "If I had to get up early for work, he'd get up too and build a fire for me so it was warmer when I got out of the shower. That's how he cared for me," she sobbed.

When their troubled friend Marcus (Jason called him "Marcosis") became drunk, morose and belligerent, Jason was the one who sat with him and drew him back from his alcohol-fueled depression. It was how Jason treated his friends.

At the same time McVean harbored a second, hidden nature that twisted his idealism into extremism and his disposition for compassion into brutal indifference. Under the calm, competent, self-reliant Jason McVean festered another personality haunted by feelings of inferiority and wretched with self-pity.

As early as high school, Jason felt he was unequal. On his entrance essay to Colorado Timberline Academy after dropping out of public school, he wrote: "The reason for my wanting to go to the Academy is that the people are a lot cooler and don't think they're better, unlike at this [Durango] high school." It was a sense of his second-class status that defined the remainder of his life, embittered against mainstream society and defiant of authority. In a note scribbled quickly to Wallace a few months before he disappeared, his sense of place in the social order hadn't changed. "Linda, I get the bad feeling you don't like me. I know I'm white trash. . . . Maybe you think I just get in your way. . . ."

Whatever may have been the basis of Jason's low self-esteem, it had blossomed into a full-blown complex shortly after he moved to

Durango at age thirteen. By the time he entered high school two years later, he had descended into self-destructive drug abuse.[1] The personality traits and belief system that would lead to his tragic crime ten years later had begun to metastasize.

Jason's childhood was spent on a small Cleburne, Texas, ranch. His parents divorced when he was four and while such a breach in a child's world can be traumatic, it is an occurrence that millions of children weather without permanent damage. In the case of Jim and Sandy McVean, the breakup was relatively benign. "It was not a bitter divorce," Jim McVean explained. "Sandy and I agreed we'd never put Jason in the middle of it and we never did. We remained friendly and kept in close contact."

After the divorce, Jason was not without family. He lived with his mom but Jim saw him often as well. Free to range across acres of countryside outside his back door, his childhood was outwardly happy, marred only by his dislike of school when mandatory busing into the city made him the country-boy target of urban African American classmates.

At the vulnerable age of thirteen, however, Jason was forced to make a decision with the potential of swamping a young life with guilt, resentment and self-loathing. It was a question with no right answer. His father was moving to Durango, Colorado. At age twelve in Texas, children can choose which parent they wish to live with. Jason, who'd vacationed in Colorado with Jim multiple times, chose to go with him.

It was a lifestyle choice rather than a preference for one parent over the other, Jim explained. "We had family in Durango and he loved the outdoors and camping we'd do whenever we came to visit. Sandy's idea of camping was the Holiday Inn. For a thirteen-year-old boy, the lure of outdoor adventure is strong."

Jim remained a single parent throughout Jason's adolescence. They moved frequently within Durango as Jim built his business as a metal building and roofing contractor, but Jason was beyond the age of neighborhood schools and friendships limited to kids on the same block. Despite the moves, his first years in Colorado were stable at Miller Middle School and he maintained a group of friends from one grade to the next. As a parent, Jim was permissive within limits and Jason enjoyed more freedom than most of his contemporaries. Expecting some wild behavior from boys of that age, Jim believed Jason was a pretty normal teenager. "He got in the kind of trouble now and then that teenage boys do, but nothing serious," he said.

Jason's police record confirms that impression. Despite his reputation throughout high school as a stoner, Jason stayed clear of the police. He was arrested for the first time at age eighteen for theft and criminal trespass. The infraction was a first-degree felony but the actual circumstances of the crime were minor. He pled guilty and paid a hundred-dollar fine. Other than that, the only notations on his police file were a ticket for driving with expired plates and a vehicle accident.

He also was not a standout troublemaker in school. He was not physically aggressive or blatantly disruptive. Instead he was quiet, polite and indifferent. One high school teacher described him as "passively defiant." He showed no inclination toward cooperation, adhering to norms or following rules but neither did he argue nor fight. His grades at Colorado Timberline Academy were mediocre but sufficient to pass. He dropped out because he hated school, not because he didn't have the grades to graduate, his father explained. Jason was blessed with natural intelligence and a somewhat intellectual bent. "Learning is no problem," he wrote, explaining his poor performance in public school, "but I'm around all these people I don't like so after a while your will to do it dies."

Other students alluded to Jason's drug use and school staff concluded he smoked pot almost every day and probably used other drugs as well although they had no specific evidence. On school field trips, teachers suspected Jason's main agenda was getting high and instigating drug use among other students. The suspicion was cemented with his antics during a trip to the Weminuche Wilderness Area in the San Juan Mountains during his senior year at Timberline Academy.

Jason was seventeen at the time. Nine years later as police scrambled to learn what made Jason McVean tick, the teacher in charge of the expedition remembered it vividly.

McVean's high school classmates hiked as a group along the mountain trail. Jason and another student walked at the rear of the class, slowing their pace until a gap separated them from the other students. Then as the rest of the class disappeared around a bend, they darted off the trail through the trees, scuttled down over a rock ledge and disappeared.

Frantic calls by school staff went unanswered. Local authorities rushed to the area and pressed the desperate hunt for the missing students to the far edge of dusk, then resumed it at dawn. Shortly before noon the second day, after having been missing all night, McVean and his tagalong wandered back to the group. He offered no apology or explanation. He didn't care, the teacher reported. For the first time but not the last, police and Forest Service rangers conducted a futile aerial and ground search for Jason McVean across rugged terrain.

Despite his indifference to the conventions of school, Jason didn't struggle at it. He consistently tested well in math and science, and over the whole of his education maintained better than average grades. The exception was the tail end of tenth grade and the first semester of eleventh when drug use and self-imposed alienation undermined his scholarship. After dropping out of public school, his grades recovered somewhat at the private Colorado Timberline Academy. A few months shy of graduation, he quit there, tested for his Graduate Equivalency Diploma and enrolled at San Juan Basin Vocational Technical School, where he pursued a two-year Associate of Applied Science degree and earned a certificate in electronics technology. He earned Bs and Cs in courses such as Technical Mathematics (Trigonometry), Conceptual Physics, Linear and Pulse Circuits, Digital Circuits and Electronic Interfacing. (Knowledge that could be used in the design and building of sophisticated bomb trigger devices.) He did well at vo-tech because at last school seemed to have some practical application for him, his dad said.

McVean seemed to have the native intelligence to master what was important to him. In addition to electronics, he had developed a wide range of other competencies in his short life. From his dad he learned sheet metal layout and steel fabrication. He was an expert with a cutting torch and various welding technologies. Working in construction, he developed solid carpentry skills. Interested in explosives, his friends said he studied the subject intently and became the trio's expert in that field. He knew about bomb design, materials and applications, placement, trigger devices and how to shape cutting charges, they said. Drawn to guns, he developed expert marksman skills. Friends who shot with him said he could hit a target from a half mile away. When it came to desert living and survival, his skills impressed even the most experienced outdoorsmen. "McVean and Mason camped in the desert every month of the year, whether it was a hundred degrees in the summer or there was a foot of snow on the ground," one acquaintance remarked. They frequently left critical equipment and supplies such as sleeping bags or sufficient food at home in order to test their abilities to survive off the land in the harshest of conditions. They submitted themselves to forced marches without water. Everyone who knew them concurred that both men could live in the desert with the barest of essentials indefinitely.

A psychological profile of McVean composed by police in the first days of the manhunt notes his unusually close bond with his mother. It was to her that he confided his innermost thoughts about his life and expressed endearment. At the same time, he nurtured a smoldering resentment of his father.

Jason's relationship with Linda Wallace was perhaps telling. They began a romantic relationship almost immediately upon meeting, exactly one year before McElmo Bridge. He was twenty-five. She was forty-three. Social observers note that some men in their twenties are attracted to older women for the simple reason that they appreciate the woman's maturity beyond the frivolity of youth. Psychologists suggest that a second reason for the atypical relationship is that an older woman represents a mother to the younger man. For Jason, his attraction to Wallace was probably some of both. "We had an unconditional love relationship," Wallace said. "If you want to, call it mothering. I'd prefer to call it nurturing and mutually beneficial. He told me no one had ever been there for him like I had. He cried to me. Told me of how miserable he was about things. How hard he worked all his life."

Whatever unresolved issues he felt regarding his mother, his relationship with his father was also psychologically troubling. At some level, Jason's solitary survivalist self-image, his independent antisociety, antiauthority creed conflicted with his continuing dependence on his father. Jim believed the bumpy periods in their relationship during Jason's high school years reflected normal father and teenage-son tension. As Jason grew up, he believed those generational issues dissipated. Jason, however, nursed the hard feelings the remainder of his life. In high school he moved out, choosing to live with an uncle and aunt. When he confided to his mother at age twenty-three thoughts that suggested his growing extremism, he demanded she not share his disturbing views with his father. "It just leaves me open to destructive criticism which is what happened with the last confrontation with my dad about how I feel," he wrote her. Throughout his adult life he complained to friends how hard he "slaved" working for his father, and six months before McElmo Bridge, he defiantly quit his job at Jim McVean's construction company.

Still, it was his dad that Jason depended upon for a job; a place to live; help with unusual expenses such as fixing his truck after an accident or medical bills; or the materials for building a shed intended as a component for the home he hoped to have someday in the desert. Even in the weeks before his rampage, when Jason learned he needed a quick influx of cash to pay an IRS debt, he partnered with his father to purchase a used auger truck with the intent of fixing it up and reselling it for a profit.

Underlying the anger Jason harbored for his father may have been a gnawing guilt he felt for having chosen to live with Jim and by implication "rejecting" his mother. From there, it was an easy jump to feeling less worthy and, consequently, less advantaged than everybody else. Whatever the formative psychology, it was clear that as he entered adulthood, Jason had divided the world into haves and have-nots, and counted himself among the latter. Despite the facts of his life to the contrary, he wallowed in his plight as one of the dispossessed.

In actuality Jason was somewhat privileged. Upon dropping out of public high school midway through eleventh grade, he attended an expensive private school. His grandmother had set up a fund to pay for his college and it was substantial enough that Jason considered a private college in California. He attended both a two-year vo-tech program and classes at a four-year college without financial assistance from the schools. He had steady work at decent-paying jobs, never having to collect unemployment compensation between them. When he began working for his dad, he complained constantly about not getting paid enough but he was earning as much as the most experienced workers on the crew, according to Jim McVean. It was good pay, he asserted. Even as an adult, Jim helped with many of Jason's nonroutine expenses. In addition, he gave his son a house trailer next to the McVean Construction metal shop, allowing Jason to live rent-free.

Nevertheless, Jason's steady drug habit plus a compulsion to stockpile arms and supplies for Armageddon kept him broke much of the time. A .50-caliber rifle he purchased with Mason cost several thousand dollars. His body armor, gear and other weapons cost several hundred dollars each. When police searched his trailer, they found over ten thousand dollars' worth of ammunition alone, plus hundreds more dollars' worth of other supplies. What was in the trailer was apparently just a fraction of the ammunition the three conspirators had fired in practice or the supplies they had buried over the past four years. Even Jason began to realize the excess of it. "Toward the end Jason thought they had enough buried," Wallace said. "It was mainly Bob who wanted to keep burying stuff. Jason complained he would rather keep some of his guns than bury them."

Just as Jason's financial woes were largely a result of his own choices, his deepening isolation from mainstream society was also self-imposed. Physically, he was a handsome man that women were attracted to. At six-foot-two with a solid hard-labor-molded 165 pounds he was often described as "thin" or "lean" but no one suggested he was "skinny." Gray eyes conveyed a certain aloof amusement, as if he was about to tease someone. His light brown wavy hair was long over the tops of his ears and nearly shoulder length in back. He wore a thin mustache and beard that framed an easy smile, giving him a roguish adventurer look. Usually dressed in a T-shirt and loose jeans, Jason seemed casual, unpretentious and friendly.

While Jason maintained an image as a loner rebel who hadn't had a girlfriend for years before meeting Wallace, the truth was he always seemed to be romancing at least a couple of girls at a time, claimed the guys who'd known him for years.

"In bed, Jason was the greatest," Wallace smirked to the investigator who asked about their relationship. "He was the most gentle lover. We had great passion. And I felt like we really loved each other and we were really connected. There were never any other women. It was a nonissue," she added confidently. "Jason was the most real relationship I ever had."

In Wallace's mind that had been the terms of their relationship from the day they met until he gave her a small peck of a kiss through his open truck window the night before he stole the water tanker, thirty hours before he killed Policeman Dale Claxton. In the months leading up to his disappearance, however, there was another woman.

Twenty-two years old and on break from college in Oregon, Rachel Jayne was just visiting Durango when her cousin fixed her up on a date with Robert Mason. The evening with the immature, rash-talking Mason, who slept with his dog in his truck, was a bust, but her attraction to Bobby's friend Jason was irresistible. Jayne would claim it wasn't the fact of McVean's general appeal to women that drew her quickly into a deep soulful relationship with the man who in a few months would be among the FBI's ten-most-wanted fugitives. It felt, instead, like they were destined for each other. Whatever come-hither aura McVean emanated, she sensed it was meant only for her.

Jayne's brief visits allowed her only a short time with McVean before she returned to school, but they maintained a torrid correspondence and frequent phone contact. In letters from Jayne found in McVean's truck and in his return letters to her they expressed their love for each other and plans to be together in the summer. McVean referred to Jayne as his "true soul mate."

"I knew about Linda Wallace," Jayne told the FBI. "Jason cared about her but he didn't love Linda. He cared about her in a different way."

Whether multiple girlfriends served McVean's self-image as a roguish rebel or he was troubled by the deceit is unknown, but Jason did seem to contemplate societal values more intently than most young men. In his Timberline Academy entrance essay, for example, he impugned the institutionalized violence of high school football, explaining how he thought differently than most other students:

They're thinking about fighting and how they smashed someone in a previous football game, how that makes them better. . . . I don't agree . . . I'd rather not think about crap like that.

It was a noteworthy insight for a seventeen-year-old dropout, but while Jason was inclined to noble ideals, he grasped them with a tainted mind. His pondering led to some distinctive conclusions. Upon those he built both a dangerous worldview and personal outlaw code of honor that demanded bold action, modest demeanor, selfless loyalty and a Robin Hood distinction between authorities, whom he considered combatants, and ordinary citizens, whose rights he championed.

On an emotional level, Jason was nonviolent. Unlike most of his peers in Durango, despite a Western tradition that reveled in the annual pursuit of deer and elk, Jason did not hunt. He lamented the sport, noting in one letter that he was witnessing "more wildlife killed by these idiots who can't live with Nature." Nor was he hotheaded and aggressive toward people. To the contrary, he was notably calm, controlled and nonconfrontational. "Jason didn't have a temper," Wallace said. "The few times we got frustrated with each other, I'd be like pounding on his chest and he'd just be very calm. If we disagreed on something he'd just say 'Well, whatever then.'" Recalling the student she had in several classes, a teacher at Timberline Academy concurred, "He didn't strike me as being violent or one who would do violent acts."

Jason believed a revolution in which citizen soldiers would wage war against an oppressive government was imminent but he didn't speak of it with excited anticipation, according to associates. He expressed neither hope that it would happen, nor dread. Unlike his friend Mason, McVean didn't make rash statements about killing cops. Nearly everyone who knew him shared the same impression: although McVean made it clear he thought of police as agents of an oppressive authoritarian state and would not hesitate to shoot them, such action would be defensive in response to a direct challenge initiated by police.

In truth, McVean kept most of his theories and plans to himself. When Mason went off on a tirade about stocking supplies, glorious revolution and shooting police, Jason would tell him to shut up or he'd move to some other part of the house and distance himself from the conversation, their friend Terry Westland said.

While McVean was reserved about his beliefs, they were well known by his closest friends. Several months prior to McElmo Bridge the three outlaws reportedly attended militia meetings in Cortez and Durango, but as far as the investigation revealed, never actually joined one of the groups. Prior to that McVean and Mason were said to have met regularly with an informal group of fifteen to twenty like-minded men in the basement of a Durango business. There they would reiterate their political views, work on their guns and train in military tactics. As far as is known, the group never gelled into a formal militia or had a specific political agenda. McVean is not known to have ever had an extremist mentor or paramilitary father figure who took the fledgling patriot under his wing.

At the McVean home, politics were never a topic of discussion, Jim McVean said. Jim described his own political beliefs as mainstream. "I'm not antigovernment. I'm a believer in our country and system. I've never felt taxes were unconstitutional or anything like that," he said.

Jason McVean was for the most part a self-taught extremist. He began with the anger and resentment fed by his childhood demons, then found a political rationalization for his acute feelings of oppression. Even a parking ticket roused his antiauthority ire. "I question the reason for the ticket; is it to give the little officer a sense of power?" he wrote challenging the ticket, ending the letter with the accusation that Durango was a "parking-police state."

At Durango High School a lot of kids had a general antipathy toward police and authority, one of his former classmates told reporters. In fact most citizens groused about one or another supposed example of government abuse. In the West such sentiments were pervasive. It was the philosophical foundation McVean needed. He read widely, mixing and matching extremist conspiracy theories, political news, urban myths and pop-sociology. In searching his trailer, police found articles on such varied topics as the death of children in the FBI Waco, Texas, siege; a history of citizen exploitation by the US government starting with the founding fathers; financial policy; and the ineffectiveness and potential threat of the United Nations. All were written with an extreme right-wing perspective although McVean would also borrow from the extreme left, particularly radical environmentalism.

The final construct was a generic antigovernment polemic. At the core was the most common of the extremist conspiracy theories, the New World Order. In its most typical variant, a small secret power elite was manipulating governments, monetary systems and global events intent on world domination. The police were willing or unwitting agents of a corrupted puppet government which had been slowly oppressing citizen rights and weakening opposition to a final assault by UN troops. In McVean's version, citizen resistance had been softened sufficiently that the final assault would occur soon. "They" would take advantage of the destabilizing effect of a catastrophic occurrence to declare marshal law, seize citizen's guns and launch the invasion. "People who aren't armed against the government are gonna be the ones that are naïve idiots, that aren't gonna be able to protect themselves," he told Wallace.

He believed several such catastrophes loomed in the near future. In May of 2000, an alignment of the planets would lead to natural disasters sufficient to cover an invasion. But even more likely, in his mind almost certain, was the collapse of modern society caused by the Y2K computer glitch.[2] Then in the spring of 1998, McVean wrote to a friend that there had been a "cosmic change." It is uncertain if he was referring to his conspiracy theory or not, but if he was, it seemed to move up the timetable.

How long McVean had been preparing for the final stage of guerilla war against the forces of oppression is uncertain. He had been storing food and ammunition for at least four years. It seems he had not started amassing an arsenal as early as Mason or Pilon but by the time of McElmo Bridge he was as well armed with two full automatic AK-47s including one with a folding stock, two full automatic M16s, a. 50-caliber sniper rifle, a full-automatic SKS rifle that Mason gave him for his twenty-fifth birthday, a Mini-14 9mm semiautomatic rifle, a .30-06 hunting rifle with a scope, a semiautomatic Colt .45 pistol, a high-tech crossbow, full body armor, hand grenades and explosives including C-4. Those were just the weapons friends who had been shooting with him could recall. At the rate the three outlaws had been purchasing arms and hiding them in the desert, most believed it was only a fraction of the firepower McVean actually owned.

The fact that none of his surviving close friends knew the full extent of his arsenal or where the weapons and supplies were stored was typical of Jason. He liked to keep things separate in his life. His girlfriend of one year, Linda Wallace, never went out with him and his other friends, whom he frequently got together with as a group. With the exception of Mason and one other individual who happened to be at McVean's trailer when she stopped by unexpectedly,

Wallace never even met any of them. "It seems like Jason lived a double life. There was a lot about him we didn't know," Jim McVean admitted years after his son vanished. "But Jason was an adult," he added. "We couldn't know everything about him." Apparently no one else did either, other than perhaps Bobby Mason.

There was one true thing that everyone knew about him. Sooner or later, everyone who knew Jason summed up his being with the same four words, "Jason loved the desert."

Jim McVean introduced his son to camping and the outdoors at an early age. But Jim was oriented to the mountains, as close to Durango heading east as the desert was to the west. Bobby Mason introduced Jason to the desert, taking him along on camping trips to the haunting, desolate landscape when the two met and became best friends in eighth grade. In all the years of their lives since then, it was where they escaped at every opportunity.

In a letter he wrote just weeks before McElmo Bridge, Jason told Rachel Jayne that he had just returned from "the same old desert" and then listed its disagreeable features such as gnats and sand. He concluded with how much he loved it and that he needed to "focus on making my own personal world."

The desert in its solitude fit Jason McVean. Despite his easy way with women, regardless of the many friends that he socialized with several times a week, irrespective of the many casual acquaintances who liked him, notwithstanding his lifelong bond with Bobby, Jason was a lonely person. Students at Durango High School and staff at Timberline Academy remembered Jason as "a loner, a kid who stayed in the background." In a record of his writing that stretched from his Timberline Academy entrance essay at age seventeen through his young adult years, Jason frequently writes that he feels apart from his peers and community. ". . . people that turn their heads when you even try to say hello. . . . There isn't any people to talk to. . . . I don't tell how I feel to anybody anymore," he wrote to his mother.

Jason wasn't the first young man to feel such isolation and the extremist response it spurred in him wasn't original political thought. The ideas Jason wove together into an elaborate conspiracy theory were widely promulgated in fringe media and extremist culture. But unlike Mason, he didn't just parrot them. He thought about them, rearranged them and validated them with the real world as he saw it. It was an intellectual process that would have made his beliefs highly personal and, in his mind, irrefutable. His inflexibility on the subject certainly limited the number of people he could talk to. Acting on those beliefs would have demanded even more secrecy and isolation.

Inherent in his beliefs was rejection of mainstream society, especially those social interests that seemed to engage his contemporaries. For Jason, fashion and designer clothes, spectator sports, and consumerism were all "crap." One of the first things he demanded to know of Linda Wallace when they met and he noticed her new TV was, "Are you some kind of material girl?" Even the structure and nature of work offended his sensibilities. "He didn't play the society game. He didn't want a real job," Wallace explained.

It was a mind-set that not only further isolated him but which often drove him to negative moods, according to Wallace. It would get started and everything was wrong—"This house sucks, the wood stove sucks, Doc [Linda's dog] is a pussy, the landlord is a dull jerk." In Jason's mind, the rest of the world was more concerned about the name on the back of their designer jeans than they were about waking up to a desert sunrise, feeling connected to nature and truly alive. They were thoughtless, "the walking dead." They were "zombies," a word McVean used frequently to describe virtually everyone from police to politicians to anyone who didn't fervently believe in the coming collapse of society. "How can you find in yourself to even care about these people you don't even know?" he asked Wallace, a radio news reporter, about the people she interviewed.

Jason, in turn, had become paranoid, concerned about defending himself against possible assailants including police. In the year she knew him, Jason never went anywhere unarmed, Wallace said. Usually that meant a Colt .45 pistol in his backpack.

Jason knew what would make him happy. He had been working toward it for four or five years and it was within his reach. He could have had it without killing anyone, without becoming an outlaw, without the deadly pursuit of hundreds of police. He wanted to create his "own personal world." He wanted to buy land in his beloved desert and live there in solitude close to nature, far from the society he despised, untouchable by oppressive authority, safe from the chaos that was certain to come. He had already stored enough food, water and supplies to live there independent of the rest of the world for years. The week of McElmo Bridge, he completed a metal shed he intended to move onto his desert land as the one half of a temporary home. He had been warning Wallace for months that he was "due for his lifelong trip to the desert."

Jason also had a second plan. His concern about individual rights, freedom from oppression and preservation of the land as God created it was great. His commitment to the cause was strong. Why he didn't just move to the desert and wait for the spark he was so sure would ignite the revolution will never be known. Perhaps it was as he wrote to his mother years before, "I've got to do something rather than nothing."

In the end, shooting his way past police who would stop him, Jason did go to the desert. "I always knew deep down inside me Jason belonged to the desert. The desert was in him. He loved it out there. He could be peaceful out there with nobody around him," Wallace said.

Years after he was last seen alive fleeing from McElmo Bridge, his bones would be found there in the desert. The flesh had long since fallen from them, dried in the desert heat and crumbled to dust. Wind, water and the hooves of passing cattle spread the dust across the landscape where it mixed speck by speck deep between grains of sand, was absorbed through the roots of sage and clung to the fur of coyotes. Jason McVean had become the desert.

CHAPTER 10
MANHUNT

West of Cortez, where the invisible boundaries of states, counties and reservations implied a pretense of civilization, the desert began in earnest. It was neither a sand desert with corrugated dunes nor an unbroken dirt plain dotted with majestic saguaro cactus. It was a meaner, more aggressive terrain; the kind of place that would cripple a Mars rover in the first fifteen feet. It was a labyrinth of twisting canyons scoured over ten thousand square miles of bone-dry earth. Within the canyon bottoms, between ragged red rock walls hundreds of feet high was an uneven landscape of jagged rock outcroppings, ankle-breaking boulder fields and patches of dense, prickly sage. Along the few streams that ran through the area, cottonwood trees and willow bushes, unwelcomed elsewhere in the harsh climate, crowded together so tightly that pressing through them was like wading against heavy surf. Branches snagged, poked and scratched. Half-inch thorns tore bloody trails across forearms and faces.

Oven-brick heat radiating from the surrounding sandstone surfaces pressed uncomfortably through the soles of boots and pounded faces with waves of thermal energy. Overhead the sun bore down with blast-furnace intensity, pushing air temperatures past 110 degrees Fahrenheit.

Lieutenant Jim Spratlen checked left and right, making sure the five other men on his team had moved past him and were now stationary, making him the point of a shallow "V." Seeing they were in position to provide covering gunfire if it came to that, he darted forward another thirty yards, crouched behind a desk-size boulder and waited for the others to again move one at a time to their new line of advance.

While others viewed his forward movement as "darting," it felt like anything but that to Spratlen. His Durango Police Department tactical squad had been humping the canyons from 6 A.M. to 4 P.M. since the beginning of the manhunt. By then, their advance through the canyons was more of a hurried trudge. Their fatigue was palpable. Spratlen pumped his legs over the jarring terrain with increasing effort. At each stop an irrepressible weariness flooded down his limbs. His muscles sagged, complaining with slight spasms of overuse.

The oppressive heat had drained what reserves of energy he may have called upon to pick up the pace. Vests designed to keep bullets out and trapped body heat in, and the shirts they wore underneath, were soaked in sweat. Faces blackened with camoflauge paint absorbed the sun's heat. Perspiration beaded their foreheads and trickled behind sunglasses, stinging their eyes. It ran down their necks and the inside of their legs. Their underwear clung and chafed. Their feet, rubbing against constantly damp socks, blistered.

Only their throats were dry. Unrelenting thirst compelled them to suck a mouthful of water from their hydration pack tubes every few minutes. Nevertheless, they often reminded each other to drink. It was a lesson as old as the prospectors and as fresh as the bleached bones of animals they'd pass; out there, dehydration could kill them as surely as a sniper's bullet.

Not only was their gear unbearably hot in 120-degree desert heat, over the course of several long days in a physically demanding environment it grew heavy and cumbersome. Most police tactical situations occur in a comparatively human-friendly urban environment rather than under rugged wilderness conditions and are measured in terms of hours rather than days. Tactical team training usually involves short bursts of exertion and seldom pushes the outer limits of endurance. A typical training day might be an hour of a mock exercise with gear in the morning, followed by a refreshment break and discussion. Then repeat the schedule in the afternoon.[1]

Body armor, rifle, pistol, ammunition and ancillary gear added twenty to fifty pounds on the officer's legs depending on the level of protection he wore. Most joining the manhunt showed up with their standard-issue level II or III body armor, an eight-pound vest designed to stop bullets from handguns and light rifle fire. Those lucky enough to have the parts upgraded their armor to level IV or V with steel plate back and breast inserts, side panels, groin and leg protection. It was capable of stopping a slug from a high-powered rifle like a .233 but the added security came with a price: more restricted movement, slower reaction time and an extra thirty pounds to hump uphill, downhill, over rocks, and through brush for ten hours nonstop.

By then, Spratlen's team had taken a cue from the unstoppable Navajo police units and lightened their gear to a day pack carrying only the minimum esentials, but the physical punishment was only half of it. The tension of being in a life-threatening situation for a prolonged period of time could deplete an officer, body and soul. The search for Claxton's killers involved an unusually high level of threat.

From time to time, Spratlen spotted other tactical teams working a parallel swatch of canyon, or a squad inserted within rifle range to search a specific site. Sometimes he spied police snipers on an overlooking ridge, or they'd cross the tracks of another team cutting through their search area. In most cases, he didn't know them. Police department SWAT teams from all over the country had joined the manhunt. Within the canyons were hundreds of police officers. Most had never trained together. Many were not even communicating on the same radio frequencies or using the same numeric radio designations. They knew nothing of each other's skills and discipline. All they knew for certain was command was chaotic; emotions were high with the vicious murder of a police officer; some were there for the glory; some were lost and not where they were supposed to be; some didn't even bother to wait for an assignment and charged ahead on their own; and almost all of them were wearing camo commando gear ready to shoot three suspects described as wearing camo commando gear. Friendly fire seemed more than a possibility.

Even more worrisome was the firepower they would face if they did find the suspects. During their escape from Cortez, the suspects had already outgunned the police by a wide margin. The automatic assault rifles they carried were bad enough but investigators had quickly determined the suspects also had another weapon that was truly fearsome. It became a key question asked of the suspects' acquaintances, "Do you know where they have the fifty-caliber?"

The anxiety over the suspects having a .50-caliber sniper rifle was justified. The .50-caliber cartridge, 5.5 inches long and almost an inch in diameter at the base, narrowly missed being banned as a destructive device under the National Firearms Act. The weapon fired a supersized projectile with extreme accuracy over a long distance. When the bullet arrived at its target up to a mile away, it would still be traveling with enough velocity and energy to penetrate a brick wall, punch through an armored vehicle or drop a helicopter from the sky. Against such a weapon, even the highest category of body armor was like wearing tissue paper.

Within the canyons, flanked on two sides by cliffs peppered with caves, nooks and outcroppings where a sniper could hide and watch the canyon floor below, police were fish in a barrel. The precariousness of their position was not lost on any of them. With just a good hunting rifle, a decent marksman could rip their ranks apart. Against a .50-caliber sniper rifle, the last of them standing still wouldn't know where from a thousand yards away came the shots that tore his comrades in half.

At forty-four, Jim Spratlin was the oldest member of his team and drove himself to keep up physically with the men he commanded. He kept in shape, worked out regularly and trained hard. His team often trained in the countryside near Durango, just fifty miles east, but even they found the canyons unfamiliar, "an unexpected, awkward evironment where we didn't know what we were doing." For many of the other teams around them, the canyons were another planet.

Tactical units from Arizona, Texas and Florida had functioned in temperatures as hot in their own turfs, but like most of the other three to four hundred officers from around the country who showed up, they were city cops comfortable in urban landscapes of streets and buildings, staircases and squad cars.[2] The desert canyons of Four Corners were unlike anything they had ever trained in, unlike anything they had ever seen. Handed a map and directed to drive to an embarkation point indistinguishable from endless miles of land stretching to the horizon beyond it, or inserted by helicopter into the middle of it, they were without warning in the wilderness; remote, harsh, unforgiving wilderness.

Some, too worn down to mind their step, too numb to react quickly, would fall among the bruising rocks and injure themselves. Others would become dehydrated. Their muscles cramped. Their pulses raced. Dizzy, ~~nauseous~~ NAUSEATED, vomiting, confused, they'd be snatched by helicopter before coma and death could claim them. Many others just wished they were someplace else where maybe they would face armed and dangerous men, but at least the environment was not trying to kill them.

Among the officers who reported to Cross Canyon the day of the shooting was Dolores County Sheriff Jerry Martin.[3] With the flatbed abandoned and the manhunt commencing in Utah, a mile west of the Dolores County line, he came to follow orders, but in the days ahead Martin and the resources he could tap would change the tenor of the search.

The illness that had assaulted Sheriff Martin's daughter her sophomore year of college was debilitating. Martin sat with her at the Phoenix clinic where she was rehabilitating when the call came from his dispatcher in Dove Creek. He'd taken one week off to care for his daughter while his wife visited relatives and suddenly his county was going to hell, dragged into a giant cop-killing, bullets-flying, car-chasing, desert-fleeing crime spree. He had to get back.

One by one, Martin called the airlines that flew between Phoenix and Durango—four calls, the same answer from each: there were no more flights that day. His fifth call was to Maricopa County Sheriff Joe Arpaio. "Sheriffs are a brotherhood. They come through for each other," Martin hoped. Arpaio did.

Martin introduced himself and explained what was happening. Three hours later, with his daughter bundled in the seat next to him, he stared down at the canyons from a single-engine Cessna flown by a member of the Maricopa County Sheriff's Office Aviation Posse. With luck, he thought, he'd spot the fugitives.

Martin's sister-in-law had barely stepped into his Dove Creek home to take over his caregiving duties when he bolted for his patrol car and raced toward the southwest tip of his Dolores County jurisdiction. A half mile further into Utah, officers were congregating around an abandoned flatbed. It would be two and a half days before he got home again and that was just for a quick shower and change of clothes.

"It looked like General Patton had arrived," Martin noted. It was about 6 P.M., five hours after the flatbed had been discovered. At the turnoff from Hovenweep Road onto the gravel route into Cross Canyon, an assemblage of patrol cars and officers congregated around a hay barn. Their focal point was a car with a San Juan County Sheriff's Office emblem on the door. The state line separated San Juan County, Utah, from Dolores County, Colorado, where Martin was sheriff. The barn sat about on the border and police milled about it wandering back and forth between states.

Martin followed the gravel road over the rim where it looped toward the canyon floor and looked down at the abandoned flatbed. Below him there were even more police than he saw around the barn. Multiple patrol cars parked along the road and dozens of officers in tactical gear moved about the crime scene. Within the short few hours since the site became the last known location of Dale Claxton's killers, an army of two hundred police had formed there. San Juan County Sheriff Mike Lacy, a man Martin had known and worked cooperatively with for twenty years, was calling the shots.

Bruce Tolzer had nodded a polite "howdy" to the fugitives that morning when they stopped their getaway vehicle long enough to let his cattle cross the road in front of them. Now he sat cross-legged on a bluff, a .233 rifle across his lap, ready to kill them. Tolzer was there as a favor. Montezuma County Sheriff Sherman Kennel had called him earlier in the evening after he returned from trailering cattle to summer range. "Bruce, I got a problem and I need your help," Kennel said. "I got a couple of boys in the area searching for those fugitives and I'd feel better for their safety if you'd watch over them for the night."

There was no moon and the gap between him and the roadblock below him was India ink. The roadblock itself, however, was illuminated in the squad cars' headlights. He could see the deputies as they stepped from the shadows into the light beams to search each of the few cars still on the road at that late hour. He watched them order motorists from their vehicles, question drivers at gunpoint, shine flashlights through the vehicles' interiors and rummage through trunks. He saw their fear spill out. "I witnessed officers getting out of line with the public," Tolzer recalled. "Some of their actions disgusted me. It was what fear did to them."

While Tolzer sat in the dark, Sheriff Lacy positioned officers on the Cross Canyon rimrock, equipped with night-vision goggles borrowed from the Blanding, Utah, National Guard Armory. Roadblocks had been set up surrounding the area and patrols moved between them. Several trailers and vehicles in the canyon that belonged to a cattle company were secured. Other than flyovers by the San Juan County Sheriff's Office twin-engine Piper Navajo, the effort that first afternoon had been to seal the area rather than search the canyon.

It was a tactic that could have succeeded only with a preponderance of luck. The canyon was over twenty miles long and ranged from a couple hundred yards to over a mile wide. It was the first in a sixty-mile-wide corridor of similar interconnected remote canyons leading more than one hundred miles west. For over a half century, beginning with Butch Cassidy in the 1880s, the canyons had sheltered a succession of notorious cattle rustlers, bank robbers, renegade

Utes resistant to white encroachment and Prohibition bootleggers, never yielding any into the hands of the law. No one person knew all the forgotten backroads and obscure jeep tracks that wound through the area. Night-vision goggles designed to amplify ambient nocturnal light had a shorter detection range on moonless, darker nights. May 29, 1998, was a new moon and the section of canyon where the fugitives struck out on foot was wide. Nighttime observers on the rims during the first days of the manhunt could not see most of the canyon floor even with night-vision goggles. Even thermal imaging was compromised. Against the hot background of the canyons' solar-heated rock surfaces, spotting the thermal image of a warm body was like finding a polar bear in a snowstorm.

By the time Lacy got to the abandoned flatbed site that afternoon, it was already swarming with people from multiple agencies. He didn't know who they were or who they claimed to answer to but there was one thing he intended to make clear right from the get-go, this was his county and there were rules for these situations. Law enforcement protocols for unified incident command put the local sheriff in charge. Most sheriffs may have yielded power to the crime-fighting prestige, resources and impudence of the FBI but Lacy was a country cop in a part of the country that was not overly fond of federal authority. No federal agent in a suit was going to run operations in San Juan County, Utah.

Four days later as the police response continued to mushroom out of control, Lacy would grudingly concede temporary leadership to commanders from distant Colorado sheriff departments as well as take direction from US Army specialists, but his cock-of-the-walk confrontation the first afternoon with Colorado FBI agents set a tone of interagency bickering, finger-pointing and lack of cooperation that plagued the pursuit for nearly a decade. Many connected to the case, from members of the suspects' families to police officials with other agencies, would label Lacy a glory seeker whose ego interfered with its resolution. The broad-based criticism of Lacy may or may not have been justified, but the truth was that interagency rivalries and resentments existed long before Cross Canyon. In the chaos of the case, there were enough miscues, petty obstructions, fumbles and blunders for every agency with a central role to take a share, including the FBI.

Despite his assertion of authority under the rules of command, Lacy's control of the manhunt during the first two days was tenuous at best. In actuality, the fugitive search was divided with Colorado-based FBI agents housed at the Cortez command post directing some of the search operations and Lacy running others. While the media was presented a picture of a massive unified manhunt, coordination between the two camps was in spirit weak and in practice shallow. That evening with hundreds of officers standing by, Lacy spread the lion's share of duties among his own deputies and the few local departments he was most comfortable with.

To his friend, Sheriff Jerry Martin, he gave the responsibility of establishing the northeast quadrant perimeter. Martin was by nature a 110 percent kind of guy, ready to help without complaint. As he told Lacy he would do what he could, he told himself the order was ridiculous. The Dolores County Sheriff's Office had five officers, himself and four deputies, one of whom was left in Dove Creek to cover the most pressing of the office's regular, ongoing responsibilities. That left Martin and three deputies to seal a fifty-mile arc of countryside from Cortez to the Utah border.

Telluride Deputy Marshal Keith Hoffman opened the back door of his squad car and motioned his German shepherd, Zeke, to the ground. He snapped a fifteen-foot tracking lead to the dog's collar and followed a San Juan County deputy deeper into the canyon. Zeke kept his nose to the ground sniffing at the two sets of boot tracks they were following.

Along much of the route the tracks had been trampled and obscured by other boots that had trod the area since the abandoned flatbed was discovered six hours earlier. They disappeared completely where the suspects had crossed wide expanses of rock. The gaps, however, didn't slow their pace. An earlier K9 team had already covered that ground and found where the tracks picked up again. Zeke went to work in earnest where the other dog left off.

The exercise had none of the rush of terriers chasing a fox, or the frenzied excitement of bloodhounds treeing a raccoon. It was a slow, laborious process that quickly wore out dog and handler. Zeke would follow the scent track for a few yards, halt, frantically nose the ground, move a few feet in one direction then return to the track to assure that at least its endpoint was still there before searching the other direction. Sometimes Keith would direct the dog to the area where geography and the suspect's direction of travel suggested they might find a resumption of the scent. Other times he let Zeke lead him back and forth across an ever-widening circle until the track was relocated. For every yard they progressed along the suspect's trail, they hiked fifty back and forth across the rugged canyon.

The conditions were poor for K9 tracking. The multiple police who had crisscrossed the area made scent discrimination difficult. The extended patches of hard-pack soil and rock coupled with sparse vegetation trapped less scent than more absorbent surfaces with grass, weeds and other low ground cover. Finally, what little track scent the desert surface did produce was quickly burned off and weakened by direct sunlight and heat.

Better at tracking in those conditions were the Navajo trackers. Much of the trail that had been discovered was found by the Strategic Response Team from the Navajo Nation's Tuba City police district, one of five Navajo Nation police districts that dispatched their SWAT teams to aid the manhunt. The Tuba City team responded from more than two hundred miles across the vast reservation.[4] Like other police units in the region, they came unbidden; part of the law-enforcement brotherhood ready to help wherever they could. It wasn't until they arrived at the flatbed that the tribal police realized they had a second rationale for being there—the manhunt was to begin on the northern boundary of their land. As they followed the tracks southwest, they quickly crossed onto the reservation and into their official jurisdiction.

Moving confidently along the trail, the Navajo trackers sensed they were gaining on the fugitives and predicted they'd have them cornered by nightfall. The possibility was too atractive. The Native Americans were called back—ostensibly replaced with white teams who wanted to be in place for the capture, the Tuba City commander speculated. Within half an hour, the trail was lost.

Now, in stops and starts, Keith and Zeke pressed the track forward. Occasionally a bootprint would confirm what Zeke's nose knew; they were still on the suspect's trail. They extended the trail a half mile and were more than three miles from the flatbed as the sun rested on the western rim of the canyon. Topside, on the flat of the world, daylight would linger for another forty-five minutes. In the depths of the canyon, the shadows darkened quickly into night. Keith and Zeke were ordered back. Before they turned around, Keith twisted a stick into the ground to mark the spot. It was where they would pick up the track again in the morning; the farthest point from McElmo Bridge that police had followed Dale Claxton's killers on the day he was murdered.

Zeke, along with several officers, slept at the hay barn command post on the eastern ridge of Cross Canyon. Some sprawled in their cars, others slept on the ground. But the night was short.

Shortly after midnight, helicopters began a methodical search pattern above the canyon using thermal-imaging cameras. The officers were roused and deployed along the main roads; positions from which they could swoop in and apprehend at the first sighting. Confidence was high that the fugitives couldn't evade the high-tech search. By morning they would be captured or dead.

The cameras did show warm-blooded movement in the canyon; bodies moving unhurriedly, aimlessly in large groups. The cattle appeared unbothered by the beat of helicopters overhead. They moved as herds, tearing at the tufts of vegetation in their path, unknowingly trampling what stood in their way. The beasts didn't understand that one stick poking out of the ground had special significance; that they should step around it. Their hooves knocked it down, crushed it into pieces and shuffled those remnants along like soccer balls until what was left of the marker lay nowhere near the spot where it had been jammed upright in the thin layer of gravel. Whatever scent still lingered from yesterday's travelers was diluted beyond recognition with the odor of bovine pounded into the earth. Any physical tracks of men fleeing justice that moldable soil may have preserved were written over.

The second day of the manhunt, Saturday, May 30, began with the parking of a small house trailer on the east rim of Cross Canyon, next to the gravel road leading down into it. Its purpose was practical and political. Equipped with generators, communications electronics, maps and emergency supplies, it facilitated tactical operations. The signage on the side—large letters identifying the trailer as the SAN JUAN COUNTY SHERIFF'S OFFICE MOBILE COMMAND CENTER—gave Lacy a little more weight in his ongoing tug-of-war with the FBI for control.

Even more contentious than his confrontation with the FBI the previous day, was Lacy's relationship with Navajo Nation Police Chief Leonard Butler. Over the long course of the case, the two men would emerge as the key commanders of the physical search for the fugitives and right from the beginning it was anything but a partnership. Despite long tenures commanding overlapping jurisdictions, the two men had met only once or twice before at regional interagency meetings, but when Butler showed up the second day, tension between the sheriff and the chief escalated quickly.[5] Butler believed his teams made a crucial contribution to core manhunt operations. Lacy, on the other hand, despite open admiration of the Navajo Strategic Response Teams by other SWAT units who watched the Native American officers perform, expressed a lower estimation of the Navajo police capabilities and, according to Butler, attempted to sideline his officers from key operations.[6]

Having grown up in white communities and endured playground tants of "Injun," Butler was hypersensitive to affronts. There had been ocassion in his career when white officers suggested he step aside from a case because he was an Indian. Rightly or wrongly, in Butler's mind, Lacy's assumption of authority and delegation of manhunt duties reflected that same attitude. Ready to protect his officers from any perceived slight in the politics of the manhunt, Butler's argument for his men seethed with unspoken accusation.

It had been less than twenty-four hours since the fugitives had ditched the flatbed and headed into Cross Canyon. On foot, in the heat of the day or traversing rugged country at night, moving cautiously to avoid detection, the suspects could not have gotten more than twenty or twenty-five miles. While that distance was more than enough for the fugitives to have climbed out of Cross Canyon and dropped into an adjacent canyon, police doubted that was the case. The fugitives would have avoided cutting across the flat, wide-open plateau between the canyons as an unnecessary risk of exposure, they reasoned. The search focused on Cross Canyon.

Among the many officers responding with unknown tactical capabilities and uncertain preparation for extreme environments were several tactical teams that quickly proved their competence. Spratlen's Durango PD team and the Telluride officers, as well as the Farmington, New Mexico, officers, a team from the New Mexico State Police and the US Border Patrol became go-to squads for the commanders. At the 5 A.M. manhunt field command briefing the first morning after McElmo Bridge, the plan was to track the fugitives down.

As Lacy settled into the mobile command center, Deputy Keith Hoffman searched for the suspects' trail lost in the wake of the cattle herd. Working with Zeke and two other K9 teams, plus a SWAT team from Farmington, they beat the edges of the trampled area for over an hour before regaining the track but soon lost it again at the edge of a swift-flowing stream. The teams split up and searched each bank for a mile and a half, but neither the scent nor footprints reappeared. The suspects had hiked in a generally southwest direction four and a half miles from the abandoned flatbed, waded waist-deep into the cold, swirling current of Montezuma Creek and vanished.

The search pitted three locals against the overwhelming resources of the state and primitive survival skills against a technological society. By the second night the police's technological advantage became even more pronounced with the requisition of Nightstalker surveillance. Controversial as a tool of domestic spying, the FBI Nightstalker program was a fleet of sixty super-quiet drones equipped with advanced optics cameras, infrared and thermal-imaging capabilities, listening electronics and tracking technology. One of the first publicly acknowledged uses of the planes was during the 1993 Waco, Texas, siege of the Branch Davidian compound, but for the most part the program's existence flew under the public's radar. It took a field office request and special circumstances to get Nightstalker surveillance. Its rapid approval for the Four Corners manhunt proved, in the era of Waco, Ruby Ridge and Oklahoma City, how troubling the militia movement was for the FBI and the priority they gave to a fast resolution.

It was shortly after sunrise, day three of the manhunt, and the tracks were not where they were supposed to be. They appeared to have been made by military combat-style boots, but that fit the general description of footwear worn by most of the officers traipsing the area in tactical gear. By now there had been dozens of tracks found that caused a flurry of interest only to be dismissed as having been made by another officer. Yet to the discriminating eyes of the Navajo trackers who found the two sets of tracks as well as forensic experts, these footprints were not another false clue; pressed into the gravel apron of Larry Murdock's driveway and in the woods behind his house was a reliable match to the tracks that led from the abandoned flatbed.

The trail of footprints veering southwest from the flatbed plus the lure of secret trails and endless hiding places in the canyons to the west, away from police, gave a presumed direction to the search. Murdock, however, lived on the edge of Cross Canyon, twenty-four miles *northeast* of where the flatbed had been abandoned, two miles north of the tiny Dolores County, Colorado, community of Cahone. The canyon was shallow there at its leading end where it crossed US Highway 666. It would have been easy for the fugitives to scramble up the short rock wall forming the east side of the canyon and cross Murdock's property to the highway. The footprints suggest that was what happened.

By midmorning, police had other signs that the fugitives had followed the canyon northeast to the Cahone area. A rural Cahone home was reported broken into sometime early that morning and food stolen. Parked vehicles were reported to have been tampered with. Searchers found human waste along a northeast route leading to the Cahone area. No one clue was definitive, but the evidence was compelling enough to shift the focus of the manhunt.

"Avoid a confrontation. Just leave your cars unlocked with the keys in them," Sheriff Martin advised the residents of Cahone. By late morning of the the third day, the manhunt had moved to his county. Manhunt field command operations shifted to the Cahone Community Center. Lacy's mobile command trailer was parked next to it. Squad cars filled the community center parking lot and a dozen helicopters came and went from the field alongside of it. Working in Lacy's jurisdiction, Martin had done what was asked of him. In Dolores County, he was in charge.

The FBI continued to shuttle tactical teams to the canyons from its command post in Cortez, but the bulk of the manhunt forces and the heart of its operations were based in Martin's jurisdiction. In an unspoken agreement, he shared command of the manhunt with Lacy. It was an easy partnership, Martin said. The two men had been sheriffs of adjacent rural, sparsely populated counties for twenty years. They had even cooperated years before in the pursuit and capture of an outlaw who had fled from one county to the next and ran for the canyons that slashed through both their territories. Broad philosophical agreement on citizenship, law enforcement and desired outcomes provided a basis for mutual support and friendship, but their styles varied greatly.

Both men realized how ill-equipped they were for the task they had assumed. "We were never prepared for anything like it. An operation of that scale had never happened before," Lacy explained. "We didn't know how to go about it. Lots of local departments didn't even have long guns. We didn't know the best size for SWAT teams. We made it up as we went."[7]

Martin was less inclined to make it up as he went. Whereas Lacy guarded his authority with a belligerency that alienated some of the officers working the case, Martin was a congenial bridge builder. Friendly, easygoing and sincere, most people would probably exclaim what a nice guy he was even as he snapped the cuffs around their wrists. Martin knew they needed help. Tapping the friendships and contacts he'd developed over the years, he went looking for it.

Through years of semiannual meetings of the Colorado Sheriff's Association, Martin had close friendships with sheriffs across the state. He called three from the eastern slope reputed to have the best tactical teams in the mountain time zone—Boulder, El Paso and Pueblo Counties.

Overwhelmed with the sheer logistics of feeding, lodging and provisioning the five-hundred-person force that suddenly doubled the population of Cahone and was now his responsibility, he called a man he'd met a few years before at a seminar. U.S. Forest Service Incident Command Systems Specialist Steve Budjack arrived the next morning. Experienced at managing logistics and support for giant forest fire crews in remote areas, Budjack was organized, regimented and brusque. Some officers would take affront at his manner, but he knew how to get the job done and stepped in without hesitation.

Finally, Martin called his most powerful contact. Colorado Governor Roy Romer's sister lived in Dove Creek, the county seat of Dolores County. Through that contact, Martin knew the governor personally and had been calling him with incident updates since he first arrived at Cross Canyon. Now he wanted the governor to send in the Colorado National Guard. Romer's verbal commitment of National Guard assistance the day after McElmo Bridge had already provided the manhunt some logistical support but Martin wanted soldiers. The massive wilderness pursuit resembled a military operation as much or more than it did a police response, Martin argued. Trained special ops forces were needed.

Martin's request was not an easy one politically. In principle, the use of the US military for domestic law enforcement violates the federal Posse Comitatus Act. It would be considered a fundamental abuse of government authority. Romer could authorize the National Guard's involvement only under narrowly defined exceptions to the law. First, National Guard units operating under state authority rather than federal service were exempt. Also exempt was the use of military personnel and resources for aerial search and surveillance. Calling up the National Guard for the manhunt blurred both lines. Even though the manhunt command center had shifted to Cahone on the Colorado side of the state line, many manhunt operations were still being conducted in the Utah canyons where Romer had no "state authority" to authorize National Guard forays. In addition, the help Martin requested was Special Forces ground troops equipped with more than cameras. Romer held back. Martin continued to ask.

On Tuesday, the fifth day of the manhunt and two days after Martin assumed shared command, as national media led with Four Corners coverage and public outrage at the vicious killing mixed with growing public fascination at the outlaws' escape, Romer acted. By executive order "declaring a state of emergency due to the murder and injury of law enforcement officers," he authorized an "order to active duty as many members of the Colorado National Guard as necessary for the purposes of response and mitigation of this emergency." Under the command of General William Westerdahl, the commanding officer of the Colorado National Guard, it arrived in force.

Besides bringing in expertise he and Lacy lacked, Martin had another reason for requesting help. He had his own perspectives on how the manhunt should proceed and wanted resources that were there at his request who he could rely on. Even the National Guard was technically under his command. Martin knew Pilon and understood that while the man may have been a screw-up in the civilized world, the deeper he got into the wilderness, the greater his comparative competence grew. Martin guessed that even if the fugitives had first fled northeast to Cahone, they had immediately reversed direction and moved back deeper into the canyons where they felt safe. It was an opinion shared by the border patrol trackers who in the days after the tracks were found in Cahone, once again began finding evidence of the suspects in the canyons to the west.

On day four of the manhunt, federal agents knew by the sign nailed to the fence post they had located the property they were looking for:

ABSOLUTELY
NO FEDERAL OR STATE INSPECTORS
BEYOND THIS SIGN

INCLUDING INTERNAL REVENUE AGENTS WITHOUT
FEDERAL WARRANT & ACCOMPANIED BY A LOCAL SHERIFF

They had come looking for an acquaintance of Pilon's who was known to share the suspect's antigovernment views. The property was a scrap of land near an area known as Bug Point. The residence was close to both Cross Canyon and Cahone. It was also not too far from the Dolores County dump where the night before there had been a confirmed sighting of two men with flashlights.

No one appeared to be home. Beyond the gate, taped to the small house trailer that looked to be the living quarters, police found a second sign. This one was handwritten on a piece of cardboard: AIN'T NOTHING HERE WORTH DIEING (sic) FOR! BOOBY TRAPPED! DANGER! In the bottom corner the author had scribbled a smiley face with the words HAVE A NICE DAY.

Fifteen yards past the trailer, in a tangle of fallen trees, a deputy with a cadre of agents and police officers looked twice at one of the tree stumps poking up among the trunks and branches. The vertical saw cut was barely noticeable. He pushed through the branches for a closer look. Poking up from the ground into the hollow stump was a three-inch-diameter PCV pipe, an air vent to an underground bunker. It took a half hour to find the entrance camouflaged with rock and brush. As one deputy lifted the door, two others stood over it and aimed their pistols into the opening. They shouted into the hole. No answer. They fired several shots into the bunker. No movement. Then CBI agent Kevin Humphreys dropped through it.

Humphreys could stand at his full height but a man two inches taller would have had to stoop. The space looked to be about ten-by-twelve feet. Stacked along the walls were supplies of food, clothing and living provisions. There were no weapons. There were no fugitives.

The morning briefings occurred an hour before sunrise. As the sky lightened, the first of the teams were shuttled to their assigned search areas. A house-to-house search south of Cahone was begun but never completed as officers left to respond to various reported sightings. None were definite. Residents were questioned, vehicles checked. The Dolores River and reservoir were closed to recreational boaters. The main thrust of the manhunt, however, was redirected deeper into Cross, Squaw, Patterson and Cedar Canyons.

The search area stretched over five hundred square miles. Some teams were inserted deep in the canyons by helicopter. Others drove to an embarkation point and hiked in. Losing teams quickly surfaced as a problem. Occasionally a team became lost within the canyons, searching the wrong area, failing to show at a pickup location. Radio communications in the canyons was often blocked by the terrain. The disappearance of a team was cause for grave concern. The possibilities were deadly, from heat stroke and exhaustion to serious terrain injury to battle. It was reason to divert other teams and send in helicopters, to stop what you were doing and focus on finding the missing officers. More often teams became lost on the way to the search area. Most of the officers were not from around there. Many had never seen such country. The few designated roads that wound through the area twisted between and through canyons on paths dictated by Eocene rivers rather than civil engineers. Crossing them were hundreds of unofficial roads and dirt tracks that were nevertheless critical for reaching some destinations. Directions that made sense to a local only confused the unfamiliar.

Many police departments sent a full SWAT team. Other officers, from as far away as Florida, took vacation time and showed up on their own or with a cop buddy. Every hour, more found their way to the Cahone command post, signing in faster than Martin and Lacy could deploy them.

When Martin and Lacy did deploy them, they did it with trepidation. After marking a search area on a map and handing the assignment to a team leader more than a dozen times in the first hour, Martin thought the knot in his stomach would ease up. Instead it got worse. He couldn't shake the feeling that some of them would die in one of those canyons. "We knew it was high risk," Lacy said. "The officers were essentially defenseless against a sniper." Where possible, they placed their own snipers on the canyon rims watching over the search teams below, but those opportunities were limited. Everyone involved understood; if a team was successful and found the suspects, it was unlikely the outlaws were going to surrender. An encounter almost certainly would end with more police fatalities.

The teams ranged in size from three to ten officers. Many went out all day, others for four- or five-hour shifts. When possible, support personnel ferried food and water to the search teams. On average, a morning or afternoon shift was enough time for a team to clear a swath two to three hundred yards wide and two miles long. A concentration of caves, abandoned uranium mines or Indian ruins in a search sector slowed progress even further. The caves and ruins needed to be probed thoroughly. Checking the mines usually went faster. In the entrance to many was an accumulation of fine soft sand that had blown into the opening. If anyone entered the mine recently, it would show there.

A suspect hunkered down twenty yards outside the search corridor would likely not be seen. Neither was there any way to clear an area and seal it. As soon as a search team was extracted, nothing prevented the suspects from moving into the cleared sector. Despite the manpower and continuous effort, the search area remained impossibly large. To the commanders in Cahone and the teams in the canyons and the police at the roadblocks and the pilots conducting aerial surveillance, the fugitives remained invisible. The search area would contort from time to time, shifting its center to where the latest set of tracks were found, but by and large one day blended into the next in an unbroken, unending, fruitless, frustrating, exhausting grind.

On the evening of the fourth day search hopes shifted twenty-five miles west to the head of Cow Canyon. Navajo trackers discovered a new set of tracks police described as "hot." They were fresh and, like the boot prints that directed the search to Cahone, an undeniable match to the suspect's tracks leading from the abandoned flatbed.

Thirty hours separated the discovery of tracks in Cahone and similar tracks in Cow Canyon; more than enough time to hike the distance between the two locations. In addition, a reported sighting west of Cahone the previous night of furtive men with flashlights and tracks discovered in the area the next morning suggested the fugitives headed that direction. It was also likely that the fugitives didn't have to walk the whole way. The flashlight sighting was near the home of a known Pilon sympathizer and police were convinced the subjects were receiving help moving from one location to another. In fact, over the course of the manhunt, searchers found several indications the suspects had visited two distant locations within an improbably short time for people on foot in difficult terrain. The only reasonable explanation was that they were getting rides. People were meeting them and helping them move ahead of the manhunt.

Throughout the next morning three National Guard Blackhawk helicopters ferried heavily armed searchers into a fifty-square-mile search area around the newly discovered tracks. Once again, police thought they were close. Once again, by the end of a grueling day, the few footprints that lured them there was as close as they got.

On the seventh day, far outside the search area, a State of Utah social worker decided to eat his on-the-go lunch at a scenic location along the San Juan River known as Swinging Bridge. By evening, the manhunt command center was relocated there.

CHAPTER 11
BOBBY

The breaths grew shallow. The brown and black fur covering the massive chest heaved less with each inhale until respiration became imperceptible. The big dog didn't thrash or snap, growl or whimper. It didn't claw for traction on the smooth stainless steel tabletop. Only its wide dark eyes betrayed its anxiety.

Dirk's death in the spring of 2007 was especially difficult for Ann Mason, more grievous than just losing a pet. The German shepherd had been her son Bobby's dog, adopted by him as an abandoned puppy and left in Ann's care when he headed out for what was supposed to be a three-day camping trip. In the nine years since, Dirk had become a living, breathing connection to the hardworking, easygoing, kind young man she knew as her son. As the dog, ravaged with cancer, succumbed to the vet's injection, Ann felt Bobby's life slip away from her one more time.

Ann and Gary Mason's recollection of their son stands in stark contrast to the creepy misfit child grown into a savage killer that emerges in police reports and FBI profiles. While it can be said that none of the suspects' parents fully knew their adult children, neither did the police reports with their focus on the dark side of their personalities. Compared to the handsome young man captured in family photos, even the WANTED poster images of Bobby Mason seemed manipulated to portray a sadistic personage who would garner no sympathy.

Naïve and easily led, Mason was the most tragic of the outlaws.

He was in many respects a reincarnation of Billy the Kid— medium height, clear blue eyes, light brown hair and a light complexion. Like the Kid, Mason's response to life betrayed little introspection, deep thought or planning; not for lack of mental capacity but due to his go-with-the-flow personality. Intensely loyal to friends, both outlaws followed others into circumstances that more thoughtful, self-directed men would avoid and, with no aversion to violence, reacted to the situation as it unfolded.

Unlike the charismatic Billy the Kid, however, Mason was socially awkward, often exhibiting a weird demeanor that unnerved people. According to acquaintances and his parents, he was very immature for a man in his mid-twenties.

Although he had the wherewithal to operate as a self-employed subcontractor and built a reputation as a conscientious worker and skilled tradesman, in other realms of adult life he was dysfunctional. To anyone's knowledge he never had a girlfriend or romantic relationship. Among his social group he was included more as Jason McVean's shadow rather than for any capacity to make friends on his own. Despite the fact that he earned decent money, he was financially irresponsible, frequently borrowing from friends and leaving credit card bills unpaid. He was homeless. His permanent mode of habitation was couch surfing at acquaintances or sleeping in his truck. Every few days he showed up at his parents' house for a meal and a shower.

By all the apparent laws of nurture and nature, Bobby Mason should have grown into a hardworking, tax-paying, law-abiding citizen, a regular guy who grumbles about the government from time to time, votes his mind and goes about his life. If a stable home with parents modeling civic behavior were a predictor of how children turn out, then the son of Ann and Gary Mason would never have lined a policeman up in his rifle sights and squeezed the trigger.

Bobby Mason grew up in as close to a *Leave It to Beaver* environment as probably existed in the late-twentieth-century middle-class

American West. Bobby and his older brother, Chuck, grew up in a pleasant two-story brick home on a shady street in a friendly neighborhood in Durango, Colorado. Gary was a soft-spoken elementary school teacher and Ann had a small retail shop on Main Street. The family's roots in the community were deep. Masons had been among Colorado's early pioneers. Mining claims and homesteads along the Colorado Front Range still bore the family name and Bobby's great-grandfather served as a county sheriff. On his mother's side was Oklahoma Choctaw. The boys and their mother were all registered members of the tribe and distinctly proud of their Native American heritage.

Bobby's life was marked by none of the unsettling circumstances that psychologists and social workers often cite as a prelude to derailment. There were no divorces, no frequent moves and separation from friends, no alcoholism, no police pounding on doors, no abandonment, no domineering abusive guardians nor indifferent permissive parents. He was neither spoiled nor deprived. There is no blatant anything on which the tragedy of Bobby Mason's life can be hung.

"Bobby had a good home," Ann Mason insists. "We stayed married. We celebrated every birthday. Made sure our kids had Christmas presents. Encouraged them at school." In fact, people who knew the Masons unanimously described them as decent people and good parents.

Not everything was perfect, however. Ann mixed the anxieties of motherhood with the daily stress of making a small business succeed. Gary, who had done three combat tours in Vietnam, bore his own symptoms of stress. Chuck recalled that the home environment could get a little tense. In addition, raising Bobby was not easy. All in all, Bobby was a good kid but right from the start, he was a challenge in school. "His behavior was never malicious, just mischievous," Ann said dismissively. "He always thought he should be the class clown." He was never diagnosed with a learning disability according to his mother, but his behavior suggests he may have been impeded by one. A pattern of inattentiveness and disruptive behavior followed him through the grades. "Bobby never liked school. His

mind was always drifting beyond the windows to thoughts of playing outside," Ann said.

Perhaps the most striking family dynamic was the relationship
between the two brothers. Chuck was just thirteen months older
than Bobby. That proximity in age didn't make them constant playmates and strengthen their brotherly bond. Instead, it intensified
sibling rivalry until their relationship was one of prolonged and often
bitter enmity.

Hints of brotherly affection and concern did surface between the
lines of Chuck Mason's police statement in the aftermath of Claxton's killing. It became apparent in the interview transcript that from
time to time Bobby had asked his older brother to go shooting with
him, a distinct honor Bobby bestowed only on his closest friends. He
also had evidently told Chuck a few details about his friends, small
boasts that could only have been an attempt to impress an older brother.
Chuck, in turn, expressed genuine dread at the likelihood that Bobby
was involved in Claxton's killing, not just because of the sorrow it
would cause his parents, but for Bobby's sake and his hope that his
brother was on the verge of maturing and finding himself.

Whatever bond existed, however, was obscured by years of Cain
and Abel animus. As both a teenager and young adult, Bobby reportedly told friends at various times he "hated" his brother. Chuck
told investigators that he and Bobby had never gotten along and they
saw each other rarely. He said they seldom spoke and when they did
it quickly degenerated into an argument.

Child psychologists posit sibling rivalry is particularly intense
when children are very close in age and of the same gender or where
one child is intellectually gifted. Bobby lost on all counts. With a
thirteen-month head start and a slight size advantage over Bobby
even as an adult, Chuck claimed the high road in the battle for preeminent offspring. As a grade-schooler, he'd be placed in classes for
gifted students. Bobby, who was equally bright according to his father,
was marooned on the program's waiting list. As an adolescent, Chuck
would endear by imitating the conservative beliefs of his father and
demonstrating Eagle Scout behavior. Even without the smugness

that typically attends such behavior, it would have been difficult for Bobby not to sense that the world regarded Chuck as morally superior. Both boys dropped out of high school; Bobby in the role of a flunked-out stoner who ended up bagging groceries at the supermarket, Chuck as a diverse thinker who needed a different learning environment and attended a private school before curtailing that too. In contrasting the brothers, a high school teacher remarked, "Chuck was exceptionally ethical." By implication, Bobby was not.

Following in Chuck's footsteps was a battle Bobby couldn't win. As is often the case among competing siblings, Bobby tended to move in the opposite direction of Chuck. After earning their GEDs, Chuck followed his inclinations to wear a white hat and found a position with the Southern Ute Reservation Police. Bobby foundered and began trash-talking cops as "pussies who need a badge and gun to feel powerful," according to Chuck's statement to police. Chuck eventually went to college and furthered his career in law enforcement. Bobby too stumbled upon a profession for which he had natural talent and which could have been the foundation for turning his life around. But his scorn for police continued to smolder, waiting to be fanned by others into a burning hatred.

Despite his virulent antipolice outbursts, Bobby's brushes with the law were few and, in a broader perspective, not particularly deviant. Other than a charge of shoplifting at age seventeen for merchandise of trifling value, the three other entries on his rap sheet were traffic violations. He'd been tagged for speeding, driving without insurance and, at the age of twenty-one, driving with a suspended license. For the last five years of his life with the exception of his gun-and-run last week, Mason had no encounters with police.

Despite his short and relatively innocuous rap sheet, it would also be incorrect to presume by Mason's sudden shooting spree that he unexpectedly snapped. In the months and years leading up to the Claxton ambush, Mason had become increasingly outspoken and hostile toward police, often going off on tirades about police abusing their authority. He carried a gun with him at all times, in his pack, toolbox or in his truck, and bragged to friends, "I will kill any cop that pulls me over." Whatever crime they had set out to commit when they drove through Cortez in a stolen water tanker, it is clear that he and his comrades were intent on a major felony and had been planning it for months.

Nor did there appear to be a precipitous incident that sent Mason over the edge. Partying with friends the afternoon before McElmo Bridge, the three soon-to-be fugitives were described as tense, but in good humor. In fact Mason, who was known to be exceedingly cheap, uncharacteristically sprang for pizza for the group.

It is difficult to isolate the dark impulses that drive a person to murder but key among the personality traits behind Mason's rampage would have been his latent aggression, compliant nature and extreme immaturity. Even those aspects of his personality didn't in and of themselves predestine disaster but they did predispose him toward a certain group of friends.

Bobby wasn't quiet about his obsession with guns. Throughout his life, in whatever setting he was in, he seemed to draw out and connect with people who shared that interest while his vocal belligerence toward police repelled more moderate friends. He'd hang around gun shops where he met fellow gun nuts. On construction sites, if there was another worker who had a bunker under his house stocked with automatic weapons, he and Bobby would find each other. In Four Corners, there seemed to be a lot of such people and their sentiments would surface unreserved. One acquaintance would introduce him to another until Bobby's entire social network was a web of people with similar attitudes. In fact Bobby seemed to have such a singular interest in guns that people were blinded to other attributes and dimensions of his personality. A local gun-shop owner described him as "a real nice guy who was mentally slow. He lived for guns, paramilitary training and hated the government. His only hope was for the world to end."

Bobby did have other interests, however: his Native American heritage and the deserts and canyons of the American Southwest. In time they would be subverted into an extension of his fascination with weapons and a stage for his violent fantasies. But in the beginning they were pure. He would never express his affinity for the desert with words of love as Jason McVean did, but the allure was there from his earliest years. In fact, it was Bobby who introduced McVean to the desert, who shared with his friend the wonder of trekking rugged wilderness canyons and camping under the desert stars. As a child, he spent cherished days following his grandfather as he hiked in and out of the shadows of towering red canyon walls, climbed wind-textured rock formations and hopped boulder to boulder across an incongruent desert stream.

Whether it was his interest in Native American artifacts that led him into the desert or his time in the desert that spurred his interest in the stone tools he'd find there, Bobby spent every free weekend of his adolescence and whatever time he could spare as an adult there, hiking, camping and searching for arrowheads. As a young adult, Bobby enrolled in Fort Lewis College, interested in studying archeology. No scholar, he lasted only a semester but the interest was genuine.

The presence of native cultures remains trapped within the canyons, even though the people disappeared centuries ago. Their pre-Columbian stone and adobe houses dot the canyon walls. Shards of their six-hundred-year-old pottery scatter across the trails. Their tools wash to the surface with spring floods. Their bones lay buried among the crevices and boulders. It was legal on public land to collect an arrowhead found lying on the ground surface. In his zeal, when profit rather than passion was the intent, Mason reportedly went further than that, often engaging in the forbidden practice of digging on the reservation.

The black market for Native American artifacts was huge. Intact pottery was by far the most valuable and while Mason and McVean purportedly often dug for pots, their friends agree they never found any. Mason did find arrowheads, however. He undoubtedly sold some to finance his expanding arsenal. But some he kept for himself, sacred objects from a time when *warrior* was a way of life.

Bobby met Jason McVean in the eighth grade. The friendship that quickly developed between the two would, twelve years down the road, be both of their undoing. Jason, whose parents had divorced several years earlier, had recently moved to Durango from Texas to live with his dad. Good-looking, smart and confident, he could have fit in with one of the more popular junior high cliques, but something about the odd kid who doodled pictures of guns in the margins of his schoolwork resonated with him. By that time, Bobby's antics in class plus his preoccupation with warriors, weapons and violence made the parents of his playmates uneasy. His fascination, they would recount years later, seemed unhealthy even when measured against the typical excesses of male adolescence. He constantly drew pictures of guns, scribbled battlefield maneuvers and talked about shooting this or blowing up that. Throughout his teens and early adulthood he was mesmerized by violent war action movies, watching videos of films like *Full Metal Jacket* or *Platoon* over and over. He was relegated to the margins of middle-school society. But Jason chose him as his best friend and Bobby reciprocated.

While parents of after-school friends had reservations about Bobby, they had none about the engaging new boy he brought with him to their homes. Ann and Gary Mason, however, were forming the opposite impression. By ninth grade Jason was rapidly becoming the poster boy for the school's drug subculture. Bobby followed suit. As the boys entered high school, the Masons began a seesaw battle with Jason McVean for their son's soul.

"Almost from the start, we were worried about Jason's influence on Bobby," Ann Mason said. "We thought Jason was trouble and tried to discourage the friendship." For a while the battle was a draw. The boys' friendship didn't falter but Bobby seemed to be keeping his head above water in the mainstream.

Police reports and friends' recollections would repeatedly label Bobby as mentally slow, but that was not the case. He had been identified at an early age as a potentially gifted learner. In elementary school he was a solid chess player and almost always beat schoolmates in other games of strategy. He had natural artistic talent and as a teenager would draw accomplished pen and ink studies of Native American artifacts and cultural symbols. Despite his disinterest in school he maintained above-average grades. As he entered high school, Bobby Mason appeared to be on track. He went out for junior varsity football and demonstrated unexpected athletic ability. It was an activity his parents hoped signaled his broadening interests and normal socialization.

Midway through his sophomore year, however, Mason's grades and his newfound interest in school activities fell off a cliff. Following McVean into the deep canyons of drug abuse, the two were stoned daily and high on crystal meth whenever they could score it. Ironically, it was their journey together into that harsh world that seemingly did what Ann and Gary Mason's prodding had been unable to do, separate the two friends. Flunking out of Durango High School, they went their separate ways. Bobby immediately passed the test for a high school Graduate Equivalency Diploma and began working low-end odd jobs. McVean attended a private high school.

Ann and Gary got Bobby into counseling. He eventually rebelled and finally refused to continue therapy, but he had at least gone long enough to get clean of hard drugs, his parents believed. He continued to smoke pot, they admitted, but more on a recreational schedule rather than as a daily habit. When he got arrested for shoplifting he agreed to help police snare McVean and his dealers. His parents signed the papers allowing police to use Bobby, at seventeen still a minor, as an informant. Nothing came of the investigation, but it proved that distance had greatly weakened McVean's gravitational pull on Bobby. It remained that way between the former friends and future conspirators for several years.

A couple of months before his eighteenth birthday, Bobby enlisted in the army. He met with the recruiter, filled out the paperwork and completed all the required steps. Only one last form needed to be signed and that was to be done the following day. Gary, a Vietnam vet who believed the army would teach his son discipline and give him a sense of responsibility, intended to go with Bobby to the recruiting station and encourage he be shipped out immediately rather than delaying his activation until he turned eighteen as is customary. Ann, however, with a mother's dread of sending her baby into combat, persevered. "With just a GED, Bobby would have ended up in a tank crew and, while US troops were not in a conflict at the time, if hostilities developed they take the first casualties," she argued. By morning, enlistment was off and in her mind Ann had kept her son from violent harm. Instead, Bobby stumbled down a path that would enlist him in Jason McVean's war until he lay dead under the desert sun.

Drifting into construction work as a laborer, Bobby moved from job to job, crew to crew picking up along the way the skills of bricklaying and stonework. True to his name, he was a natural mason. By his early twenties, he was a self-employed tradesman subcontracting out to building contractors and landscape companies. His prices were fair. He worked hard, completed projects on time and always did a quality job. In fact, some of the contractors he worked for claimed he was the best stonemason in the region and more than one remarked that he worked so incessantly they had to chide him into taking a break. During the summer building season he was in constant demand. It was sometime in this period at one of his jobs, his parents speculate, that Bobby ran into Jason McVean working for his contractor father.

They were, it turned out, still best friends. The friendship that made them inseparable buddies in junior high once again bound them to each other for the remainder of their short lives. Like Butch and Sundance, whatever wild young men did—drink beer, shoot guns, camp, carouse with the guys—they did together.

In the years they were apart, McVean had developed an elaborate belief system intertwining conspiracy theories, apocalyptic predictions, and suspicions of systematic oppression, specifically of ordinary white Americans like him and Bobby. Bobby, who still had an adolescent fascination with video violence and joystick justice, was the susceptible sidekick. He absorbed Jason's ideas and adopted them as his own. "Out of the blue he started making racial slurs," noted his shocked parents. "That was never something he heard in our home nor an attitude he grew up around." They figured he picked it up working construction. Around friends, he'd parrot more of McVean's antiblack, anti-immigrant, anticorporation, antigovernment philosophy, but louder and with more vehemence than ever verbalized by the more contemplative McVean. Less inclined to keep his extremism under cover, Mason often ended his rant with a violent resolution: "Shoot them. Kill them."

It was likely more posturing than commitment. He talked harshly about police, claimed he did not pay taxes and fumed about the specter of gun control. Unlike McVean, however, Mason probably felt little true angst over the state of the world. McVean's ideology with its end of modern civilization and leveling of society, clashes between righteous citizen warriors and evil establishment storm troopers, and its call for heroic glory was the ideal stage for Mason's video-game fantasies. It was the promise of a battle between good and evil played out in the canyons and deserts of Four Corners with a real-life role for Robert Mason.

Outside of that role, without his guns and combat gear, outside the game put in motion by the shooting of Dale Claxton, Bobby had a gentler side. The summer before he died, he got in a confrontation with a painter on one of his jobs. Careless, the painter dripped paint on Bobby's masonry work. Mason cleaned it and told the painter to watch it. Belligerent, the painter deliberately slopped more paint on the freshly laid stone, whereupon Mason shoved the man, hard. It happens in the testosterone-driven world of construction, but Bobby regretted his actions, Ann recalled. He brooded about it for days.

While McVean treated his friends with respect and consideration, particularly Bobby, the relationship was not equal. Jason led. Bobby followed. "Bobby revered Jason. He held him in a kind of awe," one of the group they hung with told police. "He was like Jason's puppy," another mutual acquaintance said. "He followed Jason's lead and whatever Jason said, that is what they did, no questions or protest. If Jason said, 'I decided we're leaving for the desert tonight' (instead of tomorrow like they'd planned), that's what they did. If Jason at the last minute changed the location where they'd intended to camp or suddenly decided to leave behind some equipment, that's what Bobby did." Ever compliant, a loyal friend with a laid-back "whatever" attitude, Bobby was happy to go along with Jason's wishes.

The two friends were much more each other's equals, however, when it came to shooting and survival skills. They were both expert. Bobby's interest in guns moved beyond the hunting rifles his dad and brother owned at an early age.[1] He was interested in the guns and gear of warriors. As an adult he acquired them as rapidly as his paychecks allowed. With no rent and few other expenses (his father helped him buy his truck), almost all of every paycheck for an estimated four or five years went to buying guns, ammo, commando equipment and survival supplies. Nobody knows how many guns Mason owned. Many would cycle quickly through a few rounds of ammunition at the gravel pit where they target shot, be cleaned, greased, sealed in PCV pipe and buried in the desert, along with giant containers of food, water bottles, crates of ammunition, explosives and other supplies. Friends that had been out shooting with him could account for only a few of the weapons he purchased: a fully automatic AK-47, four SKS assault rifles, two FN FAL combat rifles, an M16, a .308 hunting rifle, and together with McVean a .50-caliber sniper rifle and two 9mm Glock pistols, plus two bulletproof vests and a Kevlar combat helmet, grenades, and C-4 explosive. As they slipped stealthily through the desert, Mason and his comrades were clothed, equipped and armed comparable to the military's elite Special Forces.

As their son grew more extreme, Ann and Gary continued to see Bobby through the charitable eyes of parents. The camo military fatigues that had become the only pants he wore looked comfortable for around town and practical for construction work. Consistent with his aversion to the designer clothes worn by contemporaries, the camo pants were his antifashion statement. The gun, ammunition and commando supply catalogs mixed in with their mail were harmless reading and pictures related to Bobby's quirky interest. The UPS and FedEx shipments that Bobby had sent to their home, since he had no address of his own, were just cardboard boxes. Ann didn't look to see who they came from or try to guess what was in them. In the back of her mind, however, she suspected and worried. Ultimately she refused delivery.

Bobby was secretive. He told his parents little about what he did, who he was with or his plans. He stopped by home frequently but not according to any schedule. "Came by for food and money," he'd joke as he suddenly appeared at the door. He often disappeared for several days, leaving his parents with no idea of his whereabouts and no way to contact him.

Ann and Gary, in turn, didn't press him for information. "He was no longer a child. He was an adult," Gary explained. "When your children are grown it's different. We had no right to pry, no basis to command."

Besides, in their eyes Bobby was finally growing up and finding direction. He had a true job skill and had proven himself a good worker with solid earning potential. He seemed more thoughtful of others. At their home he built them a *Better Homes and Gardens–*worthy flagstone patio. It was an expression of his artistic ability, according to Ann. And a year before his last visit home, he had adopted a German shepherd puppy. He named it Dirk, the faux-name he was given in his high school German class, and proved himself to be a gentle and responsible caretaker. It was clear to all who saw man and dog interact, Bobby loved Dirk and Dirk loved him back.

Still, on the evening of Wednesday, May 27, 1998, when Bobby dropped Dirk at the Masons saying he was going camping and Dirk needed to stay with them, Gary Mason was worried. They occasionally took care of the dog, but usually when Bobby went camping, Dirk went with him.

"Why don't you take Dirk with you?" Gary demanded.

"I can't, not this time," Bobby answered.

"Why not?"

"I just can't. You've got to keep him. I'll be back Sunday night to get him."

Gary could not put his finger on it but there was something about Bobby leaving Dirk with them this time that made him uneasy. There was an unnatural tenseness about his son. Gary had a feeling something was not right about this camping trip.

Earlier in the day, Mason withdrew thirty-nine dollars from his savings account at Southwest Federal Credit Union in Durango, leaving the minimum twenty-five-dollar balance required to keep the account open. Much more money was readily available to him. The day before, a landscaper friend who Mason often did subcontract work for urged him to finish up a patio he was building before he left on his camping trip. At a party the next day, the friend again confronted him for not showing up and completing the job. Mason said he was getting supplies for the project and would complete it the next day. He had only a few more steps to lay and the job would be finished, less than a morning's work. Per his arrangement, he would have received a check of several hundred dollars for the project the same day.

In Bobby Mason currency, that was enough to buy more guns, several cases of ammunition and a couple hundred pounds of instant potatoes that could be buried in the desert where only he, Jason and Monte could find it. But the dependable young mason never went back to lay those steps or for payment for the work he had already completed. Perhaps he knew that the time of collecting and hoarding, hiding and storing was over. Practice and training was done. Tomorrow, he and his friends would start the revolution.

CHAPTER 12
SWINGING BRIDGE

Commander Greg McCain knew the minute he stepped off the bus that "it was a fucked-up operation." Within four hours of receiving a request for assistance from Dolores County Sheriff Jerry Martin, McCain and the nine members of his tactical team selected for the assignment were skimming a few hundred feet over the Rocky Mountains' tallest peaks aboard National Guard helicopters. Each man, dressed in full tactical gear for immediate deployment, carried enough food, water and supplies to last three to five days in the wilderness on his own. The 360-mile trip from Colorado Springs to Cortez with a refueling stop in Grand Junction, Colorado, had taken three hours. At the Cortez airport they boarded a waiting school bus for the half-hour drive to the manhunt command post in Cahone, Colorado.

Now as he surveyed the scene around him, McCain wondered if he should just turn around and take his team home. From what he'd been told of the situation, he knew it was dangerous. Risk was part of the bargain, but there were certain conditions, rules for the way things should be done that his team considered mandatory before stepping in harm's way.

"This was supposed to be a damn hot zone," McCain sputtered to himself. No one knew where the bad guys were or for that matter how many there were, how they were trained or what kind of weapons they had. Yet as night closed in on the Cahone Community Center, commandeered as manhunt headquarters, he saw a half-dozen SWAT teams milling about with sitting-duck nonchalance in front of the building. Eight or ten helicopters sat unguarded on the grounds. Peering farther out at the twilight perimeter of the property, he saw—no one. No one had secured the area.

Inside the command post, McCain was anything but reassured. "Some miscues and confusion are to be expected," he noted, "but this was complete chaos. Intel was confusing. Key information was not being shared. No one knew for sure where everyone was or had been, or even who they all were. Many of the squads were not trained or equipped for a wilderness manhunt. Field reports were often sketchy or nonexistent." In addition, most of the officers had shown up voluntarily and the gathering force was more like Woodstock than the deployment of a regimented army.

Martin's and Lacy's tenuous control of the manhunt was particularly troubling to McCain. At five-foot-ten with a weight lifter's build, short-cropped hair and steel-gray eyes, McCain had the bearing and no-nonsense demeanor of an elite Special Forces field officer. Over the past thirteen years, he had trained his SWAT team at the Pueblo County Sheriff's Office as if that were the case. The twenty-four-hundred-square-mile county one hundred miles south of Denver demanded an exceptionally broad skill set for SWAT operations. "We had urban tactical conditions within the City of Pueblo, but we also had mountain wilderness terrain with twelve-thousand-foot peaks on the western side of the county and prairie desert on the east," McCain said. His team trained continuously, rigorously, in each environment. As a result, it had a reputation as one of the top SWAT teams in the state.

Rivaling the expertise of the Pueblo County team was the special squad assembled just for this assignment from El Paso County. It too had been asked to help. McCain had been in the crowded command post only a few minutes when he felt someone behind him grab his arm. Turning, he stood face-to-face with El Paso County Under-sheriff Ivan Middlemiss. As sheriff office commanders from adjacent counties, the men knew each other well and shared a mutual respect for each other's units.

Middlemiss's gaze swept the room and then with eyebrows arched settled unblinking on McCain. The unspoken question was clear: "Well, what do you think?" McCain shook his head with an expression of disbelief.

With a slight nod, Middlemiss agreed with the assessment.

He had arrived with his team early that afternoon and had already had a shouting match with Sheriff Martin. "You asked for our assistance. We came and now you're not putting us out there," he growled, impatient to get his team into action.

Martin, who by midday was already taxed with coordinating teams in and out of the canyons, scrambling to assimilate field reports and struggling to maintain control, had no time to insert the El Paso squad or for Middlemiss's gung-ho attitude. His answer was more or less, "Park it. Tomorrow morning starts a new day."

By morning, Middlemiss, by force of personality and his obvious capabilities as a veteran twenty-three-year Army Special Forces commander, had tacitly taken over command.

The team commanders, sheriffs and General William Westerdahl, the commanding officer of the Colorado National Guard, met in Lacy's mobile command post house trailer parked alongside the Cahone Community Center. On the table they gathered around a map drawn by one of the suspects and found in a house search by the FBI almost twenty-four hours earlier. The manhunt commanders wouldn't have had it yet had not the previous evening McCain and Middlemiss, frustrated by the lack of good intel, sent some of their men to FBI field headquarters in Cortez to demand copies of any potentially useful information. Even then they may not have been given it, had not earlier in the day Sheriff Martin gone ballistic with the FBI for withholding information. By then, Sheriffs Martin and Lacy had heard rumors of evidence and leads gathered by the agency but not shared with them. They were sending men into danger while the investigative side of the effort headquartered twenty-six miles away in Cortez held critical information tight to their chests.

Scaled properly, the hand-drawn map closely matched the features of a USGS topo map of the San Juan River and Grand Gulch sectors; an area well outside the canyons where the manhunt had concentrated. What to do with the new information, however, quickly cascaded into a cacophony of opinions. McCain, convinced that the search should be shifted to the area on the suspect's map, resisted deploying his men into canyons which had already been swept numerous times by other teams.

Others argued that the significance of the map was unknown. It could have been drawn for a river-rafting trip the suspects had planned unrelated to their crime and escape. It also may have been part of an escape plan that had been abandoned in the face of the massive police response. "Stick with the canyon area where there is hard physical evidence the fugitives began their run," Martin and Lacy concurred.

Even though by the sixth day of the manhunt, the five canyons in the search area—Cross, Squaw, Patterson, Bug and Cedar—had been penetrated by multiple tactical teams, they were not even close to be being "cleared." The canyons ranged from ten to twenty-five miles long. The canyon floors, in some stretches over a mile wide, were strewn with house-size boulders and dense clumps of brush. Hundreds of side canyons and ravines, caves and crevices breached the canyon walls while scores of abandoned uranium mines pitted the landscape. Within the five hundred square miles of blast-furnace wilderness there were thousands of places where three killers with survival skills could hide.

There was one more reason Martin, Lacy and many of their fellow officers believed the fugitives were still in the canyons; it was overconfidence bordering on arrogance. Shortly after the suspects fled into Cross Canyon, police had thrown a wide, if imperfect, net over the area. With the helicopters and roadblocks, spotters with high-power optics on the canyon rims, high-tech listening devices and body-heat detection equipment at night, plus law enforcement's overwhelming forces, it was unthinkable that three local boys slipped the net. To admit the possibility was to acknowledge the suspects' superior skill and resourcefulness, a recognition no one wanted to give ruthless cop killers.

Still, if the suspects could move undetected, the forty-mile trek along Montezuma Creek from Cross Canyon to the San Juan River could have been done in the time that had lapsed. In addition, police suspected that during the night, sympathizers drove the fugitives to new canyon locations.

Shortly after noon, Sheriff Lacy got a call from his office in Monticello, Utah, and the debate abruptly ended.

Steve Wilcox was more than apprehensive when he left home the morning of June 4; he was scared. A caseworker for the Utah Department of Social Services, Wilcox ordinarily didn't put much stock in such premonitions, but his foreboding was overpowering. He had to visit a family in Hovenweep, the last place the murderers dominating area news had been seen. He sensed he was destined to encounter them.

Four hours later, his work in Hovenweep done and now driving clear of the area, Wilcox finally began to relax. With each mile traveled west on US Highway 162 toward an afternoon appointment in Bluff, Utah, his unsettling vision of happening upon one of the killers waned. By the time he pulled into the Musi Trading Post in the tiny Navajo town of Montezuma Creek, it had diminished to nothing more than a silly notion.

The way-stop had long since ceased operating as an official trading post and was now a ramshackle convenience store. Over a long career traveling the back roads of southeastern Utah, Wilcox had stopped there often. As usual, he bought a cellophane-wrapped ham sandwich, a can of soda and a small bag of chips. He opened the soda, set the food within easy reach on the passenger's seat and continued on. Although the water flowing along the canyon floor was seldom visible from the highway on top of the mesa, his route followed the north bank of the San Juan River.

On most days, Wilcox ate as he drove between appointments, but as he approached Bluff he noted the time—12:20. He had time to stop and eat. Slowing, he did a U-turn, doubled back a few hundred yards and turned onto a gravel road. The half-mile dirt track snaked in a backward S-curve along forty-foot red sandstone bluffs as it dropped toward the river. The bottom of the "S" paralleled the water's edge. It had been a few years, but Wilcox had stopped there once before and recalled it would be a peaceful spot for a picnic.

His descent was slow, barely five miles per hour, as he studied the graffiti painted on the sandstone walls. Someone down at the river looking up the road would have had him in sight for two or three minutes by the time he finally reached the picnic area. They would have noted the tax-exempt license plates on his white Ford Bronco and the State of Utah seal on its doors. It would be natural to assume it was a police car, especially if you were on the lookout for police cars.

As Wilcox eased gently through the final curve at the river's edge, he spotted a pair of combat boots on the bank—curious, but not alarming. Cranking the wheel farther, he did a tight U-turn in the picnic area so his vehicle was pointed back up the road and stopped. It was in that instant he saw the man out his left-side window; the man in the camo pants and white T-shirt lying prone under the branches of a Russian olive tree; the man fifteen feet away aiming a rifle at his head.

Despite his morning premonition, Wilcox's mind didn't immediately flash upon the fugitives, but whoever it was, he got the message, "Get out of here fast."

The car still in gear, Wilcox stepped down on the gas. The Bronco didn't have to fight for traction as he white-knuckled the vehicle through the rutted track into the first curve. Forty yards up the road, as the speedometer needle sliced through 35 mph, Wilcox heard the shot. A small puff of dust plumed alongside the driver's side door as the Bronco bounced around the bend and the river vanished from the rearview mirror. (A second empty cartridge later found where the shooter had been lying indicated a second shot, but if there was one, Wilcox wasn't aware of it.)

Speeding to the right when he reached the highway, Wilcox

knew exactly where he had to go. His foot pressed harder on the gas, urging the vehicle to catch up with his racing heartbeat. Flying down long straightaways of empty asphalt, Wilcox hunched over the wheel, peering across a flat landscape of sand and sage for the Highway 163 cutoff. Four minutes later he'd driven a large loop and braked onto the shoulder. He had line-of-sight transmission to the cell tower at the top of Cow Canyon.

The 911 call was picked up by the San Juan County Sheriff's Office forty-seven miles away in Monticello. "Someone tried to shoot me. Down by Swinging Bridge, a man with a rifle shot at me." Wilcox's adrenaline-driven voice burst through the phone. Then ratcheting down his excitement, he told the dispatcher what happened. The nearest deputy was a few miles away in Bluff.

It took Wilcox six minutes from the time he placed the emergency call to reach the top of Cow Canyon. He parked and waited. Two minutes latter a San Juan County Sheriff's Office patrol car pulled up. A large man dressed in ordinary street clothes got out and walked toward him. Wilcox lowered his window.

On the edge of death, the large man lying on the gurney watched the ceiling lights slip past as the EMTs rolled him toward the emergency surgery bay. "It was," he thought, "kind of ironic." He had woken up that morning fully expecting the day would bring a rushed trip to the hospital. He didn't think he would be the one admitted.

San Juan County, Utah, Sheriff Deputy Kelly Bradford had taken the day off. Thirty-four years old, married and the father of four, he and his wife were expecting their fifth child. That day, June 4, was the due date. By midmorning, his wife was still reporting no twinges of labor and Bradford, anxious and antsy, needed something to do. He decided to drive to nearby Bluff to take witness statements related to the arrest of an escaped felon there the day before. He was talking with the owner of an auto repair shop, when the call came in.

According to the sheriff's office dispatcher, the gunman sighting was just three miles east of his location. The top of Cow Canyon where Bradford agreed to meet the man who reported the incident put him halfway there.

As Bradford listened to Wilcox describe what had happened, he formed a detailed picture in his mind. He knew the Swinging Bridge area well—the curve of the road to the river's edge, the boat landing, picnic area and fifty yards upriver from there, the suspended cable and plank footbridge connecting the vast Navajo reservation on the south bank of the river to San Juan County on the north. He pictured the surrounding bluffs; the forty-foot sandstone wall east of the road, its lower surfaces eroded away by millenniums of spring floods, its upper reaches overhanging the spot Wilcox said the gunman was lying. He pictured how if he approached the area from on top of the mesa rather than the access road Wilcox used, he could sneak up on the gunman from above.

From the flats where he'd leave his vehicle, he would move cautiously down a short steep slope to the point where the wall became vertical. He would have to be extra careful not to dislodge pebbles or debris with his steps that could skitter down over the edge and alert the gunman below to his approach. Short of that mistake, he would be undetected, completely hidden from the gunman until he peered over the edge, trained his rifle on him and ordered him to give up.

Standing alongside his vehicle at the top of Cow Canyon, Bradford fastened the Velcro straps under his arms that tightened the bulletproof vest around his barrel-chested XXL torso. Even though he was dressed in his off-duty casual khaki pants and a sports shirt, with the body armor on there was no mistaking he was cop. The back and forth of other officers reporting their relative locations on the police radio competed with the sound of wind rushing along the canyon tops.

Until that moment, Bradford hadn't noticed the wind. Now as he watched, small cyclones of dust appeared where the wind swirled into momentary eddies, then just as suddenly dissipated. Here and there, a piece of broken-off, dried-brown sagebrush was passed between its green, still-rooted brethren. Caught for a moment in a tangle of branches, then at the wind's urging sent on its way, it moved bucket-brigade fashion, bush to rock to fence post, toward some infinite destination. "The wind will help," Bradford thought. Only loud noise would filter down from the mesa to the canyon floor in any case, but wind would further blanket his approach.

He slid in behind the wheel of his patrol car just as dispatch radioed that help was en route and advised that he wait for backup before entering the area.

"Proceeding to a safe vantage point overlooking the north bank of the Swinging Bridge area but will not attempt to enter the area," Bradford responded. The drive from Cow Canyon to the top of the bluff at Swinging Bridge took six minutes. Bradford used the time to visualize his plan step by step, over and over again. "It's safe," he reassured himself. "From down below where Wilcox saw him, the gunman can't see or shoot me. I'll be fine."

Bobby Mason squeezed the trigger of his FN FAL .308-caliber rifle. He was aiming toward the white Bronco with State of Utah seals on its doors, but it was unlikely that he intended to hit the vehicle or its driver. For a marksman of his skill, hitting a car at a mere forty yards would have been an easy shot. And he had already passed up even easier shots. At one point, the vehicle passed within six feet of him as he lay in a prone shooting position, rifle at his shoulder, index finger on its trigger. A few seconds later, when the Bronco did a U-turn and stopped, he had a point-blank still-shot at the driver's head.

Wilcox would always wonder why Mason didn't take that shot—why he wasn't killed that day at Swinging Bridge. The likely answer was that despite the state vehicle he was driving, it was evident that Wilcox was not a police officer. During their escape from Cortez, the fugitives had already spared other civilians who had ended up in their sights. Their personal war, it seems, was with police, not the public.

Why he did fire a shot toward the departing vehicle also remains a mystery. It may have been nothing more than a warning, "Stay away from here. This is our rendezvous location." Or by that point in the chase, with their plans disrupted and separated from his friends, Mason could have been ready for a standoff. Perhaps Wilcox was spared so he could perform the function he did—send police into the breach. Whatever the reason, as soon as he pulled the trigger, Mason had but a few minutes to prepare.

Whether or not Mason met with others that morning is unknown but by the time Wilcox arrived, he was most likely alone.[1] Nevertheless, based on Wilcox's description and evidence found at the scene, those moments and what he did next can be reasonably guessed.

Despite the public nature of the Swinging Bridge site, upon his arrival Mason showed little concern that he would be discovered as he set about catching up on some routine camping chores. Stripped to his T-shirt, he slipped off his boots; removed his sweat-soaked socks and washed them in the river; filled canteens; and made tape repairs to equipment. Based on equipment and items found at the edge of the river, he was in the midst of those activities when the sound of Wilcox's car prompted him to grab his rifle and find cover.

As the sound of the shots he'd fired toward Wilcox's retreating SUV drowned under the noise of the rushing river, Mason's unguarded demeanor disappeared as well. A trail of evidence from his dash back over the bridge to a bunker on the opposite bank suggests that he now moved with near-panic haste. Springing from his hiding place under the branches of the Russian olive tree from which he fired the shots, Mason ran barefoot to where his boots sat by the riverbank, pulled on dry socks, then quickly laced and tied each boot. The other articles of clothing he'd stripped off while relaxing by the river must have been nearby. He donned a navy blue bulletproof vest and pulled a camo field jacket over it, taking the time to fasten only the second button. Next he slipped a utility belt made of tan webbing over his left shoulder. Sewn to the belt were multiple pockets filled with ammunition.

The items he left behind were not as essential as the time it would have taken to gather them up: two canteens; the socks he'd stripped off, washed in the river and hung on the branches of a shrub to dry; black tape and an earphone cord.

Patches of damp soil along the riverbanks recorded Mason's

movement as he sprinted over the bridge. Two hundred yards long, the bridge swagged between stone buttresses on each bank and a midway support structure. Built nearly a half century earlier to allow workers to cross from the reservation to the oil fields, it had fallen into disrepair but was still used by schoolchildren and the occasional shopper heading into Bluff.

The regular rhythm of Mason's wide loping steps would have sent the bridge into a syncopated bouncing motion. At the points where the bridge sagged closest to water, the bounce was pronounced enough to threaten his balance. On some steps, planks worn smooth by thousands of Navajo feet and made slick by decades of moisture and rot suddenly dropped several inches lower than where he'd expect to touch solid. On other steps, the footbed rose and met his soles prematurely. As much as his kinesthetic sense would have warned him to break step and allow the bridge to settle, the crossing was where he was most exposed. The thought must have spurred him to hurry, urging him to slow only at spots where three or four missing planks left a gap to be straddled by stepping on the side support cable. Panting, sweating, fighting for his balance, watching for gaps that would drop him into the river where the weight of his gear would drag him to the bottom, he wouldn't have dared look back. He couldn't risk the time to separate fear from reality.

Running past the buttresses, Mason leapt from the last bridge plank onto the path angling up the bank. The toe of his boot scuffed into the upward sloping ground. He stumbled but recovered his stride, spun and dashed for trees that lined the river to his right. Flinging himself facedown behind the first bush, Mason pressed his body against the cool, moist soil and gasped for breath.

He crawled forward to the far edge of the thicket on his hands and knees. Police would later find the unusual tracks of his precaution. Halting his crawl every few feet and peering through openings in the thick vegetation, he surveyed the far side of the river. There was no police car, no patrolman leveling a rifle toward him. The enemy hadn't yet stormed the area.

Safe for the moment, Mason stood and trotted across thirty feet of open space to the bunker he'd prepared earlier. The oval-shaped natural depression was twelve by six feet, its long axis running diagonal to the river. On one end, the branches of juniper trees protruded into it. The backside met with a tangle of dense brush. On the river and clearing side it was edged with a sand berm Mason had enhanced with soil scraped from the floor of the pit. Forty feet from the river's edge, it provided a commanding view of the bridge as well as a sizable segment of the north bank.

Lying prone behind the berm, Mason lifted his head just enough to peer over the top if it. The flat-black rifle barrel poking a few inches beyond the berm would not reflect sunlight and be next to impossible to see from more than a few feet away. The flash suppressor fastened to the barrel end would even make its otherwise bright muzzle blast difficult to see. With dispassionate calm, Mason watched a man with body armor and a rifle on the opposite side of the river. As the intruder moved cautiously down from the top of the bluff toward its vertical edge, Mason's right cheek dropped tightly against the stock of his rifle.

Intent on surprising a gunman directly below the bluff he was descending, Deputy Kelly Bradford didn't stop to think that the shooter might have moved since Wilcox encountered him twenty-five minutes earlier. It didn't occur to him, as he concentrated on planting each foot firmly on the steep slope leading to a forty-foot free-fall, that 270 yards away on the opposite side of the river, a sniper was about to slowly exhale, then hold every muscle in his body perfectly still, except the index finger of his right hand.

Bradford heard and felt the shot at the same time. It hit near the neckline of his vest where the garment had no ballistic fiber and offered little more protection than a cotton T-shirt.

His first response to the sudden gaping hole into his left shoulder was surprise, uncertain where the shot came from. His second was to do as he'd been taught—dive to the ground and flatten your body as low and tight to the earth as you can. In most terrain, the move would have helped hide him from the shooter. Even on a wide-open city street, it would have altered the angle of a follow-up shot and made his body a smaller target. Pressed against the steep slope with no vegetation and the sniper directly across the river, however, the move was little different than flattening yourself upright against a building with a shooter right across the street. Bradford was a wide-open, straight-on target. Even his bulletproof vest offered minimal resistance to fire from a high-power rifle.

Clinging to the sloping ground, he was still trying to figure out what happened when a second shot punched hard into his back. The bullet drilled through the armor, shifted course upon exiting and ground toward his spine before searing its way deeper into his body.

Two out of two direct hits fired in rapid succession with open sights from 270 yards. Authorities who later studied the crime scene universally commented on the sniper's skill. "Mason was a hell of a shot," they agreed. It could be said with equal awe, that across the river from him, Bradford demonstrated extraordinary resolve to survive.

He laid still. Pain flooded his mind. Eventually fear broke through the pain. It wasn't so much a thought as an awareness: he was helpless. Any moment a third bullet could hit him. After the fear came conflict; should he lie still and hope to be left for dead or try to get to safety beyond the sights of the sniper? He decided on the second course. Inflicted with life-threatening wounds that doctors later predicted would leave him unable to walk, Bradford began the slow, painful crawl up the slope toward his car.

Propelling himself serpent-like up the steep slope, he moved forward inch by inch. From across the river, his progress, at least initially, would have been barely perceptible. His squirming would have looked more like death throes than an attempt to flee. Several minutes later, however, as he neared the top of the bluff, Bradford's movement would have been seen for the escape attempt it was. Still, a third shot never came. Another minute and he was over the edge, no longer visible to the man who had tried to kill him.

From his chin-on-the-ground perspective, the scattering of fist-size rocks in front of him looked more like boulders, but between them he saw hope—the wheels of his patrol car. He lifted his head higher to take in the whole vehicle but the effort tore at his wounds and he dropped his gaze almost immediately. Propelled by the thought of driving out of there, he pushed up onto his knees, gathered his feet under him and stood. A half step later, he collapsed back to the hardpack rocky ground. As bolts of pain rolled through his body, he eyed the twenty-five feet to his car door and thought about the son that would soon be born.

Seconds later, it was another Bradford who came to his rescue. Mike Bradford was Kelly's cousin and a Blanding, Utah, police officer. Like Kelly, he had heard the original report of a man with a gun by Swinging Bridge. Slowed and frustrated by the other cars he encountered on the two-lane highway, he floored his patrol car at every opportunity between them and covered the thirty-mile distance in about twenty-five minutes. Along the way, he'd heard Kelly Bradford relay his plan to look the situation over from on top of the bluff and headed directly to that location to provide his cousin backup support.

Mike Bradford spotted his cousin's patrol car parked a quarter mile away as he turned off the highway into the two tire ruts that led to the bluff. The twisting track cut across a gully that split the distance between the highway and unmanned vehicle. As Mike dropped into the gully, he spotted Kelly standing several feet in front of the parked car. When he popped out of the gully two seconds later, Kelly was on the ground.

His cousin must have dropped down to low-crawl to the edge of the bluff and peer over, Mike figured. Skidding to a stop behind the other car, Mike pressed the repeater button on his radio mic. "This is Blanding police officer Mike Bradford. I am at the bluff over Swinging Bridge," he reported. "I am at Deputy Bradford's location."

Releasing the repeater, he waited for the response. Other than static, none came. He tried reporting his location a second time, then a third. "Damn. No radio signal." Pulling the keys from the ignition, he jumped from the car with his bulletproof vest in hand and slipped it on as he ran to join Kelly.

"Get down!" Kelly shouted.

Startled, Mike dropped to the ground and duck-walked along-side Kelly's vehicle until he could see his cousin plainly. Twenty feet away, Kelly lay facing the vehicle, not the bluff. He'd been trying to get to the car.

"Get back," Kelly yelled. "I've been shot."

Mike turned and scrambled back to his car. Not thinking about the problem he had getting a radio call through just a minute before, he grabbed the mic and shouted, "Kelly's shot. Give me an ambulance!"

"Got that. Ambulance being dispatched to your location," the radio immediately answered.

Then, crouching low, he retraced his steps to the front of Kelly's vehicle, dropped to the ground and began crawling into the open toward the wounded man. Getting within arm's reach without drawing fire, he grabbed Kelly's hand and reversed his motion. Crawling backward, he dragged the 240-pound man back to the deputy's vehicle.

"I can't get in; hurts too much," Kelly stated matter-of-factly.

"Got to," Mike answered as he strained to move Kelly headfirst onto the rear seat. "You're going to lie across the backseat."

"I won't fit," Kelly protested.

Kelly was right; he didn't fit. Leaving the rear door open where Kelly's feet overhung the seat, Mike jumped behind the wheel and tore toward the highway. At the ravine, the car transferred a jarring bounce to its passenger. "Damn it, Mike, slow down. You're going to kill me," Kelly groaned. Mike kept moving, buoyed by the belief that implicit in his cousin's complaint was a stubborn commitment to survive.

At the highway, Mike met his chief, Mike Halliday, about to turn in toward the bluff. He handed him the department's only rifle, which he'd been carrying, and told him to be careful. The ambulance arrived a minute later.

Having heard the first police report of a gunman at Swinging Bridge and suspecting there might be injuries, the EMTs had driven south from their base in Bluff. For the past thirty minutes they had been waiting just a half mile up the road when Mike Bradford radioed for an ambulance.

It took another two minutes to move Kelly onto a gurney and into the back of the ambulance. Mike watched it speed away, then turned back toward the bluff to join Halliday. For the next five hours, the two officers with one rifle between them lay side by side overlooking the river valley and watched the search unfold.

Sheriff Lacy hung up the phone and looked at the police commanders huddled around the hand-drawn map the FBI had found among the suspects' possessions. There was no doubt the map depicted the San Juan River but there was uncertainty about what it meant. The buzz of voices within the small trailer house next to the Cahone command post subsided quickly to an expectant silence as Lacy started to speak.

"There's been a reliable sighting of a gunman on the San Juan River near Bluff," he announced. "According to the report a man with a rifle shot at a fellow who drove down by Swinging Bridge to eat lunch. The incident happened about ten minutes ago. We have a deputy in that area who is checking it out."

"I want a team in there now," Middlemiss ordered.

Stepping out of the trailer, he saw several teams on the grounds in various stages of readiness. Some stood eating pastries, their body armor and gear piled a few yards away. Others had taken advantage of the downtime to clean and repack equipment that at the moment was spread across a ground tarp. At the edge of the property, however, the Pueblo County squad was in full gear, weapons in hand, patrolling the perimeter, as their commander Greg McCain had ordered.

McCain followed the last of his team into the trailer where Middlemiss and Lacy briefed them on the sudden turn of events and response plan. Fifteen minutes later, the *whoomp* of the rotor pounded in their ears, as they hunched over and scrambled into the Huey. The 'copter could only take six plus its crew and it was decided McCain should remain and help direct the unfolding action from the command post. The team had been airborne only a few minutes, however, when Lacy got a second call. His deputy had been shot.

As quickly as events seemed to be developing, Middlemiss reversed his decision. He wanted McCain on site, directing the insertion and search.

"Take my Blackhawk," General Westerdahl offered as he waved his pilot into action. McCain ran for the chopper and took the seat next to the pilot. Lacy and Martin piled into the rear seats and the bird lifted off.

Radioing his team still en route ahead of him in the Huey, McCain warned them they were going into a hot zone and ordered them dropped on the north bank downriver from the bridge, beyond what he hoped was the sniper's target area. "Clear the area up to the bridge but do not attempt to cross," McCain warned. He then radioed Middlemiss and ordered in several additional teams. His idea was to confuse and demoralize the fugitives with an overwhelming show of force.

The first of the SWAT teams arrived forty-five minutes after Mike Bradford settled in next to Chief Halliday on the overlooking bluff. The unit from the Navajo Reservation Police parked at the highway and, gliding along the base of the parallel cliff, worked their way down the same road to the river Wilcox had followed. Breaking from the cover of the cliff, the three-man team sprinted for trees along the shoreline. As they began the methodical process of shuffling forward one man at a time, a Huey pounded down the valley crossing almost level with Bradford and Halliday. A few hundred yards downriver, it hovered twenty feet off the ground while the Pueblo team rappelled into action.

The Blackhawk swept in over the south rim, touched down briefly to place Martin and Lacy on a high vantage point, and shot back into the air. Behind it a half dozen more helicopters inserted teams both downstream and upriver in an attempt to seal off escape in either direction along the canyon floor. The nearest of those teams to the site of the shooting was the El Paso County team, inserted about the same distance east of the picnic area as the Pueblo team was west of it. Slipping cautiously from rock to tree, the Pueblo, El Paso and Navajo teams converged on the bridge.

On top of the canyon, Lacy's deputies had quickly set up a road-block on Highway 162 east of Bluff and a second one below the turn-off to Swinging Bridge. The only vehicles allowed to pass through carried police. Of those, there were dozens as word of the shooting spread and law enforcement flooded the area.

With their SWAT teams off-loaded, the eight helicopters beat back and forth along the two-mile stretch of canyon in what McCain hoped would be a disheartening display of force. As one skimmed along the treetops then suddenly shot skyward, another would dive low. One would scream across the canyon walls while another dropped close to the floor spinning a whirlwind of dust. For more than three hours, the pilots improvised the aerial shock and awe show, tense to the possibility of a midair collision within the confines of the mile-wide canyon.

McCain's Blackhawk zigzagged among them as he flew from one vantage point to another directing the ground teams. As more teams swarmed the area, however, his ability to control what was happening below him quickly found its limits.

Radio communication with the ground deteriorated as different squads tuned to their own frequencies rather than the universal channel—NLEC (National Law Enforcement Channel). Even that channel, which depended on line-of-sight transmission, had blind spots within the twisting geography of the canyon. Struggling to coordinate the influx of personnel, McCain pressed the headphones for the NLEC radio to his right ear. Against his left ear, he held the headphone for a second radio that scanned the other police frequencies. In a high-pressure game of juggling multiple conversations at the same time, he might hear, "We are approaching the bridge," with his right ear while into his left ear another team reports, "We are on the ridge."

Frantically trying to contact each team and direct it to a strategic position, McCain soon realized that even when he did establish radio contact, some teams weren't going to follow his command. Teams he'd placed at the edges of the search area to prevent escape would suddenly show up in another location. "Who took your watch on the ridge?" he'd ask a team that appeared out of place.

"Ahh—it was all quiet at the ridge, Blackhawk," they would respond. "Looked like there might be more action down here."

"Son of a bitch," he fumed to the pilot. "There's no one watching from the ridge. Those asshole glory seekers just left the position unmanned and now that's another big hole these killers can run through." Despite the manpower, the canyon was anything but sealed off, McCain realized, but by then there was no longer any point in trying to shut the doors. Determined to regain control, he focused on the teams he knew he could count on: his own Pueblo team, the El Paso squad and the few others that demonstrated the discipline the situation demanded.

Converging on the north bank at the foot of the bridge, the Pueblo, El Paso and Navajo SWAT teams established a perimeter and waited for orders. Finally, McCain ordered them across.

The first to cross went in pairs, one man from the Pueblo squad and one from El Paso running side by side. As the first Pueblo officer leapt from cover and charged the bridge, his shout captured the moment; two words that vented the pent-up anxiety of waiting to act and masked fear with lighthearted bravado. Two words that expressed sentiments of rebellion at a dangerous order yet, in the banter of men, declared their willingness to obey the man who gave them the order: "Fuck McCain!"

The battle cry was caught up by others. As the first pair reached the center of the bridge, the next pair sprang into the open, "Fuck McCain!" and they thundered onto the wooden planks. "Fuck McCain." "Fuck McCain." And eight men were across.

As soon as the first pair touched the south bank, they split in opposite directions and found shooting positions. The subsequent pairs filled between them forming a fan of riflemen in front of the bridge. A handful of officers stayed to secure the north end of the bridge. The balance stormed onto it single file, one on the heels of the other. Two minutes later the crossing officers had all found cover on the south bank and the teams began their search of the area. The boot-print tracks they had discovered on the north end of the bridge were also evident on this side. Breaking into small clusters, some men remained in position at the bridge, others moved off to the left. The main contingent followed the path and tracks to the right, into the tree line along the river.

In the trees, they could see pressed into the moist soil where someone had dropped to their knees and crawled to where the path broke into a thirty-foot clearing. Here the searchers split up, some staying in the trees as they circled around the far side of the clearing, others moving up through the brushy edge on the near side. Toward the upper edge of the clearing was a low sand berm.

From the nearside group came the shout, "Rifle." The sound of safeties being clicked off followed, as a semicircle of men swung weapons to their shoulders. Poking above the berm, pointed skyward was the barrel of a rifle topped with a flash suppressor.

A Pueblo officer slipped from the formation, moving deeper into the trees where he'd be hidden from the berm as he circled behind it. Working his way cautiously through the vegetation, he kept his rifle pointed ahead, finger on the trigger, moving silently toward the menace until he could see into the bunker.

"He's dead," he shouted.

What happened next is not exactly clear. Reports and statements by several of the police officers present differ in some significant—and in light of questions that would later surface—important details. What was the position of Mason's body when it was discovered? Some reports claim it was sitting in a semiprone position, others that he was found lying facedown, feet sprawled out behind him. Did police move the body? Some say absolutely not; that would be a breach of crime scene procedure. Some say yes but minimally, just to identify the body. Others say the body position was changed significantly from how it was discovered to how it was when crime scene investigators photographed and officially recorded it. Others go so far as to suggest that the scene was "staged" in an attempt to mislead. None of the reports insinuate Mason was not already dead when the three SWAT teams found the body at 5:45 P.M., nearly five hours after Deputy Bradford was shot.

This much, however, was clear: from the vantage point of the bunker, Mason could have inflicted heavy losses on police breaking cover on the north bank or crossing the bridge. "We're lucky he was dead. If he wanted to he could have taken us out one at a time," one officer observed.

One other fact was quickly noted; next to Mason's body were three pipe bombs. Upon spotting them, the officers backed away.[2]

With the discovery of one suspect, chaos flared across the valley. "There's a second suspect, he's moving south," someone yelled over the NLEC channel. The call shifted the attention of dozens of police. A short time later a second frenzied voice called, "The second suspect is down." Then a third sighting was reported. Police surged toward the location of each report only to find no sign of a second suspect. In the ensuing confusion, McCain concluded the reports were the imaginings of overexcited officers. "Find the guys making those reports and get them out of this valley," he ordered.

By 8 P.M., when Colorado Bureau of Investigation Special Agent Wayne Bryant arrived to oversee crime scene investigation, police presence in the valley had wound down to the original three teams supplemented by San Juan County deputies and a smattering of other law enforcement personnel. Keeping his distance, Bryant photographed Mason's body and strung a yellow tape barrier to protect the site from further trampling. Close inspection would wait until the following day, after bomb disposal technicians had rendered the site safe.

It was dark by the time McCain's team boarded a bus that would transport them to the new command post that had been relocated that afternoon from Cahone to the Bluff middle school. After a day of trying to rein in the undisciplined surge of forces in the valley, the sight that greeted him at Bluff was a final straw. Over five hundred police had descended on the post since the report of a gunman at Swinging Bridge had gone out ten hours earlier. Helicopters covered the football field. Weapons and gear were left unattended across the grounds, as officers jockeyed for food and a place to sleep. "Don't take a lot to eat," one officer warned the action-weary Pueblo team.

He had obviously just driven in that evening and had two sandwiches on his tray.

"Get yourselves some dinner and meet by the bus. We're heading home tonight," McCain told his men. He then went searching for whomever would be taking over the operation so he could brief him on that day's action. Instead he found an FBI agent and a commander of the Utah State Police in a heated argument, each claiming authority.

Mason's body was on Navajo Nation land and the rule as to who had authority over the crime scene was convoluted. In most cases, being on the reservation would put Indian police and federal agencies in charge. But the perpetrator was presumed to be white. That made the county sheriff in charge, according to Sheriff Lacy. Mason, however, was a registered member of a Native American tribe, clouding the issue further. The uncertain claim to authority between the reservation and adjacent San Juan County left an opening for the Utah Department of Public Safety (state police) to assert its right to run operations. Add to that, Lacy had already taken the unusual step of assigning crime scene investigation to an agency from another state, the Colorado Bureau of Investigation. Plus people from Colorado police agencies had, with Lacy's blessing, already commanded operations on both sides of the river.

McCain wanted no part of it. Stepping in tight enough to interrupt the argument, he leveled his stare at one man, then the other. "I don't care who wins this pissing match," he announced. "I'm out of it." He debriefed both men and left.

CHAPTER 13
UNCERTAIN DEATH

According to police records, Navajo police assumed authority for the crime scene overnight, but final authority for processing the scene and for the manhunt on both sides of the river seemingly remained in the hands of Sheriff Lacy. The refocused effort along the northern edge of the Navajo Reservation once again forced Lacy and Butler together but if anything had changed since their engagement in Cross Canyon, it was that the relationship had deteriorated further. What Lacy didn't know was that a few days before Butler had traveled to Salt Lake City where he met with the US Attorney's Office to discuss jurisdictional issues and a hypothetical action plan that circumvented the sheriff in the event Navajo Nation police captured the suspects on their own.

At midmorning, June 5, bomb specialists from El Paso County and the Colorado Springs Police Department arrived at the scene. The pipe bombs were removed first. If detonated, the devices would have spread lethal shrapnel several yards in every direction. Behind protective rocks a few yards away, a remote-controlled disrupter rendered them harmless.

With the bombs removed, police still worried that the body and gear in the bunker could be booby-trapped to explode when moved. Using the cable winch on the front of the medical examiner's SUV, the bomb techs remotely lifted the rifle and backpack from the bunker. An X-ray revealed the backpack was safe to search. Mason's body was last. With a piece of rope, they tied a sling between the utility belt Mason wore over one shoulder and his right thigh. The winch cable was hooked on the sling. As the officers watched from behind the vehicle, the winch slowly dragged the body over the lip of the berm into the clearing.

Minutes later it was strapped to a gurney in the back of the medical examiner's vehicle as the car bounced along a dirt road angling through twenty miles of reservation before turning north to Salt Lake City.

Even to the casual observer, there was something that didn't seem right about the police's hasty explanation of how Robert Mason died. It was clear that hours before his death, he wasn't planning suicide. He washed out socks and hung them to dry, filled canteens—activities that suggested he wasn't planning to end it there and if circumstances suddenly changed his mind, his police profile had him going out in a blazing shootout, not quietly killing himself.

Dr. Maureen Frikke of the Utah State Medical Examiner's Office bent close to the naked corpse on the table in front of her, dictating her observations into the microphone that hung above the body. Methodically, she examined the man's feet, legs, hands and arms, torso, and last, the bullet wound in his mouth. The meticulous external examination was the first step in each of the seven or eight autopsies she would perform that week, indeed for each of the nearly three thousand she had performed already in her career.

By that point, as she examined Bobby Mason's body, Dr. Frikke was by every standard a highly experienced, highly regarded forensic scientist. A graduate of Washington University Medical School in St. Louis, she specialized in pathology during an internship and residency at the University of Florida Hospital in Gainesville and then received a prestigious fellowship in forensic pathology while she trained and practiced with the Medical Examiner's Office in Minneapolis. She had been with the Utah State Medical Examiner's Office seven years. It is a position within the broader field of pathology that specifies that every workday, every case involves death under uncertain, suspicious circumstances, possibly a crime.

Dr. Frikke was adept at shedding light on those circumstances, weighing facts and stats to determine what did and did not likely happen. Prosecutors called on her to testify as an expert witness in court two or three times a month. Law enforcement agencies across the state unreservedly relied on her expert opinion to help solve crimes. Except in the case of Bobby Mason's death when her opinion was an unwelcome complication.

Several weeks after performing the autopsy on Mason, she conveyed to Mason's mother, "Police had already decided Robert's death was a suicide even before the autopsy." Even after her report challenging that conclusion she received only one routine follow-up call from the investigating agency. Their lack of interest in her findings was, in her word, "amazing."

The first seeds of doubt were planted as Dr. Frikke studied the trajectory of Mason's bullet wound. The path from the entry point on the roof of his mouth to the back of his skull showed that Mason's neck was hyperextended when he was shot, his head tipped back at an extreme angle atypical for a self-inflicted wound. It was even more unusual considering the Kevlar helmet Mason wore would have restricted head movement and made such a tilt unnaturally difficult. As an isolated inconsistency with the suicide theory, the tilt of Mason's head could have been shrugged off as a curiosity, uncommon but not impossible. Guided by the principle of Occam's razor—the simplest solution is usually the correct one—it could be reasonable to conclude that Mason put the muzzle of his Glock 9mm pistol in his mouth and in a final flinch at what he was about to do, tossed his head back as he pulled the trigger.

But the tilt of Mason's head was not the only inconsistency with the police's claim of suicide. By the time her diener began sewing the body back together using wide baseball stitches, Frikke had listed a string of observations unexplained or even incongruous with the speculative narrative of suicide. Police attempted to explain away some of those incongruities with the supposition of unlikely circum-stances, stacking one improbability on top of the next until the odds of it all having happened collapses the entire storyline. Other trou-bling observations were simply ignored. Step by step the likelihood that Mason killed himself receded into the realm of the improbable in Frikke's mind.

Aware that her observations ran counter to the police explanation of how Mason died, Frikke suggested ballistic tests to match the slug found in Mason's skull with the pistol found near his body. A posi-tive match would not prove someone else had not pulled the trigger, but a negative result would dramatically disprove suicide. In a letter Frikke wrote several months after the autopsy, she noted that to her knowledge the tests had still not been done. Based on a search of case records, it appears they never were.

It was not in Frikke's nature or job to speculate, to imagine elabo-rate scenarios of what might have happened. Instead, she limited her analysis to what the evidence indicated with reasonable certainty, careful not to stray beyond what science and logic support Her au-topsy report for Robert Mason lists:

```
Immediate cause of death: Gunshot wound to head
Manner of death: Uncertain
```

In that section of the report where she states her professional opin-ion, Frikke begins: "The gunshot wound to the head had many un-usual features which suggested it was not a self-inflicted injury." It is an opinion that demands an alternative scenario for Robert Mason's death, one that, although speculative, better explains all the unusual injuries Frikke found on his body; a cohesive narrative that fits the facts as a logical sequence of deliberate actions rather than a series of unrelated, improbable events. Occam's simple, likely truer solution—Robert Mason was murdered.

From his vantage point, Mason would have been able to see just the roof of one of three patrol cars on the bluff across the river from him.[1] That one had been driven there by the deputy he'd shot. He couldn't see what became of the wounded man after he crawled over the crest of the bluff. The drivers of the other two cars had stayed out of sight and taken cover opposite him. That was almost a half hour earlier. Now at the base of the bluff, a small band of police worked their way down the road the State of Utah vehicle had come down earlier.

At that point, given his skills and success at evading capture so far, Mason could still have reasonably considered slipping quietly away and escaping into the thick brush and rocky ravines of the San Juan River Canyon. Or, having already shot the first lawman to enter the canyon, he might have determined to make a stand. In either case as he lay in a prone shooting position focused on movement across the river, other men may have been focused on him. In total, Frikke's findings suggest Mason was surprised by men with lethal skills and deadly intent.

As an attacker suddenly leapt into his bunker, Mason's natural reaction would be to roll onto his hip as he pivoted to face the intruder, all the while swinging his rifle toward the man's chest. The attacking commando's first move would have been a defensive kick tearing the rifle from Mason's grip. While police never even addressed the enigma, such a scenario would explain why police found the rifle leaning haphazardly several feet from the body of a man who loved his guns and would have kept them close even unto a methodical death.

The commando's next likely moves would account for injuries on Mason's legs that police explained only with unconvincing conjecture. Halfway between lying flat on his back and sitting up, legs bent, feet apart, Mason was exposed to powerful, incapacitating kicks to the groin. But as he flailed his heels against the ground in a frantic attempt to escape his attacker, the movement of his legs would have disrupted a clean strike. The first kick brushed his right thigh before slamming into his crotch. Hoping for a better-placed blow, his attacker unleashed yet another kick just as Mason rolled left causing it to hit high on his left thigh.

The bruises on Mason's inner thighs had puzzled Dr. Frikke. Unlike other nicks, scrapes and bumps on Mason's body that could be expected after several days scrambling through brush and rocky terrain, the inner thigh is usually protected from environmental injuries.

Police suggested the bruising occurred when Mason crossed a nearby footbridge over the river. The forty-year-old bridge had several planks missing, forcing any would-be crosser to walk tightrope fashion along a two-inch diameter cable for a step or two while hanging onto a parallel waist-high hand-line. Mason must have slipped and ended up abruptly straddling the cable, bruising his thighs, they hypothesized. Such a fall, however, is unlikely according to Dean Potter, one of the world's leading slackline athletes. Renowned for record-distance slackline walks, in which the athlete walks a line that sags (like the cables of the San Juan footbridge) rather than a line stretched taut as a tightrope, Potter observed that while straddle falls are common, bruising both thighs in a fall is rare. Usually one side or the other takes the hit, but not both. Given the fact that Mason would have also been holding onto a parallel cable railing, a forceful straddle fall is even more unlikely, Potter added. Add to that the six-inch-square wire mesh stretched between the cables to protect children from tumbling off the boardwalk, and such a fall was nearly impossible.

Delivered with sufficient force, even glancing kicks to the groin would have curled Mason into a fetal position as coronas of pain burned through his abdomen and flared down his legs. Unable to even hold his hands up defensively and vulnerable to further assault, the next blow, this one to the head, could have easily fractured his skull. Frikke described hairline fractures radiating upward from Mason's eye sockets caused by blunt-force trauma to the back of the head. Based on the degree of hemorrhaging around the injury, it occurred about the time of death but was unrelated to the gunshot wound, she reported. Police suggested Mason had fallen backward and hit his head on the ground. (If the police explanation for Mason's various injuries were to be believed, the man who nimbly eluded hundreds of well-conditioned, physically fit police officers in an obstacle-course-from-hell chase through some of the most challenging terrain on the continent suddenly seemed to be falling down a lot.) Impugning the "fall" explanation was the fact that Mason was found sprawled forward from a seated position, not flat on his back with his head against a rock. Frikke also concluded that Mason's helmet would have sufficiently dampened the force of a backward fall, protecting him from the level of injury she observed.

One observation after another—an abrasion under the chin, lacerations on the upper lip, peculiarities of the gunshot wound, the blood flow pattern—indicated that something more than the simple suicide claimed by police happened at Swinging Bridge. Clinging adamantly to the story that Mason killed himself, the police neither looked for additional evidence answering challenges to their conclusion, nor offered an explanation for the injuries within the framework of a suicide. They simply ignored them.

By themselves, each unrelated detail was an unsettling anomaly, a solitary pearl suggesting a broken strand. Strung together, they form a sequence of murderous attack:

Sprawled on his back with his skull fractured, Mason, at best, would have been semiconscious, his mind lurching between panic that he would black out helpless and the enveloping urge to let it happen. In the end, as his attacker subdued him, he ceased whatever feeble resistance he had put up. His body went limp with surrender. Darkness flooded over him until the only light left was the afterburn of the western sun on his eyelids. Then that too faded to black. His head fell back slightly. His mouth slacked open an inch.

Kneeling over the unconscious victim, the commando pulled a pistol from the holster strapped to his right thigh. His left hand plumbed a pocket on the front of his vest, emerging with a seven-inch anodized black aluminum tube, 1.25 inches in diameter. He methodically screwed the silencer to the end of the gun barrel. Despite the fact that other police were in the vicinity at the time of Mason's death, none reported hearing a gunshot.

"Hold his mouth open," the commando ordered.

With one hand, a second man placed his thumb under Mason's chin, and slid the tips of two fingers into their victim's mouth along the inside of the lower lip. He hooked three fingers of his other hand under Mason's upper lip and, holding the lower jaw firmly in place, yanked the head violently backward, hyperextending Mason's neck and opening his mouth wide.

The force of the man's hold left a small round abrasion the size of a thumbprint under Mason's chin and bruises on the inside of his lips as well as a laceration where the upper lip attaches to the gum. Like the skull fracture, the injuries were perimortem. There were no marks on Mason's face that suggested the injuries to the inside of his lips were caused by an external blow, Frikke said. Nor were they caused by the gunshot wound, she concluded.

Extending the hypothesis step-by-step through the details of one man shooting Mason while another held his mouth open offers the only cohesive explanation for Frikke's observations of the bullet wound itself:

Several clues point to the fact that the gun that killed Mason was held a few inches in front of Mason's face rather than with the tip of the barrel in his mouth. Continuing the scenario of attack and murder, the commando presumably held the pistol four or five inches in front of Mason's face, lined up to fire a nearly horizontal shot between the hands of the man who held Mason's mouth open. At that point-blank range, a trained shooter could be confident the bullet would split the two-inch gap between his partner's hands without hitting them. Without some protection, however, the muzzle blast from the end of the barrel would still leave the second assailant's fingers pitted with small particles of gunpowder and soot, perhaps even badly burned. Holding the pistol steady, the commando used his free hand to release two Velcro straps securing his kneepad and held it in front of the barrel.[2]

The pistol emitted a soft "psswurr" inaudible to a person ten yards away who wasn't intently listening for it.

Such a killing would have accounted for several discrepancies from the typical gun-in-mouth suicide. First, the bullet carved a groove in Mason's tongue. Although possible in a case of suicide, the tongue wound is extremely rare according to forensic pathology literature. At that time in her career, Frikke had never seen it herself. But if the victim's head were tipped far back and the bullet fired from in front of the mouth into it, the tongue, resting on the lower teeth, would naturally lie in its path.

After plowing a five-centimeter groove in Mason's tongue, the bullet blew through the roof of his mouth. But again, the entry point and trajectory was unusual for an intra-oral suicide—too far forward and at too shallow of an angle. The extent of injury also told Frikke that Mason had not closed his lips around the gun barrel creating a seal, the common practice in such suicides.

The bullet-bored kneepad or whatever object could have been held in front of the barrel was never found but its existence was affirmed by pathologic and ballistic evidence. Imbedded in Mason's tongue were fragments of a copper bullet jacket. The projectile commonly used in modern cartridges is made of lead, but coated with a thin layer or "jacket" of harder metal. The jacket expands and loosens only *after* boring through a significant amount of bone or dense tissue, eventually breaking away from the core as it passes through the body. Frikke realized there should be no jacket fragments at the point of impact, only subsequent to it; which meant before the bullet hit Mason, it passed through an intermediate target.

Frikke's understanding of ballistics and her conclusion relative to the jacket fragments is absolutely correct, according to nationally known firearms and ballistics expert Ron Scott. A retired com-

manding officer of the Massachusetts State Police Ballistics Section,
Scott oversaw two labs and a team of ballisticians handling seventeen hundred cases annually. Now an independent ballistics consul-
tant, he conducts investigations for cities across the US, state and
federal agencies, and the US military, including high-profile cases
in Iraq, Afghanistan and Nigeria. "Jacket fragments at the point
where the bullet first contacts the body implies it hit something else
first," he agreed.

What was held in front of the barrel allowed a bullet to pass
through it without stripping too much energy from the projectile, yet
was dense enough to affect the bullet jacket as well as absorb the
worst of the muzzle blast. Intrigued, Frikke looked for traces of the
intermediate object that may have been blasted into Mason's mouth.
Laced into the wound was foreign material from an unknown
source—microscopic transparent spherical pieces as well as fibrillar
particles associated with black pigment.

What she didn't find was equally telling. Whether the pistol muzzle was in Mason's mouth or held directly in front of his mouth, he
should have been peppered with gunpowder residue, particles of un-
burnt powder and soot, Scott said. If the bullet was fired from in front
without an intermediary target to absorb the blast, powder stippling
would be extensive on his chin and lips. His teeth would have been
speckled with powder. In both cases, barrel tip in or outside of his
mouth, the entire oral cavity should have been sprayed with gunpowder residue. But there was virtually none. No stippling on the chin, no
gunpowder residue visible in his mouth, only microscopic traces that
Frikke quantified as "sparse." Not even on the hand with which he
supposedly pulled the trigger.

Following the homicide hypothesis further, it's easy to envision
actions that explain other features of Mason's body that defied the
suicide theory:

If in fact Mason was killed, he was shot in the mouth so that it
looked like a suicide rather than an execution—at least to people with
less forensic expertise than Dr. Frikke. At some point, the assassins
would have stepped away from Mason's body and begun arranging

the site for its eventual discovery by others. Mason's head remained in the unnatural extreme flung-back position in which it was held as the bullet cut through a convergence of large blood vessels in his upper neck, burrowed through his brain and lodged against the back of his skull. Within seconds, the blood pooled in the back of Mason's throat, filled his mouth cavity and began to drain out his nose. It flowed from his nostrils, across his upper lip, over his cheekbones and collected in his eye sockets until they spilled it down the sides of his head onto the ground.

Confident they had brushed away all blatant signs of their presence, the men returned their attention to the body. Placing one foot on each side of Mason's chest, one of the men squatted slightly and grabbed a fistful of their victim's camouflaged jacket in each hand. In that position, one arm's length directly over the man he murdered, he may have hesitated briefly, studying the flies already converging on the bloodstained face. Then in a sudden move, the man jerked Mason to a seated position and pivoted him so his back brushed the branches of a nearby bush. As the commando balanced the body in a slouching, semiseated position, his accomplice unclipped a combat helmet hanging from a carabiner on Mason's backpack, placed it on the dead fugitive's head and buckled the chinstrap, in the process tipping Mason's head forward. The blood in his mouth sloshed forward with it, sluicing in a broad fan of red down his chin onto his chest.

There are natural forces that can shift the position of a body. A supporting branch can yield under prolonged stress (although no one went back to check for a broken branch). The onset and relenting of rigor mortis can cause a body to shift slightly and as the stiffened body goes limp, gravity can move it even farther. If it wasn't a case of the assailant making a final artistic adjustment to Mason's pose, then it was one of these processes that eventually caused his head to fall to the right, diverting the bloody flow once again. A body shift that changes the trail of blood from straight down the chin to a trickle out of the corner of the mouth onto the right shoulder would not in itself set off alarm bells. But a 180-degree change in the direction of blood flow from the nose toward the forehead to gushing from the mouth straight down the chin was another matter. Admittedly, the body was moved substantially, at one point crudely, between the time police found it and it lay on Dr. Frikke's stainless steel exam table. The reports of several officers who found the body as well as photographs, however, show Mason's head turned to the side and facing downward, as if he had slumped forward from a seated position. The bullet did massive damage to Mason's brain stem; his death was instantaneous. How his body then shifted from the backward leaning center of gravity that can be supposed by his extreme head-back, chin-up position when he died to the flung forward on his face position in which he was found, went unaddressed.

The final clue that Mason was murdered was supplied by careless police work rather than a forensic pathologist: in a final step of prepping a murder scene to look like a suicide, one man would have drawn Mason's pistol from its holster, removed a shell from its clip and curled the fingers of Mason's right hand around the grip. He draped the left hand across the body's abdomen. Then, to obstruct attempts to match the fatal bullet to Mason's weapon, the commando picked up the spent cartridge from his pistol and slipped it in his pocket.

Unless someone removed it, police should have found an empty casing within seven feet to the left of Mason's body where his pistol would have automatically ejected the shell. Even if it hit a rock and bounced, it should have been no more than fourteen feet away, ballistics expert Scott explained. In the case of an unwitnessed shooting, finding the casing is normally a high priority, and doing ballistics to match the slug to the gun suspected of firing it as well as fingerprinting the weapon is basic police procedure. Not doing that would be extraordinary negligence, he added.

Although never reported publicly, several internal police documents refer to two sets of tracks leading west from Mason's body. During the search of the canyon, a helicopter pilot reported two men to the west of Mason's body. Responding ground forces could not find them.

Escape would have been easy: ten minutes after they encountered Mason, the two men could have trotted westward over the ridge and slipped quietly through the brush toward anonymity. Or perhaps as hoards of police arrived from the east, they simply blended in.

CHAPTER 14
MONTE

How to make T.N.T.
Take two beakers. In the first prepare a solution of 76 percent sulfuric acid, 23 percent nitric acid and 1 percent water. In the other beaker . . .
—From Monte Pilon's handwritten notes on
bomb and detonation methods.

The agents and officers working in the FBI investigation command center referred to him as "the Fat Fuck." His coconspirators with whom he killed and fled were called by their last names, McVean and Mason. The police hated all three men for having murdered one of their own but McVean and Mason, with their lean-hard survival skills, had earned the officers' grudging respect, admitted one investigator who'd been at the command center.

Alan Lamont "Monte" Pilon was another matter. At 240 pounds on a six-foot frame he was grossly overweight. Even if it weren't for a permanent limp from ankle injuries, Monte couldn't have run for more than fifty yards before collapsing to the ground where he'd lay gasping for breath, multiple friends concurred. In fact, he couldn't even walk very far. A heavy smoker and drinker, the thirty-year-old terrorist was terribly out of shape.

Besides his lack of fitness, he wore Coke-bottle-thick glasses, without which he was nearly blind. He had a bad back and a lifelong history of weak ankles, suffering his first severe break at age ten when a tractor ran over his leg. He continued to injure his legs in motorcycle accidents. The last two happened just a year or so before he disappeared, according to Keith Dahl, his employer at the time. The resulting permanent limp was pronounced. Pilon would fracture anklebones yet one more time, in the course of fleeing from McElmo Bridge. But this time it may have cost him his life.

In addition to his physical limitations, Pilon didn't seem to have the mental toughness McVean's and Mason's plans required. His former employers described him as a lazy worker who called in sick frequently, whined whenever a task required a little extra effort or groused when he had to use a hand tool rather than a power tool. "He was a big baby," one of his coworkers observed. He would often get angry at small things and sink into depression and a prolonged pout.

The more police learned about Monte, the more puzzled they became: McVean and Mason had been friends since eighth grade; Pilon became the third leg of the stool late in the game, just about a year before McElmo Bridge. How did Pilon fit in? What did he contribute to McVean and Mason's plans? Why did those two even put up with Pilon let alone adopt him as a key partner? It was a question McVean's and Mason's friends couldn't answer. Pilon had his own set of longtime friends. While they recognized Monte's belligerent anti-government attitude, his emotional instability and militia connections, they too had difficulty explaining what their fat friend was doing in the desperate, brutal circumstances he'd placed himself in.

It was for sure a question Monte had been asking himself. He had been gun crazy since elementary school. One sixth-grade classmate recalled Pilon using class presentation assignments to give technical data on guns. He had compiled his own arsenal of assault weapons and explosives years before he met McVean and Mason. He practiced shooting and participated in paramilitary training exercises with his own friends seasons before he did them with McVean and

Mason. He cursed the government and hated cops, indeed even railed, "If the shit hit the fan, I'd shoot cops" long before hearing similar sentiments from McVean and Mason. But Monte knew the difference between deeds envisioned in anger, threats spouted in frustration and the real thing. In the months before McElmo Bridge, he looked for a way out. He couldn't find it.

Pilon was the least likely of the three outlaws to plot terror or coldly premeditate murder and the first of the group you'd predict was involved in killing a cop. Unlike McVean who intellectualized the violence or Mason thoughtlessly caught up in it as a warrior action game, Pilon was volatile and emotional. Living on the edge of society, feeling picked on and dabbling in "get-even" fantasies, he could be understood as the berserk gunman who with a final provocation sets off on a mad-as-hell-and-not-going-to-take-it-anymore rampage.

Friends and family believed he was close to that state of mind when the tanker crossed McElmo Bridge and pulled to the side of the road. The provocation had arrived that week in the mail. A letter from the IRS telling him that he owed fourteen hundred dollars in unpaid taxes plunged him deep into depression and anger. But at that moment, sitting in the middle of the tanker's front seat while McVean sprinted to the rear of the truck and opened fire, it is unlikely Pilon had lost control of his emotions—only the situation.

Dove Creek was a windblown working town on the edge of the Great Sage Mesa with the forlorn feel of a set in a spaghetti Western. The short commercial district spread along Highway 666 held a post office, a few worn retail stores, a couple of ag-service businesses, a small postwar supermarket where Pilon's father worked in the meat department, and rusted bean elevators. The residences spreading up the hill behind the commercial strip were a mixed array of faded mobile homes and small ramblers, almost all in need of fresh paint. Pilon lived on Main Street, a road that was no longer a main thoroughfare for the community but which did have the distinction of leading to the school and county courthouse. His parents' home was directly across the street from the Dolores County Sheriff's Office.

Growing up, Monte would have crossed the street, running between his yard and the parked patrol cars hundreds of times on his way to school. No one could have known then that one day a man from that office would command a manhunt determined to capture him or, if he must, kill him.

The Pilon property was a three-building compound on a city-lot patch of grass. The house, a double-wide on a foundation, sat fifty feet back from the road. Forward of the house at the edge of the property was a large metal shed garage. On the opposite side of the yard was an old house trailer used by Monte's mother for her business. Rosebushes climbed the side of the trailer. A sign near the door read BEAUTY SHOP.

Hostility toward the government comes easily in the self-proclaimed pinto bean capital of the world. Although Dove Creek was home to just seven hundred people, numerous area residents were known to be Constitutionalists, militia members, and rabid antigovernment proselytizers. Throughout his adolescence and adult years, Pilon interacted with an extended group of friends and associates engaged in political fringe lifestyles and suspicious activities.

In the days following Claxton's murder, police identified well over two dozen people with sympathetic political views from the Dove Creek area with whom Monte socialized. Among them were half a dozen close friends with whom Monte had attended militia meetings, played war games in the desert, buried secret caches of supplies and talked subversion. A few knew McVean and Mason as well but only through introductions by Monte. It was Monte's group.

Upon moving to Durango to live near his place of employment, Pilon saw his own friends less frequently but socialized occasionally with McVean's and Mason's group. Some of those friends held similar political beliefs, but with the exception of Monte himself there seemed to be little cross-pollination with the antigovernment crowd from Dove Creek.

While Pilon did many of the same potentially subversive activities with his Dove Creek friends that he did with Mason and McVean, there was a qualitative difference. McVean's and Mason's exercises likely conveyed a greater sense of severity, a certain inevitability. The Dove Creek patriot resistance training, on the other hand, seemed to have had an element of paintball pretense to it. For Pilon, acting out his "get-even" fantasies may have provided relief from his frustrations without pushing him to the untenable position of acting for real. One thing was evident: in the last six months of his life, Pilon's behavior was drastically out of character. Since moving to Durango, Monte Pilon had changed and even his antigovernment and war-game buddies worried about their old friend.

"Monte wasn't the same old Monte I've always known," remarked a friend who had known him since high school.

"Monte's mind turned 180 degrees since he started working in Durango and became involved with McVean and Mason. He was heavily influenced in his last year by people in Durango," a relative noted. The change was blatant and almost everyone who knew him recognized it.

Monte had always had his crazy moments when something pushed him over the edge, a couple of which had the potential of becoming violent. Eight years before McElmo Bridge, at the age of twenty-two, Pilon sat in a room with a .45-caliber pistol in his hand threatening to kill himself. The circumstances that triggered that particular incident were lost among his several other instances of suicidal depression, but people do recall it took his best friend nearly an hour to talk him down and disarm him. Two years after that the gun in Monte's hand was pointed at someone else. Jealous and angry, he waved the muzzle back and forth, aiming alternately at a female acquaintance and the man she was with, who happened to be one of Monte's friends. The threat ended when the woman ordered him to put the gun down. And somewhere in the back of his mind Monte made a distinction between show and inflicting real harm.

He had a temper and small frustrations would make him yell and swear. At times he'd punch or kick an offending inanimate object. He was dishonest. As a juvenile, he'd been caught breaking into the junior high school and stealing electronic devices. As an adult, he was suspected of stealing tools and materials from employers, including dynamite from a construction company he worked for. He also had a history of alcohol-related crimes including an alcohol-related vehicle accident and six months later an arrest for driving with a suspended license; then a DUI and finally a felony charge and revocation of his driver's license for contributing to the delinquency of a minor when he provided booze for a party. It was the loss of his driving privileges that forced him to move into a trailer at his place of employment in Durango, just two hundred yards from Jason McVean's trailer where he became caught up in crime on a much bigger scale.

In spite of his flaws, the consensus among people who knew Monte was that he was deep down a good person. An introvert who wouldn't look people in the eye when speaking with them, he nevertheless got along with people. Nonviolent by nature, he was more inclined to sulk than confront. He socialized with a wide network of people who seemed to enjoy his company and maintained several steadfast friendships over a course of years. Even former employers who at one time were incensed by his lazy work ethic and may have even fired him, or who suspected he stole from them, softened their opinions and in the end described him in charitable terms. All in all, Alan "Monte" Pilon was a big pitiful "nice guy" with some serious emotional problems.

At least that was the Monte his friends had always known. In the last several months that anyone admits having seen him, however, Pilon became more aggressive and militant. A good friend who saw him the week before McElmo Bridge described him as unusually nervous and jumpy. His paranoia deepened and his belligerence toward authority escalated. His brooding worsened, as did his drug abuse. Many of Pilon's friends comprised a party crowd and they were not prudish about drugs, but Monte's sudden heavy use of cocaine and crystal meth concerned them. He clearly had a problem.

Pilon's personality change may not have reflected McVean and Mason's influence on his thinking as much as it did his normal response to stress. Friends and family insisted Monte had a conscience and he would eventually feel tremendous guilt and remorse over acts that harmed others. As he was drawn deeper and deeper into the trio's violent plans, Pilon's anxiety would have ratcheted increasingly higher.

Monte was not always the out-of-shape, limping, brooding wreck of his later years. In high school he was a decent athlete; played tight end for the school's varsity football team and in his favorite sport, basketball, he played guard. He camped and hiked often. Even with his poor eyesight, he was a good marksman.

Nor was his slow approach to tasks an indication that he was mentally dull. Casual, quickly jotted notes he'd written to friends showed that he paid attention in school. From the standpoint of grammar, spelling, punctuation, and sentence structure, his writing would have qualified for a top-rated college. His instructors at San Juan Basin Vocational Technical School where he leaned his trade as a mechanic identified Monte as a "bright" student and a "pretty sharp kid." The school's program was tough enough to flush 40 percent of the kids out the first year. Monte not only completed the two-year program but also was among the small percentage of students who did so earning almost all As and Bs. "He was smart and dependable. His attendance was good, here every day. He was always clean-cut. He was even keel," one instructor said.

Descriptions of his behavior and attitude during that period of his life make it hard to believe he'd grown up to be anything other than an ordinary middle-class citizen. "He was real quiet, but not antisocial. He was not aggressive. There was nothing weird about him," another instructor added. At school he neither whined and complained nor acted moody, according to their recollections. He didn't talk guns or politics and didn't display antigovernment sentiments. He didn't seem to have any problem with authority and didn't react negatively when instructors prodded him to pick up his pace. "Monte was just a regular guy," he recalled.

Although he caught on quickly, Monte's natural pace was slow. He moved slowly and worked slowly. The owners of the three businesses that accounted for the majority of Pilon's employment since he joined the working world as a certified diesel mechanic agreed that if Monte didn't have constant supervision he'd slack off but he was good at his trade. Left alone to replace brakes on a truck he'd get a snack, stop for a cigarette, chat with whoever was near, clean a tool, embark on a wandering search for parts, every movement at half speed. After more than enough time to complete the job, he'd still be on the first wheel, remarked Keith Dahl, who employed Pilon for several years at two different businesses he owned. But the work he did was done well. "I never had a problem with the quality of Monte's work," Dahl said. "He was a knowledgeable mechanic who could repair just about any type of equipment," observed Gary Crowley of Crowley Construction.

How Pilon went from the high school athlete and clean-cut, motivated "regular guy" at San Juan vo-tech to the bearded, slovenly bloated adult with scraggily shoulder-length hair and a bad attitude mystified many in Dove Creek in the days after he was named a suspect in Claxton's murder. Gathered around WANTED posters hung in store windows, neighbors murmured excitedly, tracking whom police had interviewed and what they said. After all, everyone knew the Pilons. Everyone knew everyone in Dove Creek. It was a small community where many people didn't even lock their front doors and the cluster of townsfolk expressed shock that one of their own was implicated in such a heinous crime. "He was such a quiet boy," some would exclaim. "He got in with a wild crowd," others countered.

In truth, Monte had always had one foot in each world; mainstream America and fringe society. Dove Creek exposes its native sons to both. For the most part it was a community of hardworking, taxpaying, law-abiding, salt-of-the-earth middle Americans. Pilon's parents were among those. They loved their child and wished the simple pure hope of parents everywhere, that their son would be happy. Even after the boy became a man and that goal seemed elusive, they hoped it for him.

Monte's talk of a girlfriend in the months before he disappeared was encouraging for his parents. The job that moved him to Durango in the first place had also been reason for hope, the new start he needed after years of self-imposed uneven employment. The weekend Jim and Beverly spent helping him settle into his trailer in Durango next to where he'd be working—buying groceries, hauling in housewares, cleaning and organizing, making the small trailer a home their son could comfortably live in—was poignant with caring and optimism for his future, observed Keith Dahl, Pilon's new boss. For the people who cared about Monte, it was false hope. There was no girlfriend, only unilateral attraction and face-saving bluster. And within a year of moving into the trailer, Monte would once again be fired.

While Jim cleaved roasts and Beverly colored neighbors' hair in pursuit of a simple all-American dream for their family, there was also a powerful undercurrent in Dove Creek that washed up hard against the ideals of normalcy and blurred the political dialogue. Many people in the community knew of Monte's attendance at militia meetings and engagement in paramilitary activities during the year leading up to McElmo Bridge. Most didn't look askance at it. No one reported his activities to police. No one apparently tried to redirect the young man. Extremist propaganda addressed to Monte was among many other indicators at his parents' house that their son's behavior and attitudes registered outside the normal range. Pages from *The Anarchist Cookbook*, letters from the John Birch Society, articles copied from far right media and militia membership documents didn't stand out as a warning sign. If his parents recognized Monte's over-the-top interest in guns and combat weaponry as activity associated with dangerous extremist behavior, they didn't dissuade him. Components of his arsenal were kept at his parents' home. On one occasion when Monte wanted an SKS assault rifle but didn't have the proper identification required for the purchase, his father bought it for him.

Acquaintances who'd been shooting with Pilon compiled a long list of weapons he owned. A friend who shot with him years before the Claxton murder told police that even then he had multiple firearms that were full automatics and illegal. With frequent purchases, pawning some when money was tight and secreting away weapons in the desert, a total accounting of Pilon's guns wasn't possible. During the months leading up to McElmo Bridge, however, he reportedly owned: body armor, two AK-47s, four M16s (his favorite firearm), a Russian SKS assault rifle, a Mini-14, an MK11 sniper rifle, an Uzi submachine gun with a forty-round magazine, an FN FAL .308 combat rifle, a 7mm hunting rifle, two .30-06 hunting rifles, two .22-caliber rifles, a Mossberg 12-gauge shotgun, a Winchester 12-gauge, a Luger pistol, a .45-caliber pistol, a 9mm Glock pistol, a Ruger .22-caliber pistol, a .357 Magnum Ruger Blackhawk (the only revolver in the combined arsenal of the three outlaws) and one hundred pounds of C-4 plastic explosive.

In addition to caching weapons and supplies in the canyons near Bluff, Utah, and at various sites around Dove Creek and Dolores County, Colorado, Monte also had a secret underground bunker south of Durango, according to informants. Sometime in 1996, Pilon purchased a used fourteen-by-seven-foot steel shed, added PCV-pipe gun turrets and, after friends with a backhoe buried it in a hillside, stocked it with survival supplies.

At militia meetings he participated in innocuous demonstrations on how to seal and bury food, or clean a room of electronic listening devices, but some of the training Pilon did with his militia friends was against the law. Upon being interviewed by police, several of Pilon's associates talked forthright about Monte but were guarded in their descriptions of the training they did together, explaining to authorities they feared incriminating themselves in illegal activities.

Regardless of its legality, the training had always been defensive in nature, Pilon's friends insisted. Monte never spoke to them about killing police officers or being criminally proactive against the government. Yet in the months before he disappeared into Cross Canyon, his pissed-off-at-the-world outlook intensified and his militant tendencies hardened.

Pilon's self-esteem dragged in the gutter. He once characterized himself to a friend as "fat and worthless." Yet it was the rest of the world he blamed for his problems, from long periods of unemployment to the revocation of his driver's license to his IRS debt for not filing taxes. He made no secret of his anger toward those responsible for his troubles: cops, judges, lawyers, the IRS and the government in general. The FBI sieges at Ruby Ridge, Idaho, and Waco, Texas, became touchstones in his growing paranoia. They were, in Pilon's mind, just more blatant examples of the oppression he suffered.

His bitterness likely extended beyond those specific targets. Although he was raised as a Catholic, one lead received by police suggested he had joined a Christian identity congregation. With loose connections to Randy Weaver, the embattled extremist at Ruby Ridge; the Aryan Nation; as well as many of the most virulent militia movement luminaries; the organization's religious doctrine paralleled Pilon's antigovernment views. Its racialized theology incorporated the threat of internationalism and the belief that the UN, backed by Jewish representatives of the Antichrist, were preparing to take over America and impose a New World Order. Pilon's prejudices fit right in; "he was anti-blacks, anti-Jews and anti-cop," one acquaintance explained. He and his Dove Creek associates justified their antigovernment stance and their militia activities as readiness for the New World Order invasion.

There was another consequence of Monte's low self-esteem. He liked to show off, thriving on the attention he got playing the role of a dangerous radical. Unlike Mason who spewed loud extremist diatribes to the room, Pilon would corner a single person and in contrived conversation let slip, "I'm in a militia." Or in a hushed surreptitious voice reveal, "I've got C-4." It was the lonely extremist's equivalent of Clyde Barrow asking Bonnie if she wanted to see his gun. It was an ego-need that would cause him to take an AK-47 to work in his toolbox and open it when he knew his coworkers would get a glimpse of what he had, a contrivance he plied on two different jobs.

If any of the conspirators let the secret of their plans slip, it most likely would have been Monte trying to impress his friends. It is known that on more than one occasion he at least hinted at their criminal plans. In a phone conversation four weeks before McElmo Bridge he told his best friend, who was traveling out of state, "Something important is coming up." He promised to tell him more later. To another friend he confided, "We've got something big planned." And to two others he met at a party less than two weeks before McElmo

Bridge he boasted that he and his comrades would "go from nobodies to known across the nation."

McVean and Mason grew up together. They gravitated naturally along parallel tracks toward McElmo Bridge, bound together by friendship and fate. Pilon was recruited, invited to join with the duo. Physically and mentally unsuited to the rigors of the intended crime and escape, he seems like an odd choice. Within the group of three conspirators, he could never be equal to Jason and Bobby, who respected, supported and loved each other like close brothers. He was and always would be the odd man out. Behind his back, Jason and Bobby derided and made jokes at his expense. It was not frequent and the comments were not vicious, but enough so that friends knew the three musketeers were really two musketeers and another guy. But the choice of Monte Pilon was not without merit. In fact, he brought a lot to the party.

First, the identification of Monte as a compatriot came naturally. He showed up living and working next to McVean, talking up the two subjects dearest to McVean and Mason—guns and antigovernment conspiracy theory. Impressively, he had already assembled an arsenal of weaponry equal to or better than their own and he knew everything there was to know about guns. He also had a head start on paramilitary training since McVean and Mason up until then had mainly stuck to themselves. And he had knowledge of explosives.

McVean ultimately became the group's explosives expert but up front it was Pilon. As early as 1994 Pilon had made and trained with explosives. He had difficulty developing reliable detonators but, according to some who trained with him, succeeded with homemade claymores and other directional charges. He had several books on explosives as well as many of the harder to obtain chemicals used for bomb making. When police searched his bedroom a few days after McElmo Bridge, they found handwritten step-by-step instructions for making TNT; mercury fulminate, a primary explosive sensitive to friction and shock; as well as other bomb ingredients. The notes were neatly printed with perfect spelling, even of complex chemical names. In the margins Pilon added reminders such as, "Buy a good centigrade thermometer." Hand-drawn diagrams showed how to make alarm-clock timers for IEDs and trip-wire detonators.

In any contingency that demanded extended stays surviving in the desert, Pilon's mechanical skills would be invaluable, from repairing portable generators and other equipment to keeping vehicles running that provided the outlaws mobility. In a list of supplies Pilon made presumably for their final endeavor, in addition to twenty AK-47 magazines and two dozen grenades, he listed spare vehicle parts such as "two sets of spark plugs, gas tank repair putty, tire patch kit, U-joints, belts, radiator hoses and clamps, two gas filters, an air filter, blue silicone"—whatever it took to fix a vehicle broken down in the middle of nowhere and keep moving.

He may have also provided the group some emergency medical capability. Although there was nothing in his known background indicating training in that area, it was possible he had instruction and field practice in wilderness medicine through his militia activities. The medical kit police found in Pilon's pack was extensive with advanced first-aid supplies including clamps and sutures.

Pilon also had extensive knowledge of their escape route terrain. Cross Canyon was the gateway into the entire myriad of canyons, deserts and wilderness in which they intended to hide out. As familiar as McVean and Mason were with it from numerous camping trips, it was Pilon's backyard. He had hiked and camped within its walls most of his life.

Most important, Pilon had contacts. McVean and Mason in Durango and Pilon in Dove Creek both gathered around them people of similar mind. McVean's and Mason's group consisted of ten to twelve friends with whom they partied, fired weapons, hung around and cleaned guns. They didn't gel into a formal antigovernment group with an agenda. Some of Pilon's crowd did. Pilon's group of friends and like-minded associates was more extensive to begin with. When police compiled interview lists of each subject's associates, Pilon's was twice as long as the other two combined. Some in the Dove Creek group organized and began their own militia training. Many of those people, in turn, had friends elsewhere in Four Corners that shared their ideology, people they met when they were invited to someone's home for an afternoon of dry-sealing food or survival training. One person would vouch for another until Pilon—through a friend who had a friend who knew a guy—had access to a widespread network of resources not readily available to McVean and Mason. It was through Pilon's connections that all three conspirators would attend militia meetings in Cortez.

In addition, Pilon was acquainted with the people in the area who had their own distaste for all things police. He knew the guy who years earlier had shot at a state trooper at a traffic stop, the antigovernment farmer who did time for tax evasion, the radical Constitutionalist who cut the brush down around his trailer so the feds couldn't sneak up on him, the crazies who lived in the canyon bottomland with bunkers and booby traps. Pilon was the guy who could lead his buddies through the gate, past the crudely painted NO TRESPASSING sign on the fence post with the added qualifier, GOVERNMENT AGENTS WILL BE SHOT ON SIGHT. McVean and Mason may have been able to prearrange help, but in the countryside surrounding Cross Canyon it was Pilon who could walk up to a house unannounced, knowing inside he'd find sympathizers and assistance.

Despite his bravado, the righteousness of their plans in the face of the New World Order conspiracy, and the chance for a personal jab back at the IRS and government authority, there is good reason to believe Pilon wanted out. Based on a spur-of-the-moment comment made to one of McVean's and Mason's more moderate friends when others were beyond earshot, Monte recognized months before McElmo Bridge that McVean and Mason were dangerous companions. "I'm afraid of these guys," he blurted. "I'm afraid they are going to do something bad and I don't know how to get out of being around them. Something wrong is going to happen." He sounded desperate, the friend continued. He said he was afraid of Jason and Bobby and "didn't want to get on their bad side." By that time Monte had already been to the desert with McVean and Mason and knew at least some critical elements of what they were planning, the friend surmised. "He figured if he didn't go with them, they would kill him."

As the day to implement the plan got closer, Pilon continued to make veiled pleas to his friends for some way to escape, not into the desert but from the events that would force him to flee there. Four days before the three outlaws stole the water tanker and set the plan in motion that took them to McElmo Bridge, Monte expressed his dread of their intentions one last time. To a friend he had known most of his life he explained he was caught up in a plan to do something illegal, something really bad, something really big.

"Well, let's try and get you out of it," Pilon's friend suggested.

Monte answered with resignation. "Can't. I'm in too deep."

Officer Claxton was murdered on a Friday morning. The previous Sunday evening Pilon spent time with several of his Dove Creek friends at one of their homes. It was a guarded confidence he shared that night that traveled a chain of gossip and led to the anonymous tip that gave police their first clue to the identity of Claxton's shooters.

The next night, Monday, Beverly Pilon saw her son for the last time when he left for Durango after his weekend visit. She talked to him on the phone the following evening. It was the last contact she had with Monte, she told investigators. For reasons unknown, when police spoke with the Pilons four days after Claxton's murder, it was evident that they suspected that their son had by then, died.

On Wednesday, the day before stealing the water tanker, Pilon rode with a friend to Aztec, New Mexico, and back. Mostly, he just sat in the truck, barely talking, the friend reported.

In every encounter, Sunday night through Wednesday, the people who talked with Pilon made the same observation; he was agitated, quiet and acutely depressed. Monte was on the brink, wrought between normalcy and extremism, talk and action, his conscience and an insane course of action. In a shoebox of papers found under his bed there was only one handwritten item that didn't record the day-to-day mechanics of his life: directions to friends, materials lists, gun store receipts or bomb instructions. Instead it spoke to Monte's state of mind.

Within the lyrics to Metallica's "Welcome Home (Sanitarium)." written out in his own hand, Monte found words that spoke to him.

The heavy-metal anthem to the borderlands between sanity and insanity, submission and escape, oppression and violent revolt expressed his own confusion and torment. But even those cryptic lyrics, Pilon subtly altered. Whether the changes were purposeful or subconscious, the lines that he wrote down differently from the actual lyrics are telling. Where Metallica sang, "I see our freedom in my sight," Pilon saw it in his (gun) "sights." Later in the song, Metallica Sings, "They think our heads are in their hands." Like anguish uttered by Macbeth, Monte wrote that line as, "You'd think I had blood on my hands."

Sitting in the tanker's cab, Monte must have known what the noise he was hearing meant. The automatic gunfire from the rear of the truck interrupted the low, barely discernable mix of nature and distant city usually audible at McElmo Bridge. The sharp cracks compressed into a lethal stutter with each rolling burst of shots was a sound he'd heard hundreds of times over the past few years. But all those previous times had been practice and pretend. This time he knew the shooting was real and the sound of it vibrated the last grains of hope from his soul.

Whatever misgivings he'd had about McVean and Mason months before, whatever line he had feared to cross, he was now on the other side of it. There was no crossing back.

CHAPTER 15
TIN CUP

October 31, 1999, almost a year and a half after McElmo Bridge: in the last hour of the last day of deer season on the Navajo Nation, Willie Tortalita, his son Matthew and nine buddies walked side by side in a wide line across the top of Tin Cup Mesa. It was the final sweep on the way back to their trucks but they still hadn't filled their party's tags so they'd hunt until they could see the front bumpers. If a deer bolted from a clump of scrub pine and moved sideways across the line of hunters, one of them would get it.

The possibility kept Willie alert. That's probably why he noticed the dark-colored backpack on the ground at the edge of a juniper tree twenty feet to his left. Near the pack was a second object that didn't belong there. He couldn't see it well in the dusk and deep shadow of the trees, but he could see it was a rifle. Matthew, who was closest to him, saw it too. Neither man broke step or said a word, but they were thinking the same thing. "Those killers the police looked for seventeen months ago were never caught. They were still in the canyons."

The tree and the pack and the rifle slipped between him and Matthew as the line of hunters marched forward, the distance between the men contracting as they got nearer the parking area so that they all reached the trucks at the same time. "I saw something back there," Willie said. The mystery of the remark pulled the others around him.

He told them of the pack and the rifle and their reaction was the same as his and Matthew's. They all figured the items belonged to Pilon or McVean, the two fugitives still at large. The owner was probably in the vicinity.

As soon as the idea was voiced out loud, the danger it implied exploded like a grenade in the group. The circle broke and the men stepped quickly to their trucks. "Wait! There's a big reward," one man shouted. The others hesitated. "We've got to check it out." Even the potential of a $150,000 reward didn't spawn enthusiastic consent. Grudgingly each nodded his agreement, then followed Willie in their trucks across the mesa. It was 6:30 P.M. and dark when they stopped near the backpack. They stepped from their vehicles with flashlights in one hand and their hunting rifles in the other.

Willie shined a flashlight on the rifle and breathed a sigh of relief. The rust showed it had lain there a long time. Beams from the others spilled over the pack and with overlapping circles of light illuminated the space under the juniper branches. The boots were the first thing Matthew saw. The boots led to pants, which abutted to a jacket. From the jacket sleeves hung skeletal hands. At the jacket collar there was nothing. The corpse was headless.

As was the case with all the outlaws' fates, there was no eyewitness account of what happened to Pilon in the desert. The clues left behind, however, were sufficient to form a credible picture of his final hours:

The climb out of the canyon onto the flats of Tin Cup Mesa was most certainly grueling for Pilon. In his poor physical condition the uphill exertion in desert heat with a pack on his back would have pushed the overweight outlaw to the edge of endurance even without a recent ankle injury. On level ground he could manage by limping but on steep uphill stretches he was forced to use both feet more equally. The climb likely aggravated the ankle damage and by the time Pilon stepped onto level ground at the top of the pitch, the injury may have been the source of constant sharp pain. A slow, agonizing mile or so later he stopped using his left leg at all, hopped clumsily toward a juniper tree, letting his rifle fall to the ground on the way and a few feet beyond that shrugging off his backpack. At the edge of the tree's branches, which formed a broken canopy of green, a couple feet above the ground, he eased himself slowly down to a seated position.

The mesa stretches between Cross and Squaw Canyons eight miles northeast of the Hatch Trading Post. The tree was one of a pair that sat back from edge of the bluff. Seated beneath it Pilon had concealment, shade and a commanding view of Cross Canyon below. The general location where they had abandoned the flatbed truck was a round bump just short of the horizon 2.8 crow-flight miles away. A couple hundred yards behind Pilon several large steel storage tanks held oil piped from the surrounding Tin Cup Mesa oil wells. The automated field required no regular work crew but every few days, an oil transport truck pulled up to the tanks and siphoned off a load of crude for refinement.

As the sun slanted lower, Pilon slid a bit farther under the branches. Given the peaceful pose in which he was found and the careful manner in which items were laid alongside him, he was aware that for him the run had ended. Mindful of what he'd likely asked of his companion, it seems he took a bottle of Nytol from his jacket pocket, emptied his canteen taking the last few capsules in the bottle and placed the empty sleeping pill bottle back in his jacket pocket. He placed his Kevlar helmet on the ground next to him as well as his pistol and the ammunition clips he carried in his accessory pockets. Then he removed his glasses and set them gently on a small patch of dry pine needles. Sitting in a relaxed cross-legged position, he allowed his chin to drop to his chest and shut his eyes.

Mason pushed through the tree branches until he stood alongside Pilon. He couldn't tell if his chubby friend was truly sound asleep or just keeping his eyes closed in defiance of what was about to happen. He reached down and picked up the Glock Pilon had placed alongside of him. He pulled the magazine from the pistol leaving one round in the chamber, held the gun a few inches above Monte's head, turned his face away and pulled the trigger.

The outlaw then placed the unloaded gun back on the ground beside the dead man. He gathered up the other ammo clips Pilon had set out, shoved them all deep in his pack and walked away.

Pilon's body and the clues to his actions during the final moments of his life remained undisturbed through two desert summers and one winter. Seventeen months after his death, the deer hunters who discovered his remains called the San Juan County Sheriff's Office from the crime scene. Sheriff Lacy interrupted the resident FBI agent's dinner, directed some deputies to meet them on Tin Cup Mesa and sped to the area. The hunters met them near the road and led them to the remains.

There was something spooky about finding such a body on Halloween. It was essentially a headless skeleton fully dressed in perfectly intact clothes: boots, socks, pants, jacket, equipment harness, and body armor. Its legs were crossed as if it had been sitting gazing out into the desert night but the torso had fallen back into the inner branches of the tree and rested against them in a nearly prone position. A Casio watch continued to tell perfect time on a boney wrist. Nearby the flashlights revealed three large pieces of skull glowing sun-bleached white against the dark soil. A helmet, pistol, empty canteen, and glasses with noticeably thick lenses rested on the ground beside the skeleton. Beyond the branches in open sight was a camouflage backpack, a rain tarp and a rusted FN FAL .308 rifle.

Inside the backpack police found seven pipe bombs wrapped in a parka, two empty twenty-ounce plastic Coca-Cola bottles, a new water filter still in its original unopened packaging, plus miscellaneous clothing and gear. But the crime scene was more interesting for what wasn't there than what was. There was no water, ammunition or spare clips. The Glock pistol was empty with no magazine. The rifle had one live round in the chamber and a seated full clip, but there were no extras.

The Utah State Medical Examiner took control of the remains the next day while police searched the area with a metal detector. They unearthed one item, an empty 9mm shell casing presumably from the bullet that killed Pilon, presumably fired from the pistol found near his body. The slug that seared through his brain as internal cranial pressure exploded his skull was never found.

The autopsy report was short compared to Mason's, only three pages. Half described his clothing and other external observations; the second part pathological findings. Noting the glasses found near the remains, police were certain as they struggled to dislodge the skeleton from the tree branches that the bones held together by mummified flesh were those of Monte Pilon. Dental records confirmed it almost immediately. The three large pieces of skull found near the body represented only a portion of a complete skull but they were enough to conclude the cause of death was a gunshot wound to the head. The medical examiner listed the manner of death as undetermined but police quickly took advantage of the uncertainty to assert the explanation they preferred. "Pilon," they told the media and listed in their reports, "committed suicide."

Among the medical examiner's observations of the remains upon opening the blue body bag were two that were curious but never explained, questioned or incorporated into a theory of events. In the pocket of Pilon's jacket was an empty Nytol bottle. On Pilon's feet was a double layer of socks. Both socks on the right foot were in good to nearly new condition with intact heels. The heels of both socks on the left foot were worn through.

Examination of the skeleton itself provided a general trajectory for the fatal bullet—right to left, front to back, and downward. It also revealed small compression fractures of bones in Pilon's left ankle.

The eleven Navajo deer hunters collected their reward for locating one of America's ten most-wanted fugitives. Prompt and ceremonious payment of the full reward, the FBI reasoned, would encourage others to come forward with information to root out McVean. In a public presentation with speeches, pomp and news cameras, each man was handed a check for $13,636.

Three months later University of Utah forensic anthropologist Shannon Novak finished the painstaking task of fitting together fragments of Pilon's skull; not just the three larger sections but dozens of tiny pieces sieved from the soil of Tin Cup Mesa. In the minds of many experts, the more complete skull challenged the prevailing police opinion.

Rather than being shot by a pistol held level at the side of his head, like most theatrical depictions of a person putting a gun to his temple, the reconstructed skull showed Pilon was shot at a downward angle. The hand holding the pistol and pulling the trigger was to the side and *above* Pilon's head. Such a contortion would not be impossible for a self-inflicted wound, the forensic experts concurred, but it would be improbable. It may have been even more unlikely considering Pilon's presumed state of fatigue and the extra effort the higher reach required, as well as the tangle of branches immediately above his head that would have complicated the movement. Despite the higher probability that it was not Pilon's hand on the pistol, in endless media accounts and police reports summarizing the events of the summer of 1998 in Four Corners, Pilon's death would continue to be called a suicide.

CHAPTER 16
BLUFF

Long before the discovery of Pilon's body, compelling clues to his demise lay at the bottom of a backpack found alongside Bobby Mason's body. It would be almost five years before anyone recognized the clues for what they were and by that time the suicide assertion had been planted so deeply that uprooting it would prove impossible. But at the time Mason was found shot dead, police didn't know Pilon had already come to a similar end and authorities focused on catching the two fugitives still unaccounted for.

The last hint of daylight faded slowly to purple then extinguished completely. Seven days had passed since the manhunt began and an equal number of hours since police stormed a short stretch of the San Juan River canyon and discovered the body of Bobby Mason. Commander Greg McCain and the Pueblo County SWAT team, among the last to leave the action at Swinging Bridge, stepped off the bus at the relocated manhunt command post into a crowd of five hundred officers. Beyond the elementary school where the officers congregated, the streets were quiet. The businesses were shuttered. The homes were empty. For the first time since 1879, there was no one living in Bluff, Utah.

The last of the 350 residents to leave joined the line of cars heading east about 4 P.M. and followed the procession to Monticello where shelters had been set up in public buildings. By order of Sheriff Lacy, the entire town was evacuated. Heavily armed men in black commando gear guarded the roads leading to and from the community, as others moved stealthily among its vacated buildings.

Since midafternoon, the quiet river community named for the three-hundred-foot sandstone bluffs that form a stage backdrop along its north edge, vibrated to the sound of an advancing blitzkrieg. A steady stream of patrol cars and military units hummed through the outskirts. The drone of circling planes competed with the constant *whomp* of choppers. Radio chatter too distant to be distinct but sharp enough to cut through the din of a small-town day erupted unexpected from one direction and then another. Nighttime added the sweeping beams of airborne spotlights—betraying circles of light gliding across parking lots, prying into backyards and alleyways, shining through windows.

Jim Hook, owner of Bluff's Recapture Lodge, stayed behind to house police officers in his hotel. In an e-mail diary to friends, he wrote:

> **The air is full of helicopters and spotlights, all the bridges and entrances to town are blocked and guarded. The SWAT teams have set up skirmish lines along the river next to the lodge and on top of the cliffs. They are holding positions until the sun comes up and they can see what has happened.**

Mason lay dead three miles away on the west bank of the San Juan River, his body cordoned off by yellow crime scene tape. The police logic was reasonable: if Mason was in the area, then perhaps so were McVean and Pilon. There had been several unconfirmed sightings; reports of men racing ahead of the army of police that swept the area after Deputy Bradford was shot, claims that two men escaped downriver in a boat before the first SWAT teams arrived. Authorities even found fresh drag marks where a boat or raft had been pulled into the water.

Lacy and the other manhunt commanders moved with the surge of adrenaline. After days of futile searching and frustration, they believed the quarry was close. Perhaps a couple of miles upriver, perhaps a few miles downstream, but somewhere near and soon it would all come to a bloody end.

The river attracted fifteen thousand boaters a year, most of whom did multiday float trips, camping at night along its shores. It was the height of the rafting season. Bureau of Land Management rangers dispersed quickly to launch points from north of Bluff to the downriver community of Mexican Hat, twenty-four miles southwest. Within an hour a thirty-mile stretch of the San Juan was shut down. Recreational boaters and hikers caught between the checkpoints were ordered to leave the area.

The next morning, the day after five hundred officers and National Guard troops swept through the narrow Swinging Bridge sector of the San Juan River canyon and discovered Mason's body, the redirected search began in earnest. "We have the last two fugitives cornered in a canyon," authorities told the media. What was predicted to be the final strike would involve hundreds of officers from federal and state law enforcement agencies as well as Four Corners police departments, in addition to National Guard Special Forces troops and air support units.[1]

Missing, however, were the commanders who had taken control of the chaos at the Cahone, Colorado, command post and begun organizing the searches in Cross Canyon and the surrounding area. El Paso County Undersheriff and retired Lt. Colonel Special Forces Commander Ivan Middlemiss had assumed control of the manhunt operations at the request of Sheriff Jerry Martin. At that point, Martin was sharing command with Utah Sheriff Mike Lacy. Headstrong about how the operation should be run, Lacy exchanged heated words with Middlemiss more than once. In the end, however, it was Martin's county and Martin's call. Even though Middlemiss also countermanded him at times, Martin recognized both he and Lacy were in way over their heads and bowed to Middlemiss's expertise. Now as the manhunt shifted deeper into Utah and the command post was relocated to Lacy's county, command and control authority shifted with it. The two state governors hadn't agreed Colorado police could go into Utah and Middlemiss refused to move with the command post to Bluff. He stayed in Cahone and ran search operations in the canyons with a remnant force of SWAT teams for one more day, then took his men home. The Cahone command post was disbanded completely and the remaining officers directed to Bluff.

Also gone was the competent tactical field commander Middlemiss trusted to direct the large Swinging Bridge operation. Appalled at the command disarray and lack of discipline he saw when reporting to the Bluff command post from the Swinging Bridge manhunt, Pueblo County SWAT Team Commander Greg McCain judged that staying meant putting his men in an untenable situation with unnecessarily elevated risk. In less than an hour, he pulled his team and left.

When McCain left, Utah FBI and the Utah Department of Public Safety (State Patrol) were arguing over which of them would take over. The next day the FBI established a crisis command post in Bluff with the intent of coordinating the manhunt and covertly purchased office supplies and equipment for it. Officially, however, they were only there to assist and Lacy gave no ground to either agency. As long as the manhunt was taking place within the eight thousand square miles of San Juan County (the largest county in Utah), Sheriff Mike Lacy was running it. He even claimed authority over operations on Navajo Reservation land. Navajo Nation Police Chief Leonard Butler believed Lacy's assertion of authority was an unjustified power grab and appealed to the U.S. Attorney's office as well as the FBI. Both agencies agreed with him, Butler claimed, but were reluctant to publicly enter the dispute. Instead they left the two adversaries to butt heads.

Roadblocks sealing the area netted a half ton of pot but no sign of the suspects. Trackers and SWAT teams beat their way through the heavy brush along a two-mile-wide, seven-mile-long strip of canyon bottom from Bluff downstream. Spotters lined the canyon rims overlooking the search area. Snipers along the river scoped boat takeout spots. Listening posts monitored noise and voices in the canyon. Utah Highway Patrol officers with high-power rifles surveyed the river from the bridge in Mexican Hat, while listening to a broadcast of the NBA finals between the Utah Jazz and Chicago Bulls. Planes searched the length of the river all the way to Lake Powell. At the foot of Honaker Trail, Blackhawk helicopters swooped in low over the trees overcoming two groups of campers before they could react. Battle-clad Special Forces soldiers leaned tethered from the door with assault rifles in the ready position. Within seconds the soldiers were on the ground ordering the campers at gunpoint to raise their arms while another trooper searched their tents and bags.

By Friday evening, twenty-four hours after they were forced to leave, Bluff residents returned home. The enthusiasm that began operations that morning had waned. Once again, if McVean or Pilon were in the area, they left no clear clues to their presence. Footprints had been found but there had been many hikers and boaters in the area and the match to the suspects' boot prints in Cross Canyon was uncertain. Several caches of food discovered along the river attested to the suspects' preplanning but told police nothing about their current whereabouts. "To tell you the honest truth, we don't know that they were here at all," Lacy admitted to reporters Friday night.

It was also possible that the fugitives had been at Swinging Bridge, but backtracked on foot toward Cross Canyon rather than fleeing by boat downriver into the manhunt area. It took nearly ten hours for a lead from earlier in the day to reach the FBI command post. A group of four people reported seeing two white (non-Indian) males on reservation land by Montezuma Creek about 8 A.M. that morning. The location placed the suspicious hikers on the route that follows the creek back from where it spills into the San Juan River, four miles upstream from Swinging Bridge. The men were dressed in dark clothing and were last seen hiking south into Cross Canyon.

"Tell me, little brother, what's for breakfast?" Navajo Police Chief Leonard Butler asked one of his tactical commanders over the radio.

"Scrambled eggs," came the reply.

Had the response been, "Eggs over easy," it would have meant that Butler's officers had captured at least one of the fugitives. What would happen next had been secretly planned by Butler and U.S. Justice Department officials. Questioning of the suspect would have to wait. Instead he would be strip-searched, dressed in a Tyvex coverall and shackled. Navajo EMTs would check him over and administer minor treatment as needed. He would then be photographed to document his physical condition, a hood would be placed over his head and he'd be led to an unmarked SUV with darkened windows. Surrounded by officers in the center car of a three-vehicle convey, he'd be whisked to a nearby airstrip and transferred to a waiting Navajo Nation plane.

By the time Sheriff Lacy, the media or anyone else who'd been scanning Navajo police transmissions knew of the capture, the outlaw would be safely in the custody of U.S. marshals in Salt Lake. There'd be no rescue attempt by sympathizers, no frontier justice by vigilantes, no premature news reports by the media and no jurisdictional showdown with the San Juan County Sheriff's Office.

In Butler's mind, there was no doubt the fugitives were near Montezuma Creek on the northern edge of the Navajo Reservation rather than downriver from Bluff. Despite the fact that his officers knew that country along the San Juan far better than the FBI or big-city teams from outside the area and were better prepared to operate in that environment than any other squad, Lacy had relegated the Navajo to support roles. Even more counterproductive in Butler's opinion was the fact that Lacy paid no heed to the Native American locals who populated the area. Navajo herders and ranchers were intimately familiar with the area. Not only would they be the first to spot signs of the fugitives, but they also could have directed searchers to water sources, caves and other off-the-map features men on the run may have used.[2]

Underutilized in the Bluff search where Lacy focused the manhunt, Butler's Navajo police took the initiative to search the Montezuma Creek area upriver from Bluff and Swinging Bridge.

Rookie Navajo Ranger Stanley Milford had been reassigned to

assist police from the tribe's Shiprock division. In truth, the Shiprock officers needed his vehicle more than him. As a park ranger, he had been assigned a pickup truck. It was the perfect vehicle for transporting canoes being used to search along the river northeast of Bluff. Once he got there, however, he stayed; sometimes going into the field for thirty brutal hours at a time. Just six months out of the police academy, he had never been on a real tactical mission before reporting to Shiprock, but he was soon attached to the squad under the guidance of Strategic Reaction Team (SRT) veteran Cornelius Thomas.

Navajo only on his father's side and raised in Oklahoma by his Cherokee mother, Milford didn't practice the native traditions followed by many of his fellow officers. He watched respectfully as the others prepared for their missions by fanning smoke from mountain tobacco over their bodies to cleanse themselves or offered pinches of sacred corn pollen from a small leather pouch kept under their equipment to each of the four directions to shield themselves from harm.

Milford wouldn't need such protection for his first assignment. Rather than going into the canyon where searching for the fugitives came with the risk of a gun battle, he and Thomas were assigned night watch from an observation post overlooking the San Juan River bottomland. Milford began the first shift at 10 P.M. Vehicle lights on a distant road glowed in the night-vision goggles. Status lights on oil wellheads drew his attention as they blinked on. But scanning across miles of countryside, there was nothing unusual to report—until he looked straight down. At the bottom of the bluff, on the opposite side of the river from where he was sitting, was a four-foot square of blackness, like a hole in the night. The edges of the square glowed. He pulled the goggles from his face and looked again. Nothing. Whatever he'd seen was invisible to the naked eye.

"Corny" came to the edge and looked for himself. It was like the rookie claimed; without night-vision goggles, no one looking from above could see the fire under the black tarp. Even with the goggles, a faint frame of light spilling from the tarp's edges and fleeting glimpses of two silhouettes were the only signs that someone was down there.

Tactical teams were ordered to converge from each side but thick brush blocked their progress. For much of the way, the officers were forced to slide on their bellies following a snake's path through the undergrowth. Despite their best efforts to sneak, noise of the teams' approach preceded them. They were still far apart when the light was extinguished. The next morning, peering through the scope on Corny's Remington 700 sniper rifle, the tracks were evident. But beyond the small patch of trampled earth, there was no trail to follow. Nevertheless, hints that the elusive outlaws were still in the area continued to surface and Butler was encouraged.

Despite the disappointing results downriver, manhunt command filled the San Juan River valley west of Bluff with hundreds of police the balance of the weekend, pressing the search area farther downstream each day. By that time, however, it was possible McVean and Pilon had reached Grand Gulch. The hand-drawn map found among the suspects' possessions led a team of topographers, FBI intel analysts and local outdoor guides to conclude Grand Gulch could also be the location of the suspects' master cache and a permanent hideout. Where in Grand Gulch, however, was not known. Beyond Bluff and Mexican Hat, the San Juan River enters a vast canyon system twice the area of the Cross Canyon network.

As the manhunt flowed with the river to the gates of Grand Gulch, officials decided on a new tactic. The plan was a dramatic departure from the noisy, highly visible invasion into the canyons that characterized the manhunt so far. Special Forces prepared to silently slip into Grand Gulch late Saturday night, floating in on the river during darkness, then dispersing to find the suspects unaware that a force was in the area. Officially, their instructions were to locate but not engage. Unofficially they would be fully armed.

While the Special Forces intended to move with stealth, Colorado Governor Roy Romer did not. On Friday afternoon, the day after Swinging Bridge, he showed up in Bluff, Utah, dressed in his bombardier jacket and proceeded to hold a press conference. Committed to bringing the outlaws to justice, Romer told reporters he would extend the expiring state of emergency under which the Colorado National Guard was authorized to aid in the manhunt by three days to June 10. It was a political moment and one other politician who quickly heard about it was Utah Governor Michael Leavitt. In London with a state trade delegation, Leavitt went straight for the phone. It was Saturday in Bluff when Lacy got the call from the governor's office. The conversation was not recorded but the gist of it was relayed by Lacy as he explained to colleagues why the Grand Gulch mission was scuttled. Basically the governor's questions were rhetorical and to the effect of, "What was the Colorado governor doing making political hay in Leavitt's state?" Even more important, "What are Colorado National Guard troops doing in Utah?" Leavitt's order was equally clear: "Get them out."

While the manhunt struggled, the first seventy-two hours were productive for investigators. Without a lot of easy clues, they identified McVean, Mason and Pilon as suspects in the murder of Dale Claxton. In the process they accumulated not only enough evidence to obtain arrest warrants for the men, but also to support a strong prosecution if the suspects were captured. After that, however, investigative breakthroughs were as elusive as the fugitives themselves. Even the episode at Swinging Bridge that gave renewed energy to the manhunt yielded little of value for investigators hoping to move the case forward.

Whatever small ongoing progress was made in the case came through the slow steady grind of shoe-leather police work: background checks, search warrants and questioning the men's acquaintances. (Phone taps of the suspects' families and friends proved futile.) The effort occupied a thirty-person investigative team working out of the FBI command center in the Cortez Police Department, aided by dozens of other officers from surrounding agencies.

Releasing the suspects' names didn't slow the telephone tips. Instead the callers phoned with information about the suspects: tidbits recalled from high school, where they shopped, who they hung out with, a snippet of conversation overheard. Dozens called to report sightings: "I saw Pilon in a red pickup near Blanding." "Just saw McVean with a buzz cut in McDonald's in Texas." "Robert Mason was standing on a runway at Denver International Airport with a shotgun." Other sightings were of men in camouflage clothing walking near this cabin, along that road, in a car heading one direction or another. Many were undoubtedly on-edge citizens seeing camo-clad police that had swarmed to the area to aid the search, but others had hints of legitimacy that redirected helicopters and SWAT teams from one location to the next.

On June 7, ten days after McElmo Bridge, the Cortez City Council pledged five thousand dollars for information leading to the suspects' capture. Combined with an equal amount raised so far by the Montezuma County Crimestoppers, the ten-thousand-dollar total reward registered a small uptick in phone calls, but brought in no new leads of substance. One week later the FBI chipped in another fifty thousand dollars, with similar results.

Hours after arrest warrants made the suspects' names public, Cortez Assistant Police Chief Russell Johnson sat in Francis and Beverly Pilon's living room. The room was small and modestly furnished but tidy. Francis, who introduced himself as "Jim," and Beverly sat together on the sofa facing him. Johnson had checked and knew their basic stats including their ages before he arrived, but looking at them he would have correctly guessed they were in their sixties. They were small-town folk in their manner and appearance. The stress of the last thirty hours since rumor reached them that their son was a murder suspect showed in their faces. Beverly had been crying. Johnson knew they were in a delicate state, but they seemed cooperative and compliant.[3] He checked his list of prepared questions and began asking about Monte: Did he do well in school? What were his interests? Who did he look up to? Was he suicidal?

At the same time that Johnson questioned Monte's parents in their living room, other officers combed the rest of the property. The Dove Creek home was where Monte grew up and where he still lived on weekends. Even though he claimed it as his permanent residence, however, most of the property didn't reveal his regular presence. The mobile home sited permanently next to the main house identified by a small wood sign as Beverly's Beauty Shop was just that and no more. There was nothing of Monte's in Jim's large garage that was of investigative interest. Even the house itself showed little sign of Monte actively living there, except for Monte's bedroom. It was from that room alone that police hauled away a long list of evidence. Most of it was testimony to Monte's obsession with guns. Police seized rifles, pistols, ammunition clips, multiple empty gun cartons, part of a machine-gun belt and bullets. A shoe box under the bed held extremist literature, notes taken from *The Anarchist Cookbook,* and membership documents for the secretive Four Corners Patriot Militia. All of it implied a personality that may have committed the crime. None of it directly connected Monte to McElmo Bridge, except for one item. Inside a box for a Russian-made SKS rifle was a wooden rifle stock. It was the original stock to the SKS recovered near the abandoned flatbed. The component had been swapped out for an aftermarket composite stock.

At Animas Air Park in Durango the search didn't proceed as smoothly. Deputies barely breached a shed near McVean's trailer when they pulled back and radioed a warning to the others searching the property. "Bombs! Looks like bomb-making materials here." From the edges of the property, the officers waited for the bomb experts loaned from the Colorado Springs Police Department Explosive Ordnance Disposal unit to arrive. The property held six buildings—the shop for Jim McVean's construction company, the two trailers McVean and Pilon lived in, a third trailer, a metal building McVean had recently built for his girlfriend to live in and a storage shed—plus Mason's truck. Slowed by the threat of explosives the search took three days. As was the case for most of the materials seized from Pilon's Dove Creek home, the evidence gathered from Durango didn't directly implicate any of the suspects in the Cortez shootings, but it did underscore that the men they were seeking were dangerous and planning terrorism.

Within the various buildings, searchers found fifty-pound sacks of commercial-grade ANFO explosive, hundreds of pounds of ammonium nitrate fertilizer used for making high-order explosive, dynamite, one hundred feet of detonation cord, a large supply of chemicals used for enhancing the explosive power of ANFO and for making TNT-level explosives, plus three mercury switches. In addition, police discovered an estimated ten thousand dollars' worth of ammunition and survival supplies including fifteen thousand rounds of various caliber shells, prepackaged food, clothing, tents and water purification equipment. The third camper trailer had been covered in quarter-inch plate steel. With gun ports cut in it would be an impervious mobile bunker, CBI concluded.

In the avalanche of leads from the public and the inevitable winnowing to those worth pursuing, none were overlooked that in hindsight would have broken the case open and sped authorities to a faster resolution. It was also true that in the search of the suspects' premises and vehicles there seemed to be nothing of game-changing potential missed or misinterpreted.[4] Whatever opportunities police had to learn where the suspects were hiding lay with the fugitives' associates. One by one those opportunities were lost.

Within the first weeks of the investigation and even long after it had lost its momentum police interviewed dozens of people who knew the suspects. They talked to family members, teachers, employers, casual acquaintances and close friends. They heard a remarkably consistent story: the suspects had extreme antigovernment views, were gun-nut survivalists who trained in the desert and for years had been hiding weapons and supplies in the canyons. Each successive interview added some nuance to their profiles but revealed no information that dramatically altered the conclusions of the investigation or the outcome of the manhunt.

Several weeks into the investigation, an FBI review of its Rapid Start Lead Management System resulted in a multipage list of names of people of obvious importance or potential that police failed to contact or question pointedly. Some were names found among notes the suspects left behind. Others were people identified by the suspects' acquaintances. Missed were several people whose own backgrounds and relationships to the suspects suggested they might know more about the crime. Among them were associates who shared the same extreme viewpoints and behavior.

In at least three instances, friends of the suspects rumored to have assisted them were not questioned and investigated aggressively. Among them were close friends of Pilon who joined him on weekend militia training exercises. Multiple callers advised police that one Pilon associate had taken an unusual amount of supplies on a suspicious desert canyon river trip the day after the shooting on McElmo Bridge. On June 8, police received a tip that another close Pilon friend was overheard saying she gave two of the fugitives food when they showed up at her house on the run. A third Pilon associate was accused of being an accomplice in the crime by a relative who had already provided police with reliable tips. There is no record that police followed up on the potentially significant leads to unequivocally confirm or dismiss them.

Cortez P.D. Detective Jim Shethar didn't realize it at first as he worked in the FBI's shadow but the feds' high-handed style during those first weeks of the investigation was shutting down key sources of information. Commandeering the most promising of the interview assignments—the suspects' tight-knit group of like-minded friends in Durango—FBI agents attempted to extract information with a bullying approach that proved counterproductive. "They came into a region where there is a general suspicion of the federal government and its agents, and tried to coerce information from people who have a specific dislike of the government. The interview subjects were immediately uncooperative," Shethar explained. Months later, after he had taken over the investigation, Shethar reinterviewed many of the same people. His approach was calculated. "Hey, I'm just a small-town cop. I don't know much about that stuff," became a refrain he sprinkled throughout his interviews in one variation or another. It was a friendly, you're-smarter-than-me, help-me-out style that seemed to draw out useful information even months after McElmo Bridge. Used earlier, when the information was timely, it may have changed the course of the manhunt.

Of particular later regret was that a more productive interview approach had not been used early with an individual Shethar didn't get to reinterview. The subject was a close associate of the fugitives and the one person, according to the suspects' friends and the police, who likely had prior knowledge of the crime. That he knew the suspects' plans and where they would have taken refuge was the consensus. In fact, police long suspected he was an accomplice, part of the conspiracy. It was a conjecture the individual reportedly confirmed to friends weeks after McElmo Bridge, telling them he knew what was going on but couldn't say more because he'd be implicated.

Two months after that confidence, the fourth suspect (never charged) was dead. As would ultimately be the case with his friends in the desert, police would conclude the fatal gunshot to his head was self-inflicted.

As both the tactical and investigative operations foundered, each side looked to the other for the next breakthrough. The tactical team, frustrated with the lack of progress in the field, hoped investigators would uncover a clue that would redirect the manhunt. The investigators hoped the tactical team might uncover evidence in the desert that upon investigation would propel the case forward.

On June 9, investigators thought they got the break they had been hoping for. The bullets lay in plain sight on the edge of the road a short distance from the Hog Springs rest area near Hite Marina on Lake Powell. The highway maintenance crew cutting weeds along the shoulder followed the trail of cartridges forty-five feet back from the road to a cluster of large boulders. Between the boulders, smaller rocks and soil had been disturbed. The rectangular impression of a heavy container was pressed into the ground. Broken pieces of cloth-covered wood from a suitcase were found nearby as well as shreds of ammunition boxes and plastic bags. A few feet farther along the shoulder of the road, the workmen discovered a crossbow and quiver of bolts.

CBI investigator Wayne Bryant flew by helicopter most of the distance across Utah the day of the discovery. It was dusk by the time he got to the rest area, too late to see much. The next morning, guided by the workmen who made the discovery, Bryant searched the area.

What transpired there was clear. Someone had retrieved a hidden cache of ammunition. The suitcase which was buried beneath a pile of fist-size rocks had broken apart, the cartons inside had deteriorated and shells were dropped as the hoard was carried to a car parked at the side of the road. The spilled cartridges left behind as well as acceleration tire tracks told CBI investigators that whoever had come for the cache was in a rush. Several feet down the road, a crossbow that had been set on the vehicle and forgotten in the mission's haste, vibrated off.

Hite Marina was in the direction police surmised the remaining fugitives were heading, near the Grand Gulch area that had emerged as their likely destination. The recovered ammunition was the same assault-rifle caliber the fugitives had been firing. McVean was reported to have owned a crossbow. Finally, the workmen confirmed they had last worked in that area on June 4, the day Mason was killed at Swinging Bridge. The spilled shells and crossbow were definitely not on the side of the road then; the cache had been broken into sometime within the last five days. There were several reports that at about the same time Mason was digging in for a last stand against police at Swinging Bridge, other men dressed in camouflage escaped from the area in a boat, floating to safety down the San Juan River toward Lake Powell. The timing of the cache opening fit perfectly with an escape down the San Juan three to five days earlier.

Too many pieces matched for it all to be coincidence. Bryant and his fellow investigators were confident that the person who had retrieved the cache was Jason McVean. Once again, however, the crime scene offered no clues that led further, not even physical evidence in the way of footprints or fingerprints that confirmed McVean's presence. Other than a strong suspicion that McVean had made it that far sometime in the last few days, Claxton murder crime scene #25 left police with no place to go.

On June 18, Earl Christenson, the CBI agent in charge of the investigation, e-mailed his office:

Things are slowing down around here, awaiting a good sighting of the suspects, etc. Follow-up interviews and case organization are the only tasks being performed by CBI personnel at this time. The FBI will have only one person at the command center this weekend and is scaling down next week to just a couple of agents, *unless* they put the suspects/fugitives on their ten most wanted list. I understand if this happens, they will be blessed with new resources, possibly to include an influx of new agents.

As the manhunt officially ended and the investigation ground down, Colorado Senator Ben Nighthorse Campbell announced that the U.S. Senate Appropriations Committee pledged $250,000 to the Justice Department for a larger reward in the case. On June 29, exactly one month after McElmo Bridge, Attorney General Janet Reno signed orders placing McVean and Pilon on the FBI's ten most-wanted list and authorized an additional FBI reward of $250,000 on top of the $50,000 it had offered earlier. The amount was divided, placing $150,000 on the head of each suspect. Combined with the City of Cortez and growing Crimestoppers rewards, a tip that allowed police to locate the suspects paid $325,000 or $162,500 apiece.

Eleven days after McElmo Bridge, the officers and department budgets were exhausted. More than a million dollars had been spent trying to catch the outlaws yet two of the three remained at large and police had no clues where in thousands of square miles of wilderness to begin looking for them. What had been more than five hundred officers swarming through the San Juan River canyon south of Bluff on Friday, Saturday and Sunday after Mason's body was found, was scaled back to fifty by that Monday. The manhunt command post at Bluff was disbanded, as was the one at Cahone three days earlier. Manhunt coordination was consolidated with the investigative task force at the FBI command post housed in the Cortez Police Department. Rather than a central command post that shifted location with the flow of the manhunt, each of the sheriffs in the three counties where the search had been focused—Kennell in Montezuma County, Colorado; Martin in Dolores County, Colorado; and Lacy in San Juan County, Utah—would handle operations within their own jurisdictions. Within two days, the extended state of emergency that allowed the use of National Guard personnel and equipment for the search lapsed. Various support agencies splintered off over the next several days and returned to their routine duties. Most of the volunteer officers had gone.

The remaining searchers decided to go back to square one and restart the manhunt from the site of the abandoned flatbed. For the next week there were still upward of a hundred officers in Cross Canyon looking for what they missed the first time around or in case the suspects had doubled back from Swinging Bridge. But the largest manhunt in the history of the West was essentially over.

On Tuesday, June 16, nineteen days after McElmo Bridge, it ended officially. Police announced the conclusion of that phase of the search for Dale Claxton's killers with an admission of defeat. "We're still about where we were in the search," Cortez Police Chief Lane told reporters, "in other words, no progress." Rather than a wilderness dragnet, future search operations were to be driven by information developed during the criminal investigation, Lane added, noting that the investigative side of the case remained fully staffed with thirty officers, including FBI and CBI teams. Over the course of the next few weeks, that too would dwindle.

CBI kept an agent in place through the summer. He would be a common partner for Detective Shethar as the two continued to interview and reinterview the suspects' acquaintances. The FBI abandoned the Cortez command center in August. They remained involved in the case for the next nine years but only as one more file in a tall stack of unsolved federal crimes consigned to irregular spurts of attention as leads surfaced. The specter of the crime continued to haunt most surrounding police agencies, and while their officers returned to their routine law enforcement duties, many gave Shethar's requests top priority whenever he asked for assistance in their jurisdictions.[5]

Among the fifty-one law enforcement agencies and hundreds of police officers who participated in the first frenzied weeks of the case, however, the murder of Dale Claxton remained poignant only for the men and women of the Cortez Police Department. For them, finding Dale's killers would never be routine.

CHAPTER 17
GRUBWORK

July 2, about a month after McElmo Bridge: Oliver Coho shifted his gaze lower as he opened the door. He hadn't expected the person banging frantically on his trailer home to be a child. The girl's dark eyes were wide with excitement. "I saw the bad guys," she said with a breathless nine-year-old's voice. "They were over there." She pointed beyond an uneven row of mobile homes to the edge of the trailer park where a water tanker truck was parked. Coho had noted the truck before. He didn't know if it ever moved but if it did, it reacquired its parking place with enough precision that he viewed it more as a sculpture than a vehicle. The girl he knew as one of the neighborhood children who lived in the park a couple of mobile homes down from him.

A small reservation community situated between Cross Canyon and Swinging Bridge, Montezuma Creek had been flanked by manhunt chaos. Hordes of police had passed through the town. The drone of helicopters and search planes overhead had been incessant. But all that had dissipated in the two weeks since the manhunt officially ended. The tension, however, remained. WANTED posters still hung in the gas station and convenience-store windows. Street-corner conversation seemed to include the word "killers." And while adults tried not to alarm their children, the small ones could sense the lingering unease. They still huddled near swing sets and sandboxes and talked in hushed tones about evil men lurking in the desert beyond their grass-bare yards. They were aware and scared.

The girl knocking on Coho's door wasn't the first to report one of the fugitives in Montezuma Creek. There had been a positive sighting of Robert Mason the day before his body was found nine miles downriver at Swinging Bridge. He walked out of the wash, bought food at the trading post and disappeared back into the wash heading toward Bluff and his violent, mysterious death. Coho had tracked him to the south side of the river, but by the time the significance of the sighting filtered through to manhunt command a day later, Deputy Bradford had been shot and the manhunt shifted that direction anyway.

A patrolman with the Navajo Police Department's Shiprock (New Mexico) District, Coho was in charge of the Montezuma Creek substation. Most of the residents in the area knew him as the local policeman so it was natural for the girl to have run to his trailer when she saw two men in camouflage clothing with guns. The men were trying to get into the locked tanker truck when they realized the child watching them was darting toward one of the trailers. Without waiting for an adult to answer the girl's knock, the two men turned and walked briskly away. The girl positively identified one of the men as McVean. Police presumed the second man was Pilon but in fact the girl was tentative that the man she saw looked like Pilon's picture. Once again Coho followed the footprints of men escaping alongside the San Juan River, this time losing them heading upstream toward Aneth.

Drawn from the surrounding Four Corners police agencies, the SWAT teams assembled quickly but by the time the first of them arrived, more than two hours had elapsed since the girl's sighting. By the time San Juan Sheriff Lacy had a force sufficient to even begin to seal off a sector of the canyon with teams on each side of the confluence and search the dense brush that grew along the river, four hours had passed.

Observers and snipers scrambled to positions on the canyon rim while officers with search dogs beat the bushes below. The canyon was neither as wide nor deep as the section of Cross Canyon where the manhunt began. Observers on the rim could see most of the canyon bottom, even with the limited range of night-vision goggles. Glassing over the top of the foliage, they focused on breaks in the cover where a flushed fugitive might be revealed. The officers on the canyon floor worked until dark forced them to Bluff hotels for rest. Working in shifts, the officers on the rim kept vigil for the next seventy-two hours.

Reports from the searchers tantalized. Tuesday night, the day after the sighting, Navajo trackers crept within thirty yards of two men softly talking, laughing and occasionally splashing in the closed-off river. Dense brush that limited visibility to a few feet in daylight made it impossible to see the suspects at night or establish a close perimeter. Rather than risk a blind firefight against automatic weapons, the trackers backed away and reported. The next morning, the source of the voices in the dark was gone. Left were tracks matching those at Coho's trailer park. The shared sense of things among police was that maybe, at last, they got a break; that the fugitives were trapped within a difficult but manageable-size search area.

Search dogs picked up the trail early the next morning. They followed it for more than a mile downstream; finding the infrequent footprint; questioning whether it matched what they had learned to recognize as Pilon's or McVean's. Then abruptly it ended.

The men were survivalists, practiced at disappearing. Among their training exercises was a game of wilderness hide-and-seek. One man with a half-day head start would hide in the desert. The others would have to track and find their concealed friend. They knew not to flee into the crosshairs of a sniper rifle unseen on the ridge sixty feet over their heads but instead to hide where they were. They knew how to become part of the wild canyon, blending into the environment, sliding between the rocks and shadows like scorpions.

The bad guys were still in the canyon, hiding in the dense brush, Lacy concluded. And he had had enough of their cat-and-mouse game.

Even though the search area was contained, about six miles long and a mile or two wide between the canyon walls, the ten- to twelve-foot-tall brush a half mile deep along both sides of the river was so thick that it took an entire team four hours to clear one small island. It would take weeks to search the entire area and nothing prevented the fugitives from simply moving back into cleared areas in a never-ending game of hide-and-seek.

The amplified voice from the helicopter flying low through the canyon warned of the pending fire with orders to leave the area immediately. Lacy's plan was for the chopper to make a second pass dropping fire bombs but the Bureau of Land Management which uses incendiary devices to start controlled burns had qualms about the idea and refused to supply them. Instead, as the helicopter passed by, SWAT teams rushed in under it with flares. The dry sagebrush caught fire quickly. In minutes the flames traveled in under the tamarisk and Russian olive trees that bordered the river. It was several minutes more before the building heat ignited the twiggy tips of their branches but soon entire trees burned. Plumes of dense gray smoke rose from the canyon bottom as the fire charred a swath a half mile wide and over two miles long.

Eighty snipers positioned two hundred yards apart on both rims of the six-mile stretch of canyon waited for movement below. With overlapping fields of vision and marksmanship skills that ensured any of them could empty a clip into a target the size of a dinner plate at four hundred yards, there was no place to escape the advancing inferno without being in the sights of at least two shooters. But other than the flickering flames and drifting smoke, the floor of the canyon was still. The snipers waited. The sun set and they waited. When sunlight finally inched its way down the canyon walls again and lighted the blackened bottomland, they stood down and went home.

Were the fugitives ever really there? For the police, answering "no" came easier than admitting they escaped once again.

While the tactical operation waited for leads from investigators, the investigators waited for citizens to report sightings, hoping they would be encouraged by the increased reward. It was enough to lure bounty hunters to the canyons, and send psychics and confidential informants to their phones. The discovery of Pilon's remain's seventeen months after McElmo Bridge, however, seemed to mark the end of the case—the last measure of tangible progress.

In the course of years beyond that breakthrough, reports of McVean flowed in from across the country spurred by post office WANTED posters and repeated episodes of *America's Most Wanted* and *Unsolved Mysteries* true-crime television shows. He was reported working construction in Rochester, Minnesota, and living with a woman in Charleston, West Virginia. He supposedly returned merchandise to a Sears store in San Luis Obispo, California, and hitched a ride from Ogden, Utah, to Idaho during which he casually told the driver that he was a fugitive and had killed his fellow outlaw. His likeness was seen riding buses in Salt Lake City, where his leer unnerved women passengers, and kicking back with a beer and a burger in a roughneck American bar known as Horny's in the Zona Dorada section of Mazatlan, Mexico. The FBI diligently checked all the leads, even the one from Mexico. In most cases they didn't slam down the phones and pull on their coats as they raced out the door. They fit them into their month. In some instances the subject was long gone or the retail store security video that would have conclusively confirmed the report had already been taped over. But by taking fingerprints, flashing photos or simply looking at the individual, most of the leads were discounted or at least listed as unconfirmed dead ends.

Like the sighting by the nine-year-old girl in a Montezuma Creek trailer park, however, there were some that had a tone of certainty about them, a veracity that demanded other law enforcement agencies be contacted, resources mobilized and an immediate full-scale response launched.

September 1999. The Montezuma County sheriff's deputy knew whose car he was pulling over for speeding. The driver was a person several years older than the fugitives who, according to investigation records, McVean felt especially close to. When McVean killed Officer Dale Claxton and disappeared into the desert sixteen months earlier, the man was one of several people police watched in case Jason tried to contact any of his closest friends. They knew from earlier interviews the two had discussed hypothetical scenarios and response strategies if a person were on the run from the law. Now the chain-smoking, fidgeting man who had advised Jason how to evade police appeared excessively nervous for a minor traffic stop. But what really caught the deputy's eye were twelve bags of groceries and three bundles of firewood loaded in the backseat.

Taking the man's driver's license and stepping back to his patrol car supposedly for a routine check for warrants, the deputy instead relayed a call to Cortez P.D. Detective Jim Shethar.

Shethar raced for his unmarked car, drove to the eastern edge of Cortez and waited. The deputy handed the man his license with a warning and admonition to slow down. When the man pulled onto the highway, the deputy pulled out behind him, following at a short distance to make sure he continued heading west out of Mancos, Colorado, then nonchalantly turned off.

The man stole furtive glances from his rearview mirror, still nervous with the deputy behind him. Then he saw the patrol car's turn signal, the gap between their vehicles widened and finally he relaxed. He didn't see that as the deputy turned, the officer brought his radio mic to his mouth. "He's on the way, Jim. Should pass you in fifteen minutes."

As the suspicious man drove through Cortez, Shethar slipped into the traffic behind him and tailed the car unnoticed for the next two hours to Kayenta, Arizona. From there aerial surveillance tracked the vehicle to Page, Arizona, where National Park Service rangers took over until FBI agents out of the Flagstaff office could get there.

The man checked into a Page motel and waited for two others to join him. The rangers had already determined the three close associates of McVean had arranged to rent a forty-six-foot Lake Powell houseboat. The craft was substantially larger than what was normally used by three people; the rental arrangements were made recently, without the usual advance reservation; and the two people joining the man for the trip were much younger, closer in age to the fugitives themselves. The group seemed an odd lot for vacation friends. Their most logical connection was Jason. In addition, there had been at least two unconfirmed sightings of McVean being met by individuals on the south side of Lake Powell in the past year.

In the first two days out, the boat traveled an erratic path; movements authorities interpreted as an effort to evade surveillance. The third night out the group lit a campfire on shore. Then between 11 P.M. and 2 A.M., a person on the boat shined a spotlight into the air at regular intervals while calling out toward shore. No reply from shore was detected and as the group off-loaded the next day, authorities overheard one of the boaters comment to dock attendants that they had supplies left over because they were supposed to meet a fourth person but did not.

The trip thrust the boaters under the scrutiny of the FBI's National Center for the Analysis of Violent Crime (NCAVC). The group studies behavioral patterns and concluded the three boaters likely had contact with McVean, directly or indirectly, or at least knew something of his survival and whereabouts. One of them, police determined, had already lied regarding her relationship with McVean. In fact, their relationship was such that analysts identified her as a person McVean would reach out to and she as someone who would surreptitiously assist him. The man police followed to Lake Powell, according to sketchy intelligence, had made an unusual withdrawal of funds from a retirement savings plan in the early fall of 1998 when McVean had been on the run for three months. The third person had been identified some months earlier by a reliable FBI informant as a person to watch in connection with McVean. Checks of the individuals' travel and phone records increased suspicion, showing a pattern of movement and contact dramatically different than any of them had described to police in previous interviews.

The plan was for FBI agents to arrive simultaneously at the homes or workplaces of all three people from the houseboat as well as others linked to both them and McVean. The people involved were spread from Durango to the West Coast. The hope was that the sudden, simultaneous interviews would prevent the subjects from anticipating police questioning and aligning their stories. The execution of the plan in December 1999 was imperfect. Some interviews ended up several days apart. Some of the subjects dodged the questioning altogether. Otherwise police heard the boat trip was a vacation and "No, Jason has not tried to contact me since the shooting and I don't know where he is." Nevertheless, authorities would continue to watch the group and hope that someday one of them would lead them to the last remaining fugitive from McElmo Bridge.

One year led to the next; personnel in the Utah FBI offices, where the case resided, came and went, but the case remained open. Each new agent assigned the file would initiate a renewed but short-lived effort at solving it. A 2003 Social Security number search for all three fugitives turned up no suspicious use of Social Security numbers assigned to Mason and Pilon, known to be dead. McVean's Social Security number, however, had been used six times in the last two years. Agents across the country attempted to locate the individuals who listed the number as their own but Jason McVean never answered their knock on the door. Maps drawn by the suspects and aerial photos of the canyons were forwarded to land-navigation and map-reading analysts hoping their expertise could discern clues to the fugitives' cache sites that others missed. Phone records were reexamined as the agents looked for new contact patterns and potential sources of information. Other agents new to the case would take a fresh look at existing evidence and propose alternative ideas about McVean's movements in the first days of the manhunt, suggesting new areas to look for clues. Still there was no progress in the case.

Budget and resources increasingly became part of the consideration when evaluating leads. The cost of thirty-five hundred dollars for renting a helicopter from the National Park Service to fly an agent to search a potential cache site was debated. The NPS and BLM sympathized but no longer had money in their budgets for the flight. A request for a Nightstalker flyover of another area of interest was denied as too costly given the uncertainty of a lead that key investigators considered worthwhile.

For Shethar and the Cortez P.D., every reasonable lead was a stone not to be left unturned. They could not cover as much territory as Nightstalker surveillance, but they would do their best. Reduced resources were not their only obstacle. San Juan Sheriff Mike Lacy was, by that time, reluctant to pursue any but the most certain leads himself and warned others not to follow leads into Utah without his permission. Whether the Colorado officers entered the canyons on official police business or were following leads "on their own time," they would be illegally violating his jurisdiction, he claimed. Vocal critics have interpreted Lacy's objection to Colorado police officers conducting business in San Juan County, Utah, as an expression of the sheriff's ego and belligerence, but in fairness, it had a legal basis. There are questions of liability that could arise from officers working outside their jurisdictions, although they could be overcome between cooperative agencies.[1]

Cortez officers went anyway. Multiple trips over the years into the Utah canyon country to check out a lead or search for new clues were essentially black ops. It was Shethar and Cortez P.D. that never put the case on the back burner. The file was never allowed to be a "cold case" tucked away in a seldom-opened drawer labeled "unsolved." For nearly a decade they pursued it as an active investigation.

In August of 1999 there were two independent sightings of McVean in Monument Valley, Utah, part of the canyon country that was McVean's comfort zone. A Navajo sheepherder said a man approached him and asked about a road down to the San Juan River. Later that day a woman reported the same man in front of her house. Their descriptions of the suspicious stranger were identical and both said he resembled the photos of McVean that police showed them. Three years later there was a second case of two independent sightings. The first came from a man who walked into the Arcata, California, police station and reported that he had just dropped off a suspicious hitchhiker he picked up in Colorado. En route the hitchhiker talked about a "shoot-out" he'd had with police in Cortez, Colorado. A photo was faxed from the Cortez P.D. and the man identified his rider as McVean. Three weeks later a woman reported seeing a man she identified as McVean panhandling at a rest stop south of Roseburg, Oregon. Both witnesses described the same man—Jason McVean but now with short hair rather than the shoulder-length hair shown in his police photos. Colorado to Arcata, California, and up the coast through Oregon would be the natural route McVean would take if he was heading to see his old fling Rachel Jayne, then living in Portland.

As the case grew older and colder and new leads became infrequent, Shethar went back over old ground, looking for any detail they may have missed. He reinterviewed and then reinterviewed again the suspects' acquaintances hoping time would lower their guard or the reward money would lessen their loyalty to the outlaw. Occasionally he would be led to someone new whose association with the outlaws was previously unknown. He would glean a little more background information, a fact or rumor that incrementally added to his understanding of the outlaws, but the pieces failed to answer the question: Where was Jason McVean?

There was one other law enforcement agency that kept true to the wearing, lonely, dangerous pursuit of one man hunting another in a hostile environment. As Shethar stayed on the investigative trail, the Navajo Police Department continued to trail McVean through the canyons of the Navajo Nation.

With the official end of the manhunt, the jurisdictional struggle between Navajo P.D. Chief Butler and Sheriff Lacy became moot. While the Navajo continued a proactive search for the killers within the bounds of the reservation, Lacy's department went into a reactive mode, waiting for leads from other sources and assessing which they thought merited an urgent response. Dismissing most of the leads reported by the Navajo as false, Lacy's deputies ventured less and less onto the reservation in connection with the case. Butler's and Lacy's departments would each continue to play a role in the search for the fugitives over the years, but separate from each other.

The Navajo sheepherder who found the tracks knew by then that if there was a sighting, Oliver Coho usually got it. Most of the time, people along the northern edge of the reservation just called him directly but for some reason Henry Tah called the Shiprock station and the captain called Coho. Coho stuffed a sandwich, apple, water bottle and extra ammunition clips in his pack, and grabbed a rifle.

At forty-two years old, Coho didn't find the fifteen-degree temperature—that with wind chill felt like minus-five degrees on his face—any more agreeable than the hundred-degree temperatures he endured walking the same arroyo when the manhunt began eight months ago. It was damn hard country summer or winter.

Now Coho and his guide stood at the lip of a steep bank, Henry pointing toward a stunted juniper. The top of the tree had broken off and was probably hauled away for firewood years ago. The broken trunk remained ragged but its raw core had long since weathered gray, blending with the bark. Sighting along the sheepherder's outstretched arm, Coho saw the suspicious footprint Henry had discovered early that morning.

Most of the time a sighting started with the appearance of a suspicious stranger, but sometimes it came from people intimately familiar with their environment noticing something out of place—rocks that had been shifted, litter that wasn't there yesterday, the ashes of a campfire. This morning it was a footprint where someone who had been stepping from rock to rock slipped into the snow, followed by smudges on the first few boulders where he recovered his catlike footing.

A lot of the time Coho followed indistinct or partial impressions a mile or two before finding a complete footprint and discovering he was tracking the wrong guy. More often than not the sighting turned out to be some hapless soul walking where he didn't belong. This time he was starting with nearly a complete boot print and he knew right away Jason McVean had left it.

There were other Navajo trackers who also picked up a trail after reported sightings but Coho was the only person to have seen McVean's footprints after a confirmed visual sighting, so most of the calls came to him. It was a distinction bestowed by a nine-year-old girl who banged on his door after seeing McVean and another man trying to steal a water truck in the Montezuma Creek trailer park where Coho lived. That was one month after McElmo Bridge. Since that time there had been more than a dozen positive sightings and Coho had learned much about his quarry.

Coho had checked the weather on his drive to Henry's hogan. The snow had stopped about 3 A.M. The track had been made after that. Judging by the agility the boulder path required, he guessed it was light out when McVean passed through. The crispness of the print's edges, a feature that would steadily deteriorate in the wind, told him the track was laid down four to five hours before.

Coho knew this single misstep by McVean was the biggest break he was going to get all day. McVean was as good as they get at covering a trail. By then Coho knew a lot of McVean's tricks, which helped him pick up a lost trail faster, but the fugitive was good at mixing it up. He'd keep to the rocks when he could, walk backward, cross cattle-trod areas on tiptoe so his own prints would blend with hoofprints, wade streams. Much of the time Coho was following little more than scuff marks and misplaced pebbles. On one occasion, Coho had discovered only two complete footprints over a course of three miles. The snow would help but McVean was careful. The signs of his passing would be minimal, never a cigarette butt or a candy wrapper, nothing but the faint impressions of a ghost.

Coho was used to running outlaws to ground. He'd been a lawman on the reservation for eighteen years. There had been a lot of cases of burglary and theft that involved tracking suspects across the desert and he almost always got the culprit. He was good at it. During the manhunt, a lead agent from the FBI was awed by the skill of the Navajo trackers, calling them the best in the world. CBI agent Kevin Humphrey was equally impressed. "I got to spend a couple of days with them and it was an education. What they see that others don't and are able to interpret is truly amazing," he said. Coho had survival training in the military but it was growing up on the reservation near Gallup, New Mexico, that taught him to follow a trail most people couldn't see.

Tracking was part of a boy's everyday life herding sheep, cattle and horses, Coho said. It was a background common to most of the Navajo trackers, according to Navajo Police Chief Butler. They grew up learning to pick out the tracks of their specific horse running in a herd of twelve. Tactical tracking—man hunting—is different, Butler added, but a lot of those reservation skills are transferable.

Coho avoided stepping on McVean's tracks as he followed the fugitive. At any point he might lose the trail and need to come back to his last positive print to pick it up again. He'd been at it three hours and covered an equal number of miles. A hundred yards ahead, he knew the trail would end. A wide expanse of flat rock blown bare of snow stretched to the horizon. There would be no more tracks. From there it was a hunch and trying to think like McVean. He didn't know that area as well as he did other sections of the reservation but there was one spot not far away that made sense for a man on the run. It was rugged higher ground with lots of large boulders and caves. He moved toward it hoping that McVean had done the same.

The location was in the general vicinity of an area east of Montezuma Creek, where he guessed, based on previous sightings, that McVean was wintering. The fugitive seemed to wander a wide circle with some sightings forty or fifty miles away but this area seemed to be his comfort zone. It would have made sense to search the area regularly with airborne thermal imaging. The suspect's heat signature would have shown up better against the cold winter background than it did against the hot rock canyon floor of summer. But those funds had been depleted long before the first flakes fell.

At the edge of the boulder field that led deeper into the lair, Coho halted behind an eight-foot rock outcropping that offered some cover from a shooter waiting up ahead. He'd reached this point in the chase before. From here he had to move by instinct and his instincts were telling him to back away. Sometimes he partnered with Special Forces tracker Don Bendahl but today was more typical: he was alone, at least two hours from backup support, as usual his radio didn't work this deep in the canyons and he was in uniform—a big target for a cop killer. Facing upward terrain, he wasn't about to catch someone by surprise. On the contrary, the hairs on the back of his neck told him he was being watched.

Even if his radio did work and he was to wait behind cover for backup, the closest officer was probably a San Juan County sheriff's deputy cruising somewhere in the vicinity of Bluff and at that Coho wasn't confident of the deputy's response. Pooh-poohing reservation sightings as "the Navajo hallucinating," Lacy claimed the reports were usually a waste of time. Navajo officers, on the other hand, claimed San Juan County deputies often took too long to respond to a McVean sighting and in a couple of instances didn't come at all. In their estimation, the lack of speedy support from the sheriff's department not only blew opportunities to finally corner McVean, it also put their lives at greater risk and created jurisdictional risk. Without county sheriff backup, if Coho pressed the search off reservation and ended up in a confrontation, he was in the wrong place.

In truth, reservation sightings were far more likely to be genuine than sightings elsewhere. The reservation was a large part of the territory where the fugitives disappeared and supposedly hid out. If they remained in the canyons, they inevitably were on the reservation much of that time. It was not a place where they could blend in with the crowd. First, there was no crowd. The Navajo Nation lands were sparsely populated. There were often miles between residences. Second, even if there were a crowd, the outlaws would not have blended in. Any white stranger was noted with suspicion. Dress him in camouflage fatigues, add a backpack and assault rifle and the needle was tilting toward fugitive. Throw in a resemblance to the photos on the hundreds of WANTED posters hanging throughout the reservation and the report, in light of all the effort spent on less promising leads, should have been recognized as a worthwhile possibility.

In one instance Coho received calls from several residents near Aneth reporting two people coming down off the mesa at night with flashlights. He called the San Juan County Sheriff's Office but it was three hours before deputies showed. Whoever had been there was gone. The next morning, Coho found McVean's tracks and a military night-light that must have bounced loose and fell from one of their packs as they descended the rugged slope. "It was timing that killed it," he lamented.

While Coho was dead certain of McVean's footprint signature, he was never sure who left the other boot prints sometimes found next to McVean's. The girl who positively identified McVean trying to break into the water truck at Montezuma Creek hesitated to say the second man was Pilon. It was generally assumed that was the case but Coho also had reason to doubt it. Often McVean's tracks showed he was alone. Other times, however, there was a second set of prints alongside his—prints that differed from time to time. In a couple of instances there was evidence of two people with McVean. Coho guessed the outlaw had four or five different acquaintances who would join him for a short while. It was a theory that had visual confirmation when McVean was reportedly seen north of Montezuma Creek one evening drinking beer with three other men in front of a Jeep. The tracks were two days old and crumbling by the time Coho got the report, but once again, he'd crossed paths with the man nobody could catch.

In time the sightings slowed down. McVean seemed to be spending less time in the area. Nearly two years after McElmo Bridge the sightings ceased. In all, Coho believes sixteen to eighteen of the sightings he followed up on were legitimate. If McVean had remained active and the sightings continued, he believes he would have found him; perhaps not on the nineteenth sighting or the twenty-fourth but the day would come. He agrees with every other officer involved that the manhunt was flawed from the beginning by poor communication and even worse cooperation between agencies. But in his opinion, the white police agencies lacked an even more critical attribute—patience. "From the FBI down, the attitude was hurry up and catch them and get the glory," he said.

The last thing police knew with certainty about the suspects' movements was the fact that at least two of them drove to the bottom of Cross Canyon, ditched the truck they had commandeered at gunpoint and disappeared into the desert on foot with a two-hour head start. The head start grew to days, weeks, months and, in the case of McVean, years. He had vanished, leaving police with two choices: toss the file in a drawer and hope someday someone in a distant city would report his whereabouts, or try to move the investigation forward by taking Jason at his word. Even after years of making no substantial progress on the case, Cortez P.D. was not about to let it rest.

Their only option was to believe Jason's claims to friends that he loved the desert, wished to live a survivalist lifestyle in the canyons and had stockpiled enough supplies to sustain him there for years; that he'd stayed put. Find out where he hid his supplies and Jason would be there, living in a cave on the side of a wilderness canyon in southern Utah. Finding McVean's cache sites became the thrust of the investigation.

The hand-drawn map found in McVean's trailer in the first days of the investigation convinced police the suspects' master cache was in Grand Gulch. Multiple sources confirmed the landmarks drawn on the map matched Grand Gulch topography. The dots, police assumed, had to mark cache sites. Given the scale of the map, however, a dot designated a large area rather than a precise coordinate. Months afterward, in the course of reinterviewing one of McVean's and Mason's closest friends, Shethar came away with a description of the fugitives' wilderness hideout: a cave partway up a sixty-foot red sandstone cliff with a large rock overhang above. There were large boulders on the slope below it. It was near a natural stone arch. Shown photographs found in Pilon's trailer, the subject suddenly pointed at a picture of a stone arch. "That's it," he cried, the same photo Mason had shown him six months before the shooting as he described their hideout. Police still didn't know where it was but they knew what it looked like.

At about the same time, the Phoenix FBI office began working with a confidential source who, driven by the reward money, had been undertaking extensive searches for the suspects. But he wasn't starting the search blind. He was described as being in a unique position to have knowledge of where McVean and Mason had been caching supplies, a position that prevented him from testifying against the suspects. He was in fact a close friend of McVean's and Mason's. During a 1996 camping trip with them in Grand Gulch, McVean left camp one morning and returned with an armload of supplies. When Cortez police learned through their own investigative efforts the identity of the source, the FBI fumed, claiming a confidential source they had used for years had been compromised.

The informant narrowed the location for McVean's Grand Gulch hideout to a remote twenty-five-square-mile area known as Slickhorn Canyon. Traces of human activity in the area were minimal, evidently left by someone with survivalist training rather than ordinary camping skills. Both the informant and an FBI agent who was searching the same area a month earlier, after aerial photos showed evidence of human activity, reported hearing gunshots.

Once again, Cortez P.D. and Colorado FBI asked Sheriff Lacy for help. Lacy and Salt Lake FBI refused, claiming a search of such a large area was not worthwhile, considering the resources it would require, nor did they trust the informant. In the same letter Lacy advised through the San Juan County Attorney that "Colorado authorities do not have peace officer powers in Utah," followed by a warning of civil liability and a terse statement to the effect of, "If we want your help, we'll ask for it." Colorado authorities organized a force of fifty officers and slipped across the state line. The search continued off and on for nearly a year with no results. But a growing list of circumstantial evidence convinced them they were close to finding McVean's master cache and hideout. Whether that meant they were close to finding McVean was another question.

Finally in November 2004, six and a half years after McElmo

Bridge, a hiker in Grand Gulch spotted the corner of a blue tarp that had washed from a crevice in the canyon wall. It wasn't the master cache. There was no hideout nearby. And Jason McVean was nowhere in sight. In fact, the discovery was made in Steer Gulch canyon rather than Slickhorn Canyon. But it was a large cache and authorities were certain the suspects had hid it there. The hiker judged that it hadn't been opened since it was buried. It took him and a buddy with an ATV two days to move it out. It held two thousand rounds of .308 shells, hundreds of rounds of 7.62-caliber cartridges (the size fired into Claxton), and an equal number of shotgun shells. There were several two-liter bottles of salt, a gun-cleaning kit and a 1996 gun parts catalog. The catalog was published during the time Mason and McVean were actively burying supplies. Unfortunately, the gun parts company had purged all customer files earlier than 1999 and couldn't tell police if any of the suspects had ordered from them.

Police didn't learn of the find until March of 2005 when an FBI agent based in Monticello, Utah, received a tip that a man was attempting to sell a large quantity of ammunition he'd found in the desert.

By that time sightings and mobilization to capture McVean were infrequent. Even Cortez Detective Shether would often hear about them only after the fact and informally. In early 2005, the FBI received a tip that Jason McVean was at a house near Flagstaff, Arizona. Drive-by surveillance appeared to confirm it and hours later SWAT teams descended on the residence. The home's occupant bore a striking resemblance to Jason McVean and for a brief time police believed they had finally captured the last of the Four Corners fugitives. Fingerprints, however, soon proved they had the wrong man; one more false lead in a long line of disappointments.

Seven years after McElmo Bridge, it was the last significant police action in the search for the man who jumped from a stolen tanker truck with an assault rifle and killed Officer Dale Claxton. Jason McVean remained at large.

Cowboy Eric Bayles holds a rusted AK-47, found with McVean's bones. Cross Canyon, June 2007. (Photo courtesy of Lyle Bales)

McElmo Bridge crime scene hours after Police Officer Dale Claxton's patrol car is parked alongside the road at the far end of the bridge. (Photo © copyright *Cortez Journal*; used by permission)

Slain officer Dale Claxton's funeral procession along Main Street, Cortez, Colorado.
(Photo © copyright *Cortez Journal*; used by permission)

One of dozens of roadblocks across Four Corners in the search for copkillers who vanished into the
Western landscape. (Photo courtesy of Dan Bender, La Plata County, Colorado, Sheriff's Office)

Police spotters on canyon ridge not only watched for the fugitives, but were ready to provide sniper protection for manhunt teams searching the canyon floors. (Photo courtesy of Dan Bender, La Plata County, Colorado, Sheriff's Office)

View of manhunt terrain from a helicopter deploying the La Plata County Sheriff's Office SWAT team. The labyrinth of remote desert canyons stretched for thousands of square miles. (Photo courtesy of Dan Bender, La Plata County, Colorado, Sheriff's Office)

Helicopters at the manhunt field command post in Cahone, Colorado. In addition to aerial search and support, the choppers transported ground search teams in and out of the remote canyons. (Photo © copyright *Cortez Journal*; used by permission)

Bobby Mason was characterized as extremely immature. In the time before McElmo Bridge, his parents saw hopeful signs that their son was finally becoming a responsible adult. (Photo provided by Ann and Gary Mason)

Swinging Bridge. Deputy Bradford was shot on the bluff in the foreground several yards to the left of the frame. Mason was found dead across the river. (Photo courtesy of Gerald Trainor)

A few days before Officer Claxton disrupted his killers' plans, Alan "Monte" Pilon told friends he was about to do something that would make his name known across the nation.

Monte Pilon's view of Cross Canyon from the spot on Tin Cup Mesa where he was shot. Cross Canyon Road cuts through the center of the frame. The fugitives abandoned the flatbed just above the road toward the right side of the picture. McVean's remains were found just beyond the left edge of the picture. (Photo courtesy of Gerald Trainor)

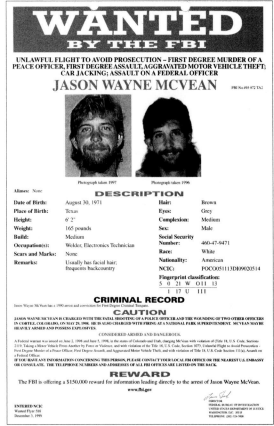

One of the FBI's "10 Most Wanted" fugitives, Jason McVean's whereabouts were a mystery for nearly a decade after he escaped into the desert.

Jason McVean's skeletal remains and equipment found buried in a desert wash nearly a decade after he and two fellow fugitives vanished into the remote canyons of Utah. (Photo courtesy of Lyle Bayles)

South end of McElmo Bridge, Cortez, Colorado, where the violent murder of Police Officer Dale Claxton triggered the largest manhunt in the history of the West.

The burning of the San Juan River canyon floor in an effort to smoke the fugitives out. Police snipers lined the canyon rims. (Photo courtesy of the San Juan County, Utah, Sheriff's Office)

CHAPTER 18
PATRIOTS

Two cop killers in the southwest
Put the pigs and feds to the test.
For a month and half
They just sit back and laugh
Because Monte and Jason are best.
 —Anonymous limerick mailed to police six
  weeks after McElmo Bridge.

The community response to Claxton's murder and the wounding of the other officers was "overwhelming," Shethar recalled. "The outflow of kindness and support was unbelievable." The City of Cortez shut down and thousands of its residents turned out to pay their respects to the fallen officer. Claxton's family was besieged with expressions of sympathy and offers to help them cope with the ongoing tasks of daily life. Hotel rooms and restaurant meals were donated to officers arriving from outside the area. Equipment and supplies were loaned to aid the police effort. Volunteers assisted with behind-the-scenes duties. A steady stream of casseroles and baked goods showed up at the station for weeks. But citizen support was not universal. The investigation and manhunt were also hampered by those rooting for the outlaws.

The suspects' prowess at avoiding capture frustrated police, but it fascinated the public. The longer the two fugitives remained ahead of the law the more they took on the romantic persona of outlaw heroes. After years at large, McVean became in some quarters legendary. Articles in national magazines and episodes on true-crime TV shows inevitably used phrases like "outwitted the largest manhunt in Western history and baffled police for eighteen months—two years—five years—almost a decade." Virtually every story also made the comparison to Butch Cassidy and the Sundance Kid, who eluded the law in the same canyons. For most Americans, the ability to outwit authority and escape society's grasp was captivating, especially in a Wild West setting, but in the end the outlaws were still the bad guys.

Those who did wholeheartedly side with the outlaws usually did so for reasons beyond outlaw hero romanticism. At some level, they shared the fugitives' animosity toward authority. From the beginning police received hate mail that in the circumstances was particularly bruising. Several police stations were mailed a photocopy of a newspaper photo showing a tearful officer at Claxton's funeral. Below the photo the sender had added a handwritten caption, "Waaah!! Ah shucks, Sarge. We can't find them two boys. We need more donuts." (Mason was already reported dead.) Another anonymous letter was titled "Keystone Cops" and derided police as "comic book cops totally baffled . . . outwitted by two to your two hundred." "So who is smart now?" the writer asked. And one day in July as the search for the fugitives struggled onward, police turned onto Highway 140 in La Plata County to find spray-painted across the southbound lane KILL MORE COPS. In extremist Web sites and newsletters around the nation the killers were applauded as "true American patriots." Locally several residents expressed their support for the outlaws by claiming they and their neighbors were leaving their cars unlocked with the keys in them.

The fugitives' animosity toward police and government agencies was extreme but it wasn't radical in Four Corners. Hostility toward government authority was endemic to the area. "The region has more than its share of residents who proclaim their dislike of the government, protest paying income taxes and refuse to put license plates on their cars," Chief Lane explained.

For Westerners, particularly those living in the rural interior, antipathy toward the government reflects the feds' historical control of the region, confounded by a bite-the-hand-that-feeds-you resentment of their dependence on Uncle Sam. More so than in any other part of the country, the federal government is lord and master of the West, owning 44 percent of the land, compared to just 4 percent in the rest of the lower forty-eight states.[1] Even more domineering was Washington, D.C.'s assumed predominant control of the region's other critical resource—water. Accumulating deeper and deeper behind every Bureau of Reclamation dam, surging through its irrigation channels was federal power to control the region. As a result, the federal government seemed to be in the face of rural Western residents at nearly every turn.

Most citizens objected within the system or on bad days by cursing the regulators. But some believed patriotism was found in extreme deeds. Militia activity was prevalent to the point that a broad segment of the population had some firsthand experience with the movement. They knew someone involved or had encountered men playing war games while on a family outing. So when news reports described the fugitives' military attire, weapons and tactics, in the mind of police and citizens alike the connection was clear. Among the hundreds of leads police received in the days immediately following Claxton's murder, dozens reported militia activity. "There's a group that meets in a Cortez home." Or, "My family was hiking near Black Steer Canyon and a paramilitary group threatened us from the area." Or, "I sold some land near Soda Canyon to a militia group. They use it for war games and maneuvers." Other callers pointed their fingers at people they knew who belonged to militia groups, suggesting to police that the vicious crime was consistent with the individual's militia mentality. "My neighbor's nephew is in the Dove Creek militia. He might know something." "A guy I work with joined a militia two years ago. He could have done this."

Identifying the suspects did little to dispel the widespread belief that a militia organization was behind the shootings. Colorado Governor Roy Romer surmised the shootings were connected to a militia-launched plot right from the beginning. Seven days into the manhunt, after police had already learned a great deal about the suspects' backgrounds and activities, Romer continued to believe it. "They [the suspects] had in mind either one or more series of operations. This is typical of a paramilitary operation," he told reporters. Whether in fact McVean, Mason and Pilon were members of a larger paramilitary group and, more important, if their presence on McElmo Bridge that morning had something to with a grander militia-conspired plot remained unclear. There was no doubt the suspects thought, dressed, trained and acted like militia members. They also had numerous ties to militia groups and known militia members, according to their friends. One acquaintance told police McVean and Mason frequently met twenty or so other guys in the basement of a Durango business for white supremacist and militia-type activities. Another acquaintance told police all three men attended meetings of the 4 P.M. militia for a while."[2] Pilon's friends were unequivocal, "Alan joined a militia." Pilon's uncle admitted, "My nephew has been involved with a paramilitary group in Durango."

Even if they were militia members, did they act on their own or at the direction of others planning armed revolt? Part of the confusion lay with the nebulous nature of the militia movement. Some were formal organizations with charters, written rules and organizational charts (commonly modeled after military command structure). Others formed more as social groups—people with a common interest who get together frequently to pursue their hobby, in this case firing automatic weapons and prepping for the invasion of the New World Order.[3] Some were large with many members, branch organizations and affiliations with other militias. Most were small cells independent of other groups operating in kind of a loose confederacy of extremists.

One thing police were keenly aware of: even if the suspects acted alone, they weren't alone in their beliefs. There were many who would assist them and some who could rally organized armed support for their cause. If they weren't acting alone, the threat was even more alarming: Were McVean, Mason and Pilon the vanguard of a much larger army of extremist citizen soldiers—armed, trained and ready to kill? Was McElmo Bridge just the opening skirmish to a much bigger, blood-in-the-streets citizen war?

Jason McVean, Monte Pilon and Bobby Mason believed in such a war. According to their friends, sometime around a year before McElmo Bridge the outlaws' extremist rhetoric underwent a subtle change. They spoke less and less of Y2K meltdowns, cosmic alignment and other looming apocalyptic blasting caps that would ignite a revolution. There was less talk of events that would trigger a black-helicopter invasion drawing patriots to the barricades. Instead they talked more of inciting rebellion; not waiting for some external initiator but being the catalyst for the cause.

A chemist friend explained to them that the catalyst gets destroyed in the reaction.

CHAPTER 19
DAM

Dear old God, you know and I know what it was like
here, before them bastards from Washington moved
in and ruined it all. You remember the river, how fat
and golden it was? Remember the cataracts in Forty
Mile Canyon? Well, they flooded out about half of them
too . . . Davis Gulch, Willow Canyon . . . Listen . . .
there's something you can do for me, God. How about
a little old *pre*-cision earthquake right under this dam?
—Seldom Seen Smith praying on Glen Canyon Dam
from *The Monkey Wrench Gang*

What McVean, Mason and Pilon were up to when Dale Claxton
spotted the stolen tanker truck remains hidden. In the early days of
the investigation, however, rumors and hearsay did reach police—
fragments of overheard bar conversation between the suspects, third-
hand gossip that reportedly originated with someone who had advised
the conspirators on some detail of the plan—small tidbits of information that hinted at a sinister plot. Disrupted at McElmo Bridge, it
never came to pass, but a worst-case scenario of the plan fulfilled was
plausible and frightening. It began with the theft of a water tanker.

Had Mike Overright continued to assume that an acquaintance borrowed his tanker truck and not reported it stolen until the next morning; had Dale Claxton not spotted the stolen tanker as it clipped the corner of Cortez, the likelihood of it later being stopped by police on the sparsely patrolled rural roads of Four Corners was slight. If not for the killing of Officer Claxton, the theft wouldn't have been part of a larger crime that drew in the CBI and the FBI, setting in motion an intensive investigation. It would have been just another vehicle theft routinely followed up in due course, and by that time the tanker and conspirators would have vanished into Utah's canyonlands, winding through a desolate country that has hidden outlaws since the days of Butch Cassidy.

Any number of ideas as to the fugitives' original intent were voiced, most unsubstantiated and seemingly contrary to the known facts. A common tip was that it was all related to a drug deal gone bad. It was a theory that never gained traction with police. It didn't explain the water truck, the years of hiding supplies in the desert, or the paramilitary training. While all three used recreational drugs—McVean and Mason primarily pot and peyote, Pilon methamphetamine—there was no evidence they were dealing drugs.

Police suggested a second possibility with enough frequency that it became the official unofficial explanation for the crime, ultimately reported by the news media as a fact. The three men were planning to rob the Ute casino a few miles south of Cortez, police surmised. The water tanker was supposedly chosen because it was bulletproof from the rear. It was an explanation first forwarded by Mason's brother when he spoke to police the day after McElmo Bridge. At the time he mentioned it, he told police it was completely hypothetical. It occurred to him, not because he had any reason to believe it was his brother's plan, but because a casino robbery was a scenario he had pondered when he worked with the Ute police force. Chuck Mason also held his brother and McVean in low regard, suggesting they were unintelligent and incapable of masterminding anything more than a sloppily conceived heist. It was an assessment of the suspects and explanation for the crime that served the officers' psychological need to debase the outlaws. "They weren't sophisticated criminals. They were smash and grab punks," CBI agent Wayne Bryant said. The explanation countered the public reaction that irked them most; that the fugitives were daring outlaw heroes with a higher cause. For the officers who had to confront the bullet-ridden body of their comrade, it would have felt good to believe it.

As the case progressed, however, most of the officers doubted the theory. The fugitives continued to elude one of the largest and most technologically sophisticated manhunts in US history. Evidence of long, detailed planning emerged. And the fugitives had clearly developed unique skills and expertise. Claxton's killers, police had to conceded, were smart criminals. They were capable of planning and, except for intervening fate in the guise of a Cortez police officer who happened to extend his patrol a half mile beyond the city limits that morning, may have had the wherewithal to execute a complex crime. The casino explanation also didn't fit Pilon's claim to friends that they were planning something that would make their names infamous throughout the nation. There was only about $220,000 in cash at the casino; not enough to explain the crime, Detective Shethar said in discounting the casino heist motive. In addition, the water tanker would have been an obviously poor choice for such a crime. It was incapable of more than 65 mph, lacked maneuverability and was less than ideal for an off-road getaway. McVean and Pilon were skilled welders and metal workers. Police discovered a camper trailer they were in the process of converting to a mobile bunker covered with quarter-inch steel plate. They could have easily modified a faster, more agile, cross-country-capable getaway vehicle, making it bulletproof from more angles than just the rear.

There was another plot police believed might have been the fugitives' intent—blowing up Glen Canyon or Hoover Dam. The theory was mentioned in multiple FBI and police memos and had never been dismissed as improbable. In the beginning, the possibility that the target was Hoover Dam was announced publicly and reported by the media. In time, despite accumulating evidence that made other theories less reasonable but kept dam sabotage on the table, it was mentioned less. Not only did it capture the public's imagination, cast the outlaws as bold criminal masterminds and inflate their reputations, it also revealed a significant vulnerability in America's infrastructure.

The day after planes flew into the World Trade Center, the Glen Canyon Dam Visitor Center was locked shut, public tours of the dam were abruptly suspended and access roads leading to it were blocked. Federal agencies scrambling to identify possible terrorism targets realized that there in the middle of nowhere, surrounded by remote canyons and desert, stood one of the highest-value targets in the nation. The dam would have qualified for increased security on the basis that it is a power plant, but, in truth, its contribution to the grid was not the primary concern. The amount of electricity generated there was not critical to the nation's power supply. Nor was it located in a large vulnerable population center, although experts did suggest that a collapse would likely have a high fatality rate. What placed Glen Canyon and Hoover Dams near the top of the target list was the widespread, long-term economic and environmental devastation that the nation would suffer if either structure failed.

Using Hurricane Katrina as a basis of comparison for the impact of various terrorist attack scenarios, testimony before the Senate Subcommittee on Terrorism in 2005 noted that only a handful of US targets posed the threat of destruction over as broad a geographic area. The two dams were among them. In addition to wiping out river towns like Laughlin, Nevada; Bullhead City and Yuma, Arizona; Needles and Blyth, California; a breach of either structure would cripple the metropolitan areas of Las Vegas, Phoenix and Los Angeles as supply canals were pulverized and those cities' primary source of water surged into the Gulf of Cortez. Thousands of acres of farmland would be flooded for as long as three years and when the water finally evaporated, much of what was the most fertile soil in the Southwest would be barren salt flats. A successful attack upon the dam would be "catastrophic" according to government assessments, meaning the economic consequences would remain severe and unabated for more than a decade.

Undiscovered, the outlaws would have had several days to execute their plan. The roads they would have followed since entering the canyons were remote. The best of them were long-forgotten narrow tracks of broken asphalt. Most were gravel trails, some just parallel tire ruts. In other places they'd drive across flat open country simply steering toward a distant landmark. The large tanker made for oil-field terrain with its dual-wheel, twin rear axels; oversize tires; and low-gear ratio could rumble across it without hesitation. Their path would have been purposeful, leading from one cache site to the next as directly as geography and subterfuge allowed.

Police never learned exactly what, where and how much the fugitives had hidden in the desert, but they did know it included weapons, ammunition and explosives and there was a lot of it. If the dam was the target, the supplies their plan demanded were voluminous; hiding it all represented dozens of "camping" trips in the canyons. Given the rigorous planning suggested by the detailed material lists and carefully drawn maps police discovered, the supply caches also would have been strategically placed, leading sequentially to their ultimate destination. The last and largest according to the maps may have been hidden deep in Grand Gulch, a few hours' drive from Lake Powell National Recreation Area and the Glen Canyon Dam.

Of the two dams, Glen Canyon was by far the softest and most likely target. Choking back a trillion cubic feet of water, Glen Canyon Dam was one of the most massive man-made structures on the continent, a tapered block of concrete 710 feet high and 1,560 feet long at the crest, wedged tight between nearly vertical walls of rock. In June, fed by the snowmelt across the 108,000 square miles of the Colorado River basin above Lake Powell, the reservoir was at its highest level. At the time of McElmo Bridge, the water lapped within eighty-eight feet of the dam's crest. A mere twenty-five feet wide at the top, the dam appeared too thin to withstand the pressure of the 186-mile-long reservoir piled against it; as if it were stressed to the point that one good jolt would be enough to break it. It looked assailable, but below the surface of Lake Powell, the dam sloped outward to form a base three hundred feet thick. It was primarily solid concrete except for a narrow core of 528-foot-deep elevator shafts, corridors, equipment vaults, control rooms and a lower cavity of hydro-turbine generators.

Glen Canyon Dam's mass, however, paled in comparison to its downstream older sister and police reports mentioning the inviolable Hoover Dam may have been intentional misdirection. It was true that it would have been easier to place the bomb on Hoover Dam. Traffic at that time drove across the top of Hoover Dam but at Glen Canyon was routed across a bypass bridge a hundred yards downstream from the structure. Other than that feature, however, Glen Canyon was the more accessible of the two for terrorists. Even then, Hoover Dam had its own police force and a semblance of security. Overdesigned and one of the most massive age-hardened concrete structures in the world, even a powerful explosion on or near the dam would have left only superficial damage. That was not necessarily the case with Glen Canyon Dam. The design and placement of the dam had been challenged by engineers and geologists from the beginning, security was weak, and, most important, Glen Canyon, not Hoover, was the ideological target.

Destroying it was the Holy Grail of environmental extremism, an act that in some minds would make the saboteurs outlaw folk heroes. The dam had been called "the most hated man-made structure in the nation" and its detractors were legion. Other than Bureau of Reclamation officials and lobbyists for agricultural conglomerates who purchased its water below cost, few people who studied the project believed it worthwhile. In the minds of many, it was "an engineering abomination—an ill-conceived, unneeded pork barrel project" and, according to Sierra Club statesman David Brower, "America's most regretted environmental mistake." The dam reservoir, the second largest in the US after Hoover Dam's Lake Meade, flooded out thousands of miles of pristine wilderness canyons, destroyed an entire ecosystem, ruined critical wildlife and aquatic habitat, and submerged hundreds of archeological sites. Downstream it choked a natural current powerful enough to carve the Grand Canyon to a placid trickle, disrupting its flow cycles, altering the canyon's ecology and pressing endangered species closer to extinction. The damage came with questionable gain. The amount of hydropower produced at the dam was insignificant. Because of Lake Powell's large surface area, high elevation and desert environment, water storage was compromised by significant loss to evaporation and bank seepage, enough to meet the annual water needs of Los Angeles. Finally, what small benefit the dam did provide was possibly short-lived. Government officials predicted the dam would remain serviceable for eight hundred years. Other scientists, however, claimed silt levels in Lake Powell would be high enough within eighty years to render the dam useless and dangerous.

Many who once supported the construction of Glen Canyon Dam, including its political patron, Arizona Senator Barry Goldwater, later regretted the decision as a "terrible mistake." Many called for the dam to be decommissioned and Lake Powell drained. Others just wanted to see it gone.

Timothy McVeigh had proven the sophistication of militia bomb-making capability three years earlier. Loading seven thousand pounds of ammonium nitrate mixed with fuel oil (ANFO) and ammonium nitrate nitromethane (ANNM) into a Ryder rental truck, McVeigh destroyed one third of the nine-stories-tall, city-block-long Alfred P. Murrah Federal Building in Oklahoma City. The blast killed 168 people, flattened or damaged 324 buildings in a sixteen-block radius, and left a crater thirty-five feet wide and eight feet deep in the asphalt where the truck sat.

The ingredients for making ANFO and ANNM could be purchased at almost any home and garden store followed by a stop at the corner filling station—ammonium nitrate fertilizer and diesel fuel in the case of ANFO, fertilizer and industrial solvent or drag-racing fuel for ANNM. Despite their home-brew accessibility, however, both substances were high-order explosives widely used for commercial blasting. Properly prepared, confined and detonated, ANFO's detonation velocity approaches that of TNT and some military explosives, sufficient for penetrating and cutting charges. ANNM is more powerful yet. ANNM is also significantly wetter than ANFO. It is, in fact, a slurry, making a tanker truck an ideal vehicle for making a large bomb.

Detonation, however, is tricky, especially in confined, large-volume charges, according to John Nixon, an explosives expert utilized by the US Department of Defense, the UK Ministry of Defense and NATO, as well as a qualified expert witness on explosives in federal and state courts. A secondary booster charge is commonly added to the detonation system to assure all the explosive material propagates and the device achieves it maximum blast potential. Detonation is the step where less knowledgeable bomb makers often fizzle, Nixon said. McVeigh not only obtained and knew how to use commercial detonators such as Tovex as a charge booster, he knew how to shape the charge toward the building for greater cutting effect. "He was knowledgeable," Nixon noted. After years of study and practice, access to a wide range of commercial and military explosives, contact with militia expertise and the opportunity to study testimony and information from McVeigh's 1997 trial, McVean was knowledgeable too.

Given that knowledge, the process the fugitives might have followed as they prepared the tanker was predictable: it would have been that activity that explained the ladder the conspirators had made a point to take from Jim McVean's shop. Eight feet was just long enough to provide McVean, the trio's explosives expert, access into the vessel through the top portal.

With the passage of several days since the truck was stolen, the tank would have been dry but working inside it would feel like laboring in an oven. In the center of the cylinder, daylight could penetrate hazy and bluish from the manhole overhead. The ends, however, would remain dark and McVean would need a flashlight to complete his task.

Along the bottom of the tank, spaced at even intervals, McVean would place several bundles of Tovex Blastrite Gel sausages. In the center of each bundle, he'd have wired an electric blasting cap in parallel with the caps in the other bundles. The bundles in turn would be buried like bean seeds in a five-hundred-pound furrow of Tovex, running the length of the tank. The leads from blasting caps would be threaded through a small hole drilled in the tank then caulked watertight. From the tank, the wires would run under the chassis where no one would see them and feed through the cab floor far under the seat. Unlike McVeigh who used a lit fuse to initiate the Oklahoma City explosion, McVean would have chosen an electrical charge. At the blast site, one of the leads would be attached to a packet of dry cells, the second to a mechanical timer. They had tested the design dozens of times and knew it was reliable.

Rigging the detonator would have taken several hours; the final step much longer. The volume of supplies stockpiled at the last cache site on the route to the Glen Canyon Dam would have been sizeable. In one of the hundreds of caves or abandoned mines pitting Grand Gulch, the terrorists would have had to have stowed nearly two dozen fifty-five-gallon drums of drag-racing fuel or industrial solvent and as many as 250 bags (ten tons) of high-grade prilled ammonium nitrate fertilizer.

In the agricultural community of Dove Creek, fertilizers were used in large volume. Purchases by the tons were common, as was the opportunity to steal sizeable quantities. In addition, Mason worked with landscapers who had supplies of fertilizers. McVean and Pilon, on the other hand, had access to nitromethane industrial solvents through their places of employment. Over the course of several months the materials could have been shifted to the mine, four or five drums of nitromethane, twenty bags of fertilizer at a time.

The final step would have found the trio mixing fertilizer and nitromethane in an empty plastic drum. The liquid explosive could be transferred to the tank using the truck's vacuum pump. Smaller batches could be passed in buckets man-to-man up the ladder and spilled through the access portal until the tank was full. When the portal was finally closed and sealed the truck would not just be carrying a bomb; it was the bomb.

———

As Timothy McVeigh was propelled to terrorism by reading *The Turner Diaries*, McVean, and through him his coconspirators, was inspired by another work of fiction, Edward Abbey's 1975 cult classic, *The Monkey Wrench Gang*. The book's antiheroes, like McVean, had an affinity for the natural landscape of the American Southwest. In defense of their primal world, the fictional characters engage in a guerrilla war of sabotage against the government projects and corporate spoilers of the land. What started with pulling up survey stakes and pouring Karo syrup in the fuel tanks of earthmoving equipment escalated to dynamiting power plants and coal trains, culminating in a blazing gun battle with authorities. The ultimate goal of the eco-saboteurs, with which the book begins and ends, remained unfulfilled—blowing up Glen Canyon Dam. On many high school required reading lists, the book is an entertaining warning against unrestrained industrialization and the degradation of the natural world, a modern-day Wild West *Walden*.

Douglas Brinkley observed in his introduction for the novel's twenty-fifth-anniversary publication, "*The Monkey Wrench Gang* is far more than just a controversial book—it is revolutionary, anarchic, seditious, and, in the wrong hands, dangerous." For Jason McVean, *The Monkey Wrench Gang* was more than wild satire. It was a call to arms. He read it and reread it; according to friends, at least seventeen times. He'd cite it more often than Billy Graham did the Bible, they said, often referring to it to explain his beliefs or justify hypothetical actions. Police would find a worn dog-eared paperback copy among his possessions with passages underlined and handwritten margin notes. In time, McVean would even confide to a friend his desire to blow up Glen Canyon Dam.

McVean was not the only one influenced by the book or to share its characters' malevolence toward Glen Canyon Dam. Abbey's novel became the manifesto for environmental extremism and an instruction manual for radical eco-activism. In 1981, Earth First! went public with a prank from the pages of *The Monkey Wrench Gang* when members unfurled a three-hundred-foot black plastic streamer down the front of Glen Canyon Dam that looked like a deep crack in the structure.

The world can only guess what Jason McVean, Robert Mason and Alan "Monte" Pylon would have done had not Dale Claxton intervened. But with their choice of a water truck; their training and preparation; their antigovernment convictions, conspiracy paranoia, revolution and apocalyptic visions; and their obsession with *The Monkey Wrench Gang*, the best guess is they wanted that crack in the Glen Canyon Dam to be more than a black plastic streamer.

Had the conspirators made it through Cortez, converted the stolen tanker into a bomb and parked it near the Glen Canyon Dam, their chances of causing any significant direct damage to the structure would have been slim. But if unlikely aligned with unknown, the result could have been catastrophic.

Glen Canyon Dam opponents, by and large, would have been as alarmed at the prospect of terrorism as any other citizen. But the depth of their commitment to seeing the awful structure decommissioned was conveyed by Edward Abbey's jest when a reporter asked if he really advocated blowing up the dam. "No," he replied. "But if someone else wanted to do it, I'd be there holding a flashlight."

The truth is, Abbey could have left his flashlight at home; sabotage of the dam barely needed the cover of night in the pre–9/11 era. Today, armed guards watch visitors from strategic positions around the site; security cameras pan the facility; no bags, packs or even small purses are allowed in the visitor center or on the dam; tours of the structure are limited to small groups, begin by walking through a metal detector, and are guided by Bureau of Reclamation employees. Drawings, plans and construction details are classified. Roads leading onto the top of the dam and the tunnel leading to the base are controlled with key-card-activated gates and patrolled 24/7. In 1998, a saboteur could have put fifty pounds of plastic explosive in a backpack and dropped it unchecked into the bowels of the structure on a self-guided tour.

Even with all the monitoring upgrades and access controls instituted since 9/11, a 2008 assessment of Bureau of Reclamation efforts to guard its facilities found security at Glen Canyon Dam "brittle and lacking depth." At the time of McElmo Bridge, it was hardly more than an unguarded gate secured with a padlock.

Even with the minimal security, however, the tunnel to the base of the dam was the only feasible approach for covertly maneuvering the truck close to the structure and the assault undoubtedly would have occurred in the dead of night.

Pilon probably would have separated from the others someplace short of the dam. Overweight with a permanent limp from ankle injuries, there was no way he could keep up with McVean or Mason after they parked the tanker, set the timer and raced from the area on foot. Pilon would have understood; whether or not he was there to help set the charge made no difference at that point. McVean and Mason may have believed they could live anonymously in the desert, that no one could connect them to the crime. Based on comments to friends the week before McElmo Bridge, Pilon was sure police would figure out who did it. When they did his name would be right up there with the other two; McVean, Mason and Pilon—the three baddest men in America.

A mile west of the tunnel gate the lights of Page, Arizona, add a soft glow to the sky but in 1998 the tunnel access road at night was dark and deserted. Mason probably would have doused the head-lights on the tanker when he turned onto it from Highway 89 and navigated the short stretch to the tunnel entrance, squinting through the blackness. They'd have found the gate locked but the hasp would have yielded to a bolt cutter or chisel in a matter of seconds.

With the gate closed behind them the tanker could then slip out of view into the tunnel and the breach would have gone unnoticed by anyone making a cursory inspection. The tunnel descended at a steep 8 percent grade, dropping seventeen hundred feet in two miles. It was a single lane wide, but generous enough that oncoming vehicles could pass if they each slowed and squeezed close to their respective right-hand walls. That would not have happened. The power plant night shift parked on top of the structure. The tunnel to the base of the dam was seldom used at night.

Every five hundred feet along the left side of the tunnel an adit had been blasted through the canyon wall for ventilation. To someone who happened to be looking east from the visitor center on the opposite side of the canyon or from the dam itself, the headlights from a vehicle in the tunnel would appear like a bright flash as it passed each adit. Sequentially they would form a line of tracer lights angling down the canyon wall, pointing to the vehicle's arrival at the base of the structure. The tunnel could be driven without headlights, however, using the narrow beam of a flashlight directed low where it wouldn't show through the adits.

The tunnel ended at a small parking area forty feet from the transformer deck that spanned the arch of the dam like a bowstring. A roadway ran across the front of the deck but the dam curved back away from it, leaving the ends of the structure where it abutted to the canyon walls, the only places where a vehicle could be parked close to the dam. Those options were further restricted by a high concrete garage on the tunnel side that forced a saboteur wishing to get close to the dam to cross the transformer deck roadway to the west side of the canyon. The deck and road ended at the sheer canyon wall. There Mason could have parked with the tank portion of the truck broadside to the dam, thirty feet from where the concrete seamed against the rock face.

As practiced as McVean apparently was at the task, it would have taken only a few minutes to connect the leads from the detonator to the timer and battery pack, then hide the whole works under the seat of the cab. If the sabotage had gone as planned, ten minutes after they had driven from the tunnel at the base of the dam, McVean and Mason would have been jogging back up it. And in the dark of night, no one would have noticed a tanker truck parked at the base of the dam.

Three decades before the Glen Canyon was completed, the Bureau of Reclamation had built the crown jewel of its Western water management projects. The Hoover Dam was an engineering marvel. Wrought from Depression-era angst into a New Deal expression of America's can-do spirit and the unlimited promise of our technological future, it became an enduring symbol of national pride. The Glen Canyon Dam was to be the postwar reassertion of American might. At first glance it seemed to be Hoover Dam's near equal, a twin sister in America's triumph over the forces of nature, one half of a technological duo that would alter the landscape of an entire corner of the country. Built three hundred miles upstream from Hoover Dam, it tamed the same wild serpent of a river, the legendary Colorado. It stood nearly as tall, only sixteen feet short of Hoover Dam's once record height of 726 feet. Filled, its reservoir was almost equal that of Hoover Dam's Lake Meade. Both the site for Glen Canyon Dam and the structure itself, however, had inherent weaknesses opponents to the project warned of right from the beginning.

Of gravest concern was the rock formation through which the canyon had been gouged. Unlike the hard, erosion-resistant, impermeable black granite walls into which Hoover Dam was wedged, Glen Canyon cut through the Southwest's great Navajo Sandstone formation. The rock that formed the canyon walls was nothing more than compressed sand dunes, grains of quartz weakly cemented together with loosely compacted lime. The soft, highly porous rock absorbed water readily, eroded rapidly and, under the force of high-pressure water, crumbled easily. In the spring of 1983, when Bureau officials miscalculated the mountain snowpack runoff, they were forced to increase the flow through the dam's spillway tunnels. Within days the structure began to vibrate as loud booms echoed through the dam. The torrent through the spillways had eaten away the tunnel's three-foot-thick concrete lining and was tearing away the soft sandstone beneath it like a wolf ripping into fresh meat. Pieces of the canyon wall the size of a Volkswagen washed through the rapidly enlarging pathways and ejected in a broad arc across the face of the dam. White-knuckled engineers frantically improvised to reduce spillway flow and avoid a dam failure, but in the end disaster was averted because Mother Nature relented. The reservoir inflow peaked six feet short of the top of the dam and then receded. The scare underscored how quickly the rock upon which the dam leaned would yield to flowing water.

Of equal concern was the tendency of the canyon walls to fall away in great slabs. The soft Navajo Sandstone was by nature profusely jointed. Diced with fissures and easily eroded by seeping water, it was common for huge slabs to slide from the canyon walls into the river below. It made for an unstable surface in which to anchor a dam. To compensate, the dam builders bolted the canyon walls together with hundreds of forty-five- to seventy-five-foot-long bolts drilled deep into the face and grouted in place.

Despite the weakness of Glen Canyon's rock walls, the dam was built dependent upon them. With a massive base nearly as wide as the dam was tall, engineers estimated that Hoover Dam could stand in place and hold back the reservoir pressing against it by its sheer gravity and wide stance. Glen Canyon Dam, on the other hand, was about as tall as its downstream predecessor but less than half as wide. If it weren't for the walls of Glen Canyon holding it up, Lake Powell would push it on its face.

Even at that, Glen Canyon Dam was an imposing structure. Unlike buildings, which are essentially a shell surrounding hollow space, the dam was 10 million tons of monolithic concrete. Filled with ANNM explosive and properly detonated, the tanker stolen by McVean, Mason and Pilon would create an explosion five times more powerful than the one that destroyed the Alfred P. Murrah Federal Building in Oklahoma City, according to engineer and explosives expert John Nixon. The force of the blast, however, would be less focused, Nixon added. Whereas Timothy McVeigh arranged thirteen barrels of explosives in the back of a Ryder truck in a specific pattern that directed the primary force of the blast toward the target, a tanker bomb offered no opportunity to shape the charge. Unless it exploited a preexisting weakness in the dam in an unpredictable manner, it was doubtful that even a bomb with five times the destructive potential of the Oklahoma City blast would cause more than superficial damage to the dam, Nixon estimated.

The power plant at the base of the dam, however, was another matter. A scenario of destruction was easy to imagine: the large explosion of the tanker would be followed by a chain of lesser but still powerful blasts as the transformers along the deck at the base of the dam blew up in rapid succession. Beneath the cloud of smoke and dust that obscured the site, the devastation would have been massive. Authorities rushing to the scene would see twisted ends of rebar protruding from what was left of the transformer deck. Toward the center, slabs of sagging concrete would have hung from the shattered roadway but the western end of the structure that was directly under the bomb would have dropped completely into the river. Large pieces of transformer would sway and shift in the rushing water. Lighter pieces of debris would be carried downstream until the river slowed and allowed them to sink gently to the bottom. Pieces of tank, hood, cab, radiator and dashboard, all too small and twisted to identify, would splatter the western canyon wall as high as forty feet where the blast had driven them into the soft sandstone.

Damage to the power plant would possibly have been severe, requiring several months of around-the-clock construction before the dam would generate electricity again. But the dam itself would have still stood. With almost absolute certainty it can be predicted that no giant crack would have spread across the face. No gusher of water would have blown a giant hole in the center. No part of the crest would have broken away and plunged into the water below. Not even a small leak would have shown anew. Initial assessments would show that the dam itself was undamaged.

It is often the case with disasters, however, that events cascade beyond predictive models, defy probability statistics and expose vulnerabilities that are recognizable only in hindsight. The outcome of a powerful bomb blast against soft irregular stone riddled with steel rods and weakened by the erosive effect of continuous water seepage would have been uncertain.

It might be three days after the bombing, or three weeks or three months—it might not happen at all—but in just the right circumstances disaster may reassert itself: redirected by the heavy truck chassis along the bottom of the tank, the greater force of the blast would have been upward, hard against the canyon wall where the dam abuts. The shock wave—transmitted by the steel bolts sunk deep into the rock—would travel unevenly through the abutment and between points where the stress differential was greatest, a crack might form, a tiny fissure spreading from bolt to bolt. Water from the surrounding stone would flood in and begin working them. As the shattered rock began to loosen, the bolts would no longer pin in place slabs likely to calve from the wall. Instead, they would define the edges of pieces about to give way.

If water did infiltrate and erode cracks deep in the canyon wall caused by an explosion, then one day, just maybe, the rate of seepage around the dam through the porous sandstone of the west canyon wall might suddenly double. The difference, spread over a wide area of perpetually draining rocks, would be noted only with the most precise measurement instruments. Suspended in the water that trickled from cracks in the rock, the measurements would find a higher than normal percentage of fine grains of quartz sand, particles of the rock itself.

If circumstances had allowed such events to transpire, it is not hard to then imagine that one day, barely audible above the roar of water escaping the dam's spillways, was the crash of a massive rockslide. Slabs of sandstone perhaps twenty-five feet long and more than eight feet thick would have slid down the west canyon wall tearing more loosened rock with them. The event would have ended a few seconds after it began as the last few pebbles to break free of the formation clattered down the cliff and bounced off the larger pieces that preceded them into the river. Above the tons of talus at the base, rock bolts would protrude several feet from the face like spines on a giant saguaro and a broad void in the canyon wall would expose a section of the dam that had leaned unseen against the rock since its construction thirty-five years earlier.

The hypothetical chain of events that could begin with a tanker truck bomb detonated at the base of Glen Canyon Dam may end there, but perhaps it wouldn't: with less of a seam between the concrete and the canyon wall, the patience of water could complete what the force of explosion began. Water from Lake Powell forcing a path around the edge of the dam would squirt from a slit measured in inches between the concrete and new rock face. One hour or so after that, erosion of the soft sandstone would have doubled the opening as other leaks opened along the seam. By the time workers noticed the leaks, they would have joined to form a hole around the edge of the dam several feet long. The water gushing through it would tear away at the sides of the sandstone channel it had excavated and spray in a broad reddish fan across the face of the dam.

As the gap widened, the rate of erosion would increase exponentially. Among the half-millimeter grains of sandstone that colored the emerging water, fist-size pieces of canyon wall would appear, then pieces as large as a soccer ball, a microwave, a sofa.

With the leak unabated, the outcome would be inevitable. Within a few days after water carved a channel around the end of the dam, news media from around the world would perch on the east canyon rim above the certain catastrophe, ready to film the dam's collapse.

While the outcome of a powerful explosion directed against the dam's abutment may have been uncertain, multiple experts have predicted what would happen if the dam did break: an inland tsunami five hundred feet high, traveling 30 mph, would surge through the Grand Canyon scouring its course bare, killing every living thing in its path. It would flatten as it roared into Lake Meade, which could absorb 20 percent of the deluge before overflowing Hoover Dam by 230 feet. Twelve miles beyond Hoover Dam the water wall would enter a broad floodplain and slow before the channel narrowed again and the advancing disaster regained its energy. It would reach Laughlin, Nevada, later that same night and move on to Bullhead City, Arizona; Lake Havasu City, Arizona; Needles, California; Parker, Arizona; Blythe, California; Yuma, Arizona, and into Mexico and the Gulf of Cortez. Along the way in domino fashion, it would tear out Davis Dam, Parker Dam, the Palo Verde Diversion Dam and Imperial Dam, adding the waters of Lake Mohave, Lake Havasu, the Palo Verde reservoir and Imperial reservoir to its flowing mass of destruction. Floodwater would sweep through the homes, workplaces, and schools of three hundred thousand people. The canal headworks providing water to Las Vegas, Phoenix, Tucson, Los Angeles and San Diego would wash away, crippling the water supply of 25 million people. Crops providing 25 percent of the nation's food supply would be underwater or doomed to wither due to lack of irrigation. Much of the land upon which they had grown would remain unproductive for decades.

As for the terrorists themselves, had they remained undetected long enough to see their plan through, police would know little more about them than they did after McElmo Bridge. Within hours after the bombing, police undoubtedly would have recovered enough of the tanker truck to identify it as the one reported stolen from an oil brine disposal site near Ignacio, Colorado. A woman who lived near the site would in time provide police with the license number of a blue Nissan pickup truck she saw in the area about the time the tanker was stolen and that slim lead would ultimately point to three area men as persons of interest. Other than their strident antigovernment views and apparent practice with explosives, there would be nothing to connect them to the terrorism. Except the entirely circumstantial fact that the leader of the trio was reportedly obsessed with Edward Abbey's *The Monkey Wrench Gang*.

CHAPTER 20
FINAL BONES

It had been nineteen days since the fugitives had fled into Cross Canyon. The hound moved carefully along the creek but gave no sign she found what she came looking for—decomposing human tissue. If there was any within several hundred yards of where she stood, Cissy would find it. The five-year-old bloodhound owned by the Montrose County (Colorado) Sheriff's Department had been searching for dead people since she was nine months old. Even if the corpse was buried or submerged under water, Cissy could find it. If it was only a small piece of a corpse—a fingertip, a bloody bandage, just a knife with human blood on it—Cissy could find it. If the corpse had been moved, Cissy could find where it once was.

So far, the survivalists had avoided the largest manhunt in the history of the American West and left not one solid indisputable clue to their whereabouts. Now, just in case the reason police couldn't trace their movements was because they had crawled in a hole and died, authorities searched the same canyons for bodies. If any of the suspects lay dead in areas where Cissy sniffed the air, whether they died two hours after ditching the flatbed or expired that morning, Cissy would find them.

Cissy and her handler attempted to cover broad sectors of the canyon following a standard search grid as closely as topography allowed.

They paid particular attention to the area along Montezuma Creek where there had been a concentration of sightings and suspicious activity. After a week of brutal dog days, Cissy's search for dead men concluded the same as the manhunt—nothing.

Cowboy Eric Bayles watched from the unofficial side of the yellow crime scene tape that now circled his discovery. The area was within four hundred yards of where Cissy had sniffed nine years earlier. Within the yellow-tape circle, on a green plastic tarp, investigators laid the bones of Jason McVean as they picked them from the gravelly soil. There were not many. The tarp held only disarticulated pieces—five vertebrae, a few broken-off inches of arm and leg long bones, sections of the cranial vault, a half-dozen rib bones, a clavicle, scapula, remnants of the upper and lower jaw with a few teeth and miscellaneous fragments.

Nonanatomical evidence was equally scarce. An AK-47 was rusted beyond any hope of providing a ballistic match to Claxton's murder weapon or even a serial number. There were a few rotting shreds of clothing and a backpack with extra banana clips for the AK-47, five hundred rounds of ammunition, five pipe bombs, three water bottles that still contained water, clothing, camping gear, a windup wristwatch and a business card.

Bayles's discovery began with almost as small of a clue—a corner of camouflage fabric under his horse's hooves as he herded cattle along Montezuma Creek on a hot June morning in 2007. Dismounting he saw the frame of a backpack poking from the ground and within the pack found ammunition and pipe bombs. He was five miles from where the fugitives had abandoned a stolen flatbed truck nine years earlier; a little over three miles from where Monte Pilon's mummified remains were found seventeen months after that.

San Juan County sheriff deputies and a team of FBI forensic investigators out of Salt Lake combed the site for two days, finding fragments of bone and cloth spread two hundred yards along the wash. A search with metal detectors added nothing more of interest.

The medical examiner had little to work with. Teeth recovered with the remains showed evidence of dental work matching McVean's dental records, providing positive identification. Enough of the skull existed that pathologists could guess with reasonable certainty that McVean sustained an "explosive injury to the head, consistent with a gunshot wound." There were no bone fragments, however, with direct evidence of a gunshot wound such as traces of lead. Also missing from the recovered skull fragments were pieces revealing an entrance or exit wound and the projectile's trajectory. That information could only be guessed based on the splintering of facial bones and the recovered skull pieces that at least told them where the bullet didn't penetrate. The suggestion that the muzzle of the gun that fired the fatal shot was in McVean's mouth was presented as tentative. Beyond that, their analysis suggested the body had been in the desert five to ten years and the victim was thirty to forty years old when he died.

But the thing Eric Bayles's discovery was most stingy with was answers. The bones, bombs and bullets found in Cross Canyon nine years and a few days after the outlaws vanished into the West left the story hanging. Those connected to the case emotionally or by years of futility called the finding of Jason McVean closure. It was enough to know that all three bad guys were dead and accounted for, they claimed. But the questions still nagged.

The authorities admitted their curiosity, a wish for a true accounting of the days that began with the murder of a brother in uniform, tore them from their families and plunged Four Corners into martial chaos. But they dismiss the questions with a tight-lipped no-one-will-ever-know shake of the head. In the vacuum of uncertainty they tell their own face-saving theory of how the fugitives evaded detection and eluded police.

It is a story that strips the desperados of their cunning and redeems the police from colossal inadequacy. It is a theory summed up in Lacy's assertion upon the discovery of Pilon's remains on Halloween 1999 that the outlaw committed suicide. "He chose death over capture," the sheriff intoned as if capture was inevitable and imminent when by then events had proved it was neither.

Years later, in June 2007, when Eric Bayles led police to McVean's sun-bleached bones, the story was the same. Hounded by the swift, massive police response, McVean killed himself before the manhunt really even got started. Desperate with the realization that he was trapped, worn and crazed by the unrelenting pursuit through the inhospitable environment, he sat down and put the muzzle of his AK-47 in his mouth sometime within the first thirty-six hours after the trio fled into Cross Canyon. "There were so many of us out there, so many helicopters and so much activity that he probably thought, 'I just can't get away,'" Chief Lane surmised.

The evidence of the fugitives' early demise was the proximity of their remains to the abandoned flatbed and a wristwatch found among McVean's bones. The watch had stopped ticking at 6:35 with a "30" in the date window. Although the thirtieth of a month had occurred 104 times between McElmo Bridge and the discovery of McVean's remains, police claimed the watch stopped on the first occurrence—May 1998, one day after McElmo Bridge. They were all dead within seven days, Lacy contended. Pilon killed himself or was killed by McVean on the first day. McVean killed himself by the second day. Mason had struck out on his own when he was thrown from the flatbed as it turned off Hovenweep Road into Cross Canyon and unintentionally separated from the others. The splitting of the trio explained why only two sets of footprints led away from the abandoned truck; why police were unable to apprehend anyone else at Swinging Bridge (Mason had never been able to reconnect with his friends); and the injuries found on Mason's body. Seven days later, with no friends and police closing in, he too killed himself.

With such a theory all the sightings, all the footprints that multiple experts agreed matched those leading from the abandoned flatbed, all the signs that redirected the efforts of hundreds of people and enormous resources were false. Millions of dollars were spent, local law enforcement budgets were decimated, a town was evacuated, a canyon bottom ignited, area residents frightened—chasing ghosts.

It may have happened that way, yet the explanation feels wrong. At its roots it assigns the suspects personalities and an abridgement of competence contrary to everything police learned about the three. At the same time, it implies the self-serving premise that in the opening hours of the manhunt, police cowed the outlaws with unbearable pressure.

In truth, there was no reason to believe the outlaws felt trapped. They had already demonstrated their cool resolve and daring as they shot their way past a parade of oncoming police cars to escape Cortez. With over a two-hour head start into wilderness they knew well and in which their pursuers were neophytes, the manhunt began with miles of separation. On the first afternoon of the search, the police penetrated a little less than five miles along the fugitives' tracks. Even if Pilon was slowed by an ankle injury, their cushion widened. Within those intervening miles were thousands of unassailable hiding places. Nighttime searches were ineffective in the canyons and by the next day, the potential search area had widened farther yet. At no point were they spotted, surrounded or pressed. Even after the manhunt had grown in force and was better organized, Mason slipped through it undetected to show up forty miles away.

It is also unlikely they became despondent from loneliness and isolation. Right from the start, the possibility that the suspects received assistance from a broad group of sympathizers frustrated efforts to tighten the search area around a recent sighting. Virtually every law enforcement official involved with both the manhunt and the investigation was convinced it was happening almost nightly. The evidence was compelling: signs of them having been in different locations within a time frame that implied the fugitives were driven the distance between them, confirmed tracks out of a canyon or across a mesa that upon reaching a highway disappeared, tips that various individuals met up with them. Several people reported two men in camouflage escaping down the San Juan River in a raft shortly before Mason was killed at Swinging Bridge. Police assumed it was McVean and Pilon, unaware that Pilon was already dead. In the year after he disappeared, Coho tracked McVean walking with different companions and there were sightings of him with multiple unidentified people.

Some suggested that it wasn't just the helicopters and SWAT teams that drained the fugitives of their will but the hostility of the environment as well. That may have been true if the fugitives were anybody else. Jason McVean, Robert Mason and Alan "Monte" Pilon chose the desert for their escape. It was where they had trained, survived and were comfortable; where the environment equalized the superior force and technology arrayed against them. These were men who for recreation trekked into the desert with minimalist gear and survived for weeks at a time—summer and winter. To test their skills they submitted themselves to death marches in which they would walk into the desert as far as the water they carried would last. Then, with no water left, they'd turn around and make their way back. As brutal as the desert canyons were for the police, for the outlaws they were home.

Nor were they caught unprepared and cornered unsupplied when their plans collapsed on McElmo Bridge. Both McVean and Mason were found well armed with plenty of ammunition, food rations and water reserves. All three men had large packs full of clothing and survival equipment.

The police's key argument that Pilon and McVean died within hours of entering the canyon was a twisted syllogism of proximity: a person can walk five miles within a few hours. Pilon's and McVean's remains were found within five miles of the abandoned truck. Therefore Pilon and McVean died within a few hours. In truth, the men could have circled the globe for years and later died where their bodies were found. The Navajo police and trackers who maintained the hunt for the killers long after others quit have always disputed the claim that McVean died shortly after the manhunt began.

In the weeks and the months following McElmo Bridge there was accumulating strong evidence that he lived. Some was based on collaborated sightings and evidence uncovered by the Navajo, especially in the later months when other police forces were no longer scouring the canyons for clues. Much of it was dismissed out of hand. If anything, the source should have given it increased credibility. The Navajo Nation Police Department was by far the largest local police agency. With federal assistance its tactical units were among the best trained in Four Corners. The skill of its trackers was unquestioned. In addition, given the area within which all involved believed McVean would hide, a person would expect legitimate sightings on the reservation.

There was other evidence of the suspects' movements during the first weeks discovered by various agencies and agreed as legitimate by multiple experts. It was examined by both CBI and FBI forensic experts, as well as other sophisticated crime analysts and declared positive enough to refocus the entire search. The level of mistakes and false starts by law enforcement did not inspire confidence but it would be a stretch to believe they were all wrong in every instance.

Eight years before McVean's bones were found on the edge of Montezuma Creek, Oliver Coho, the Navajo police officer and tracker most familiar with McVean's alleged movements during the first couple of years after McElmo Bridge, identified the Montezuma Creek area as the outlaw's home territory. Coho made the observation based on sightings and evidence he'd come across but, thinking like McVean, it was also a reasonable assumption. It was an area he was intimately familiar with, having taken an untold number of camping trips there. It was near friends and sympathizers who would assist him. And it was both remote and rugged with many caves and hiding places suited to his survivalist advantage and at the same time livable. Cross Canyon, through which Montezuma Creek ran, was one of the few major Utah canyons with a good supply of water, including potable water from improved wilderness springs. That McVean's bones should be found in that area was unrelated to how long he survived.

Last, there is reason to question the assumption that McVean was in the flatbed at the time it was abandoned. The theory that Mason split from the group and that it was McVean's and Pilon's tracks that led from the flatbed is based solely on the police's inability to catch one of the other fugitives at Swinging Bridge where Mason died. It was an arrogance that by that time, given the fugitives' ability to elude them, they should have been embarrassed to say out loud. If one of the others had been with Mason, goes the reasoning, they would have caught him. Mason had to be the one separated from the others when the flatbed was abandoned. They clung to the idea in the face of evidence to the contrary.

In all instances where police have reliable witnesses, Mason was the group's driver. He was positively identified as the driver of the tanker and of the flatbed as it sped through town and darted into McElmo Canyon. Tourists in two vehicles passed by the flatbed near Hovenweep Monument, moments before it turned into Cross Canyon, and described the man in the back of the truck as "heavy-set" or "chubby," a description that matches Pilon more so than Mason.

While there is no evidence that anyone was thrown from the truck,[1] there is reason to believe that upon turning the corner onto Cross Canyon Road, McVean got out, leaving the other two as Pilon shifted to the truck cab.

Pilon's ankle injury was an aviator fracture, a subacute fracture of the talus often seen in vehicle accidents when the victim is held stationary by a seat belt and the foot jams against the floorboard. The injury was common to WWI pilots trying to manage a crashlanding with a rudder foot pedal. The force of the avionic belly flop was absorbed by the foot. Pilon experienced a similar force on his foot when the truck flew from the canyon road and belly flopped onto the gravel berm.

The most compelling evidence of who was with Pilon was in Mason's pack recovered at Swinging Bridge. Pilon was found with no spare clips for his 9mm Glock or his FN FAL rifle, nor did the pistol at his side have a magazine in it. Pilon should have had at least one magazine for his pistol. In addition, carrying extra clips was standard practice and he almost certainly would have started out with some. While McVean, who usually carried a .45-caliber pistol and was found with an AK-47 would have had no use for Pilon's extra magazines, Mason was found with an FN FAL .308 rifle and a 9mm Glock, the same weapons Pilon carried—almost. Pilon's spare rifle magazines would have fit Mason's rifle. But the Glocks were different models. Pilon's Glock had a shorter pistol grip made to fit a fifteen-round magazine. Seated in the pistol, the bottom of the magazine was flush with the bottom of the pistol. If the shooter wanted a couple of extra shots, he could use a seventeen-round magazine that when seated would protrude below the pistol grip. Mason's Glock fit only a seventeen-round magazine. Loose in Mason's pack was a fifteen-round clip that would not even have worked at all in his pistol but was made for Pilon's. In addition, all the spare magazines on Mason's accessory belt were loaded one bullet short of full, a practice of some shooters who believe it saves the magazine spring. In the bottom of Mason's pack was a leather pouch with 9mm bullets and two seventeen-round magazines fully loaded with seventeen rounds. Had Mason loaded them according to the pattern found in magazines that almost certainly were his, they should have had just sixteen rounds each. Most likely, they were Pilon's extra clips.

The fifteen-round magazine that didn't fit Mason's Glock was also loaded a round short. The missing round would have been the one that killed Pilon. Mason, it seems, was there when Pilon died. It was he who gathered up Pilon's spare clips and shoved them in his pack.

The footprints seen in Cahone and then the surrounding area apparently heading back toward Cross or Squaw Canyons most likely belonged to Pilon and Mason. The ankle injury Pilon suffered—evident in his autopsy—was painful but initially not incapacitating, although prolonged walking and weight bearing could have aggravated it. He could have walked several days before it became too painful to continue. A common symptom of the injury is deep ankle pain after a day of walking on it, enough so to disturb the sufferer's sleep. It could explain why Pilon had Nytol with him. He may have gotten it in the Cahone/Dove Creek area. There had been police reports plus rumors among his old crowd that Pilon did show up in Dove Creek in the days after McElmo Bridge and approached a few people he hoped would help him. At one residence he was supposedly fed. At another he asked for money and was turned down.

Police had also surmised that Pilon died within the first day because his water filter for purifying stream water was still in its unopened store packaging. That speaks more to the idea that Pilon remained in the area than it does the timing of his death. Cross Canyon has fresh water supplies in remote locations that usually can be accessed unnoticed. Refilling water bottles in Cahone or Dove Creek would have been easy to manage and if, as police to a man believed, the fugitives were being assisted by friends, water would have been part of the assist. In addition a two-man team would likely use just one filter. The water filter Pilon carried, like the parka in his pack, was for a future time.

The timing of Mason's arrival at Swinging Bridge on the seventh morning of the manhunt also fits the distances better if he is placed hiking between Cahone, Dove Creek and Cross Canyon for four or five days first.

Finally, at some point all three men had to obtain the backpacks and supplies they were found with. Paul Iberra, the witness who watched them transfer from the tanker to the flatbed reported seeing them move two duffle bags from one truck to the other. The duffles were found with the abandoned flatbed. Iberra's statement, however, said nothing about backpacks.

The forensic evidence speaks against the assertions that Mason and Pilon committed suicide. While there is reason to believe that McVean was shot in the head, there is no way to know whose finger was on the trigger. Without further evidence, police went with suicide but questions remain.

Troubling is what was not found among McVean's bones. Certain heavier items resistant to the elements that McVean is known to have carried should have been found near the remains. A Kevlar helmet would remain intact indefinitely. A knife that would have been standard survival equipment should have been located in the metal detector search, as would have been the Colt .45 pistol he always had with him.

There is also something about the items that were found that doesn't feel quite right. Police claim the evidence that cinched the identity of the remains before the dental records proved it was a business card for Pilon found in the pack. It was a peculiar find. Keith

Dahl, Pilon's most recent employer and the only employer he had for several years, said he doesn't recall providing Pilon with business cards. He was a shop employee who didn't have customer contact. He had no need for a card, Dahl explained. Nor was there anything in Pilon's background that suggested he was involved in some other moonlight enterprise. Even if Pilon did have a business card, why would McVean have one in his pack? Before McElmo Bridge, he lived next door to Pilon, worked next to him in the same building, and went out with him after work. Pilon didn't even have a phone. After McElmo Bridge it was unlikely Pilon would be at the number on the card.

The wristwatch feels equally contrived. Neither McVean's parents nor his girlfriend, Linda Wallace, recall Jason ever wearing a watch. It is possible he purchased one specifically for coordinating the execution of their plan, but that would have meant Mason should have had one too, and he didn't. A windup watch would also have been an odd choice for a careful planner like McVean if it was purchased for timing a mission that would unfold over a course of a few days or weeks. Pilon's digital watch was still keeping time when his remains were found seventeen months after they disappeared.

Making the watch seem even more contrived is a long-after-the-fact report of a gunshot from the area where McVean's body was found. Among the contemporary reports filed by the dozens of SWAT teams and individual officers in the field during the manhunt were reports on spotting footprints, cigarette butts, pop bottles, fallen tree branches that someone thought might be lying in an unnatural position—virtually anything that in a stretch of imagination may be a sign of the suspects. On about the same day that police claim McVean supposedly killed himself, a pile of shit found on the canyon floor was enough to divert dozens of officers, a handful of helicopters and a couple of search planes. But there were no records of a gunshot.[2] McVean's remains were found six hundred yards from where police maintained a roadblock during the first days of the manhunt. In a massive manhunt for *gun*men, it is incredible that a *gun*shot within a few hundred yards of a group of police officers would go unreported and uninvestigated. The claim that residents who lived near the edge of the canyon heard a gunshot on May 30, 1998, between 6 and 6:30 P.M., was announced nine years after it supposedly occurred. The timing of the shot was poetic coincidence, too prophetic. McVean's life and his wristwatch just happened to wind down at the same moment.

Eighteen days after McVean supposedly died, Cissy passed near where McVean's body would have been in an advanced state of decomposition. Cadaver dogs are so sensitive to the smell of decomposed human tissue that they will alert on the grave of a Civil War soldier. Cissy kept walking.

The bones were found buried in what may have been a collapsed shallow cave-like impression in the bank of a wash. Police theorize that McVean hid in the hole, took his life and the bank eventually caved or washed in over him. His bones, however, were notably sunbleached and showed evidence that carnivores had attacked the body. For a prolonged period McVean's body must have lain in the open, exposed to the sun and become buried later.

The autopsy report also estimated McVean's age at the time of death using two different methods. The Lovejoy method, which is considered most reliable for young adult skeletons, estimates age based on the degree of closure along cranial joints and the texture of joint surfaces. Had he died in May 1998, McVean would have been twenty-six years old. By the Lovejoy analysis, however, experts judged the bones to be in Phase III (thirty to thirty-four years old at the time of death) but more toward the upper end of that range or perhaps Phase IV (thirty-five to thirty-nine years old). Adding a couple of years to each end to compensate for inaccuracies in method or observation, the pathologist estimated McVean's age at death between thirty and forty years old. The bone structure was notably more advanced than would be expected in those of a twenty-six-year-old.

Finally, McVean was not packed with the calculated efficiency of a person heading out for a prolonged wilderness survival experience. He was packed casually; a large soda bottle, one whole backpack pocket devoted to packages of fast-food ketchup. It would be an odd choice for a highly experienced survivalist preparing for a flight on foot into barren wilderness. He was packed like a person who was relaxed about his immediate future. It was more as if he'd been meeting others who kept him resupplied and provided items that improved his life on the run beyond raw survival. Had he died when police suggested, he would not have yet connected with friends who, perhaps, in response to his casual gripe about a bland diet of military rations, brought him a handful of foil ketchup packs.

At best, the oddities that surfaced with Jason McVean's bones challenged the assertion he died soon after the manhunt began. At worst, the implications were sinister, posing a new set of perplexing questions: how did McVean's remains end up where Eric Bayles found them—who, when, and why?

With the discovery of McVean's remains, the FBI as well as local and state agencies officially closed the case. At CBI, the accumulated files were stuffed into three large banker boxes, sealed with red tape and labeled with a black marker CLAXTON MURDER, 1998. CLOSED. Anxious to purge reminders of a painful chapter in its department, Cortez P.D. quickly destroyed case records. With all three suspects dead, there is no one to tell the real story, and they all sighed.

It is how they hoped the case would be remembered and, as soon as possible, forgotten—the bad guys acted alone; police chased them into the desert where they quickly died. End of story.

But there may yet be people who know the real story. There may be people the three confided in before McElmo Bridge, sympathizers who aided and abetted the fugitives afterward, and accomplices who were part of the original criminal plan. Even after the plan was foiled by Officer Claxton, and Pilon and Mason were dead, McVean may have regrouped with accomplices hoping to reboot. A month after their plans came apart and they had to ditch the water tanker, McVean and another man were seen trying to break into a second tanker. Later, police believed a third attempted theft of a tanker in Durango was connected to McVean.[3]

Police received tips that acquaintances of both Pilon and McVean were part of the original plan. The accusation against Pilon's friend was never followed beyond an interview and denial. Authorities were particularly suspicious of McVean's friend. His name was mentioned consistently by acquaintances of McVean as a person likely to have been involved. It's known he trained and shot with the suspects and was one of the few friends trusted to go into the desert with the trio. Many of the supplies, including ammunition, mail-ordered by the suspects were delivered to his house. Bragging to a friend, Pilon described one of the guys training and planning with them as a former Green Beret. Among the fugitives' close associates, the description fit only that individual. Finally, after Mason's death he reportedly told others he knew what was planned but couldn't talk about it because he'd be implicated.

Four months after McElmo Bridge he was dead, shot in the head as ultimately all the suspects would be. Police ruled it a suicide. His parents agreed. Despite their denial that he had anything to do with the crimes of McVean, Mason and Pilon, police remained suspicious. The most likely fourth suspect, like the other three, would never talk to police, but someday other confidents, sympathizers and accomplices might.

McVean's bones shattered the myth. As police raked the banks of a dry desert arroyo and placed what remained of him on a green tarp, the question formed: What happened to him? It was the same question many asked about his best friend Bobby Mason.

The easy answer was that they committed suicide. Fearful and overwhelmed, the forces of society apprehended them psychologically even if it was unable to do so physically. Perhaps it was true but there was reason to question those conclusions and ask: If they didn't kill themselves, who did force guns in their mouths and shoot them?

Police have naturally been defensive about that question. Their over-the-top response seemed more than a quest for justice. Many entered the canyons emotionally charged. Some were out of control. Several teams acted on their own. Commanders didn't know for sure how many officers were there or who they were. They admit there were renegades among them. It is also true that within their ranks were some with conditioning and wilderness commando skills equal to those of the suspects.

Even Sheriff Lacy, who has been most assertive of the suicide theory, admitted he doesn't really know how either Mason or Pilon died; only that they were dead when police found them. His strongest reason for sticking with the suicide explanation is a weak one. "If a cop killed them, he'd have bragged about it by now," Lacy explained.

Greg McCain, whose Pueblo County SWAT team found Mason's body, was particularly emphatic he doesn't know if Mason was a suicide or homicide, only that Mason was dead when his team reached him. The question of whether police chose to kill rather than capture Mason was voiced immediately by investigative agencies but more as a routine question than an accusation. It was an acknowledgment that the question was obvious, so it was asked up front and the answer made part of the record. "Did you kill Robert Mason?"

But the team that stood around Mason's body upon its discovery at Swinging Bridge answering he was dead when they got there was only a small fraction of police swarming through that section of the canyon that afternoon. And in the five hours it took hundreds of police to find a body only three hundred yards from where the search began, other teams could easily have entered and exited the area unnoticed.

Rumors that the police executed Mason spread almost immediately, not only whispered among the public but also within their ranks. Two years after Mason's death, spurred by comments from a well-placed source, the FBI quietly interviewed some officers with that question in mind.

While police immediately fell under suspicion, there may have been others with equal motivation and opportunity to have killed Mason. If in fact the suspects' conspiracy involved others with similar skills, resources and ruthlessness, the botched plan may have compromised their anonymity, drawing hundreds of police into their area and risking discovery of their activities. Some witnesses claimed that two men escaped down the San Juan River as police moved into the area. Seen from the bridge in Mexican Hat, the one who looked like McVean appeared distraught—seated with his head hanging between his knees—as an unidentified man, also dressed in camo-military attire, guided the raft.

Even more persistent was the rumor that citizen vigilantes had dealt out justice the old Wild West way. Sheriff Jerry Martin's advice to the citizens of Cahone to leave the keys in their unlocked cars and avoid contact with the fugitives at all costs didn't go down well with many of the surrounding ranchers. At the time, one area resident told reporters that he and his neighbors had armed themselves and were ready to defend their property. He harshly commented that the suspects deserved to be killed.

Years later one resident noted that there has always been an unmentioned understanding within the community "that those boys died by frontier justice." Citizens agreed to watch for anything suspicious. They lived on ranches a half mile or more from each other, so "a phone tree was established and the word was if anyone spotted them, don't call police; call the tree—the neighbors would take care of it."

"It's not that we were siding with police, we didn't know the cop that got shot. It was more like three of our own kind going rogue. We've got land and livestock. If they'd kill a cop over a stolen water truck, they'd kill and butcher our livestock. We still think of that as a hanging offense in this part of the state," the longtime Cahone area resident explained.

If Mason and McVean didn't die by their own hands, then their killers are still out there. And no one is looking. No one is talking. What we are left with is pure conjecture; nevertheless it is a story that fits the facts—what is known and what makes sense—better than the story told by police.

The story goes roughly like this: as Pilon jumped from the truck bed to take his place in the cab, McVean jogged across Hovenweep Road and disappeared east following an irrigation ditch among newly planted crops, rolling hills, and dense patches of scrub evergreen. With the tanker truck plan disrupted, they focused on an emergency escape plan. The plan was to meet at Swinging Bridge in a week; from there they would travel by boat until they were well beyond the search area. From that point a vehicle would help them reach one of their ammunition caches quickly, then disappear into an even larger wilderness area. The boat was already in place. Two weeks before McElmo Bridge, Mason and Pilon were seen trucking in an aluminum flat-bottom river boat into the Swinging Bridge landing. Police who eventually heard of the boat from witnesses who knew and recognized Pilon, presumed the men hid it near the footbridge. Transferring to a vehicle rather than staying along the river was a last-minute plan change. McVean needed to contact a friend with a vehicle.

Mason and Pilon continued in the flatbed into Cross Canyon. Near the bottom, before the road leveled out, Mason steered into a dry wash, hanging the truck up over a berm of gravel. They quickly covered it with brush as best they could and headed into Cross Canyon on foot. At Montezuma Creek, they waded into waist-deep water and sloshed downstream, leaving no tracks to follow.

Had everything gone right they'd be deep into Utah with the tanker heading to the first supply cache. Instead, Monte was hurt, limping more than his usual everyday limp, and they had to stay ahead of police pouring into the canyon. Needing help, they doubled back and made their way northeast toward Pilon's friends in Dove Creek. Hiding during the day and hiking at night they moved slowly up Cross Canyon to Cahone where they crossed over the mesa top to Dove Creek.

The bolder of Pilon's friends fed and hid the two fugitives for a night. In their medicine cabinet they found some Nytol to help Pilon sleep through his ankle pain. The second night Mason and Pilon began the journey south, this time following Squaw Canyon down. After several hours they climbed out of Squaw Canyon intending to cut across Tin Cup Mesa. From there they'd drop into Cross Canyon and follow Montezuma Creek to the San Juan River and Swinging Bridge. As they approached the steep downhill scramble into Cross Canyon, Pilon was unable to go on.

Sitting cross-legged on the edge of Tin Cup Mesa, Pilon scooted his body farther under the juniper limbs. He and Mason had talked about this moment more than once since fleeing into the desert. He could feel the Nytol taking effect and fought the drowsiness just long enough to look out over Cross Canyon where he camped as a teenager and played war games as a young adult and as a man buried weapons and conspired revolution.

As Pilon fell asleep, Mason shot him in the head, placed the Glock alongside of his dead friend, gathered up the extra rifle and pistol clips Pilon had set out, dropped them into his pack and walked away.

It had taken McVean a couple of days to make contact with one of their conspirators. Together they made their way to Swinging Bridge approaching from downriver and met Mason as planned. McVean and the other man loaded quickly into the boat. Despite McVean's urging to come with them, Mason had decided to stay.

Nearly an hour after the boat had disappeared down the river, a white SUV bounced down the road toward the river. Mason didn't aim for the driver or the vehicle but fired two shots to scare him off. The deputy showed up next. Him, he shot to kill. More enemy would arrive soon. From where he lay, he could kill a dozen cops, maybe more before they got him.

Mason waited. His favorite movie line surfaced through his thoughts—the words spoken by Spock in *The Wrath of Khan* when he was about to sacrifice his life: "The needs of many outweigh the needs of the one."[4] He took comfort in his role as a noble warrior. "The needs of the many . . ." began to replay in his mind one more time. He didn't hear the men closing in behind him.

Below Mexican Hat, McVean and his comrade abandoned the boat and made their way to a side road where they had left a pickup truck. Near Hite Marina on Lake Powell they stopped along the shoulder long enough for McVean to uncover a cache of ammunition and then headed back east.

Over the course of the next year McVean hid out in series of caves in the canyons around Montezuma Creek. He was comfortable in the area and it wasn't even true wilderness survival. Friends would visit from time to time. They didn't know where he stayed but if they came to the area and waited, he'd find them. Some would stay for an hour or two, others would camp with him for a couple of days. To those who were part of the original plan, he talked of trying again; getting another water truck and starting over. All the supplies they needed were still hidden, waiting for them.

By the second year he'd shifted west into the more remote Grand Gulch area where he had even more supplies hidden, but it was only a base from which he traveled. Once he went to California, then up the coast, possibly hoping to visit a girlfriend who lived in Portland. Most of the time he moved about in the Four Corners area, usually in the canyons where he felt safe.

In the fifth year after McElmo Bridge, they at last caught up with him. His Colt .45 and knife were taken. The end of his AK-47 was pressed into his mouth and he died. After a long time had passed, whatever remains the elements and scavengers left to find were buried in a small depression on the side of a wash flowing into Montezuma Creek, waiting for a lone cowboy rounding up cattle to spot a ragged corner of bulletproof vest below his horse's hooves.

EPILOGUE
LOBO 11

In a land of legendary outlaws and lawmen, manhunts of mythical dimensions were inevitable. But in terms of sheer size, none before or since compared to the Four Corners manhunt of 1998. More than five hundred officers from fifty-one different federal, state and local agencies plus National Guard troops surged after Claxton's killers, supported by two hundred additional law enforcement personnel in administrative and investigative roles. In terms of aircraft and advanced search-surveillance technology, few other US criminals have been the subjects of such intense focus. Yet the effort failed to achieve the historic success of Pat Garrett and John Poe chasing down Billy the Kid or Wyatt Earp and Bat Masterson tracking down the killer of dance hall legend Dora Hand.

For many of the officers involved, the manhunt became a circus, three rings of blunders, posturing and chaos. To observers it looked like a massive, inescapable force of men and machines that after futile days seemed more like the false saloon façade on a Hollywood Western set. Radios didn't work. There was no universal communication frequency. SWAT teams were tracking each other. Local officers familiar with the canyons were assigned support roles while glory-seeking FBI and big-city tactical teams, whose officers had never even seen a desert canyon, led the way into them and inevitably lost the trail. Ultimately in the chaos, one FBI SWAT team opened fire on another. The best that could be said of the manhunt, most commanders agreed, was that no one else was shot.

"The manhunt was a joke," cowboy Bruce Tolzer claimed. While the police were searching the Utah canyons, Tolzer rode the rimrock of lower McElmo Canyon on horseback looking for tracks, making sure the fugitives didn't backtrack near his and his neighbors' ranches. There were lots of cowboys in those canyons at that time of year gathering cattle, he explained, yet there were no reports of the police seeing any of them. Tolzer said that was because the police stayed near the roads and their refreshment stations. "Real cowboys go into those canyons and work all day carrying a small canteen and some chewing tobacco. They don't need water flown in to them. The police were out there in hundred-and-eight-degree desert days in their damn black polyester uniforms. Hell, everyone in this country knows to wear cotton shirts because they're cooler."

Even the local police weren't up for the job, according to Tolzer. The local forces were made up mostly of town kids. Missing from their ranks with few exceptions were "country boys who grew up chasing their brothers around those canyons on a mule." Police today are trained to catch outlaws by surrounding houses and blocking roads, he added. "Out here we got no houses and roads. They know nothing about tracking and hunting a man down in open country."

Even though he might flinch at Tolzer's criticism in light of the devotion, suffering and effort many officers put into the manhunt, Sheriff Martin didn't necessarily disagree with Tolzer's point. He and Lacy concurred that the manhunt was a tactical nightmare, the scale of it quickly exceeding their experience and management resources.

The suspects knew what they were doing, former Special Forces commander and El Paso County Undersheriff Ivan Middlemiss noted. "Their plans and escape were thought through. There was nothing haphazard in their actions. They had the right equipment and a common mind-set. They had trained together a long time, knew each other's strengths and weaknesses. They were very effective."

Acknowledging that more effective organization doesn't always translate to success, Middlemiss still contended, "If there had been an experienced large-scale crisis action command on the ground day one, we may have gotten them."

Martin and Lacy had the opposite approach in mind. Their discussion kept returning to the idea of forming a small, manageable manhunt. The idea was to form an old-time posse—guys with Vietnam experience, cowboys who knew the area. In the end, the idea was scrapped as too dangerous for civilians. "The risk of getting a civilian killed was too great," Lacy said.

Had they done it, there would have been a different result, Martin insisted. A Western history buff who sits at his desk beneath a wall-mounted nineteenth-century Winchester, he claimed the manhunt would have had more of a true Western ending. "We'd have rode out and returned leading the wanted man, dead or alive."

Tolzer and Martin may have been right—in Four Corners, the West remained wild and even at the end of the twentieth century, justice in those parts required nineteenth-century lawmen.

On May 29 of every year, flowers and wreaths appear along the dusty shoulder of Montezuma County Road 27 at the south end of McElmo Bridge. They lean against a sign marking the spot where Dale Claxton died. The sign has Dale's name, the date of his death and his police call sign, "Lobo 11." It was a dispatch recording of Dale's voice played during his funeral—"This is Lobo 11 signing off"—that brought three thousand mourners to their knees. For many people there is no signing off from that summer of 1998. The legacy of McElmo Bridge is long.

Confronted with the inadequacy of their response, police departments across the West have developed resources and trained for wilderness manhunt scenarios. Most have acquired weapons and equipment more appropriate for search operations in extreme environments such as desert canyons.

There have been various official acknowledgments of Dale Claxton's service and death, including a mention in a speech by Vice President Al Gore. Congress passed the Officer Dale Claxton Bulletproof Police Protective Equipment Act of 2001, providing funding for local police departments to purchase bulletproof vests. On August 31, 2004, US Senator Ben Nighthorse Campbell presided over the dedication of the new Dale D. Claxton Federal Building in Durango.

All three suspects, but especially Jason McVean, developed a cult-like following with hundreds of thousands of mentions on the Internet and a continuing stream of articles in national media and magazines. In 2000, popular author Tony Hillerman published *Hunting Badger,* a bestselling novel based on the manhunt.

The FBI, in a move that further colored Westerners' opinion of the federal government, decided to pay Eric Bayles only half the reward it had promised. It paid the full reward years earlier for the discovery of Pilon's remains but determined against all logic that since McVean's remains closed the case, there was no advantage to paying the full amount. It was a Washington, D.C., decision that angered local officials and citizens and undercut federal agents in Four Corners. "The federal government in general is viewed with distrust. . . . Failure to award the full amount advertised would surely be represented regionally as a failed promise by the FBI and the US government," the local agents warned. It became one more headline that fanned anti-government sentiments; attitudes that at their extreme can lead some to cross McElmo Bridge.

The former Cortez patrolman whose shift Dale had taken as a favor the day he was killed, left the department and moved to California. Six months after Dale's murder, he attempted grisly suicide. Rather than dying, he found help from psychotherapist Sara Gilman. The following spring, the former officer asked Sara to accompany him back to Cortez as he confronted his final obstacle to closure—standing once again on McElmo Bridge.

By then, nearly a year had passed but when Gilman stepped into the Cortez police station, she found an entire department still in a state of shock, suffering from post-traumatic stress disorder (PTSD). There were suicides waiting to happen. One by one the desperate officers pulled her aside and told her of the nightmares and flashbacks and insomia. "I have to take care of my men," Assistant Chief Russ Johnson pleaded. Gilman volunteered to help and over the next few months would make multiple trips from Califonia to Cortez to work with department personel as well as others in the community traumatized by the tragedy.

Detective Jim Shethar was away at a conference when Gilman first arrived, so she called to talk to him long distance. At the end of the call, Shethar sat outside the seminar room and cried. They had all been holding it in, holding it together, but they were falling apart inside, Shethar said. Assistant Chief Johnson would shut the door to his office and sob. Chief Roy Lane waited two years. In the privacy afforded when his wife and kids left him home alone for a weekend, he broke down in uncontrollable tears. It was cathartic.

Using what was then a controversial treatment, Gilman brought the men and women of Cortez PD back from the edge.[1] Today they are coping, but the pain remains and what they want most now is at last to stop talking about it; to finally stop thinking about it.

Sue Claxton is one of the people who leaves flowers at McElmo Bridge where her husband was killed. She found the strength within herself and the support of her community to carry on. In the first weeks and months after the shooting, an endless supply of Tupperware meals arrived at her door. Local contractors and builders showed up at her home to finish the remodeling Dale had started. And the Cortez Police Department became part her enduring family, bound together over the years by a shared tragedy. In the small steps of ordinary life—work, raising children, community involvement—she moved forward.

Todd Martin underwent multiple operations and through a long and painful rehabilitation recovered use of his wounded leg and arm. He did leave the Montezuma County Sheriff's Department as he had planned to do on the day he was shot, and the following year picked up his life plan where he'd left it months earlier, bleeding nearly to death under a bullet-ridden Jeep. He graduated at the top of his class from the Colorado State Patrol training program and became a motorcycle trooper with the agency in western Colorado.

Deputy Jason Bishop underwent minor surgery two days after the shooting to remove the bullet from the back of his head and recovered quickly from his wound without complications. He has since left law enforcement for other reasons.

San Juan County Deputy Kelly Bradford underwent emergency surgery upon his arrival at the Grand Junction, Colorado, hospital where two days later he was wheeled into the delivery room to witness the birth of his son, Porter. Bradford's full recovery was unexpected. Even as the doctors took him off the critical list and announced that he would not die from the wounds he received at Swinging Bridge, they predicted he would not walk again. Six weeks later Bradford returned to work.

For the families of the suspects, the pain continues as well. The Pilons continue to live quietly in Dove Creek in the home where they raised Monte, wishing to remain outside the glare of their son's infamy.

It took Ann Mason two years to gather her strength and find the words but she wrote letters to the Claxton family and each of the wounded deputies apologizing for their son's actions and the pain he caused. Unlike the parents of soldiers killed in action who at least are provided the peace of couching their grief in their child's service to a noble cause, Ann explains, "My son was one of the bad guys."

Despite that admission and her letters reaching out to the victims of Bobby's murderous transgressions, Ann has alienated many of the police involved in the case with her persistent questions into Bobby's death. Suspicious that her son was murdered, she has, as a *Denver Post* reporter noted, spent more time viewing gruesome crime scene photos of her son's body and autopsy reports than any mother should ever have to. "Bobby never had his day in court and the police should explain the unusual circumstances of his death," she said.

For Ann Mason, a mother's hopes are simple. "My only hope is that before I die, someone with a conscience will come forward and I will know what really happened to Bobby."

Jim McVean still speaks of his son's innocence; claiming that in the police's urgency to find who killed Claxton, Jason and his friends on one of their usual weekend camping trips in Cross Canyon were convenient people to blame and frame. Months after Jason's remains were discovered in 2007, he received a copy of the autopsy report in the mail. He couldn't bear to look at it. The nine-by-twelve envelope lies accessible in his desk drawer, unopened.

Jim McVean always enjoyed the outdoor camping experience that captivated Jason. It was the father and son time they'd shared camping that, after Jim's divorce, brought Jason to Colorado to live with him. But Jim had always been oriented to the mountains rising thirty miles east of Durango. Now, every year on June 5, the anniversary of the day Jason's remains were discovered, Jim and his brother head west, out into the desert canyon to the spot where Jason had lain for so many years. They spend the night there under the stars and wait for the sun to rise brilliant over the rim of the canyon and angle onto the canyon floor, for the earth to warm and a new day begin. "It is really peaceful and beautiful out there," Jim said. "I can see why Jason loved it."

Caitlin Claxton, like her mother was at the time of Dale's death, is a teacher married to a Cortez cop. "We talked about it before we got married," her husband, Patrolman Robert Brewer, said. "Knowing what happened to her father, I asked her if she was sure she wanted to do this, be married to a cop."

In 2008, the boy who last saw his father when he jumped out of Dale's patrol car and ran into school for his final day of sixth grade became a Cortez policeman. Today Corbin Claxton reports to work at the police station named after his father.

The average annual rainfall in the canyon country that anchors the Utah quadrant of Four Corners territory is less than ten inches. Most of it comes in April. And when it falls, it doesn't soak in; it pools in the low spots of the sandstone surface until those depressions over-flow from one to another, displacing increasingly more water from each successive puddle. The trickles zigzag their way around pebbles and barely noticeable high spots on the rock surface until they merge to become small streams coursing through gullies and troughs across the mesa. The streams combine to form torrents, gushing over the rim of the high plateau where gravity drags it down narrow crevices amplifying the current so that anything loose in its path is caught up and carried with it . . . logs, gravel, rocks the size of baseballs. As the rain subsides, the water slows, dropping its load. By May, the water is gone and along the paths it followed tons of sand and gravel have been repositioned; in some places uncovering long-hidden secrets, in others burying the truth.

Such is Four Corners . . . a hard country, part real, part illusion.

As it was then. As it remains today.

NOTES

CHAPTER 5. MARTIN

1. Some people believe the number 666 has Satanic connotations thus the highway was known as the Devil's Highway. It has since been assigned a different number—491.

CHAPTER 6. ESCAPE

1. Police found empty beer cans in the abandoned flatbed truck that belonged to neither Bob Williams, the owner of the truck; nor Paul Iberra, the Williamses' employee using the truck at the time it was jacked. Jason McVean was a heavy beer drinker and, anticipating a long, relaxed cruise into the desert on a hot day, it is possible he brought beer with him in one of the two duffle bags Iberra saw the fugitives load onto the truck. Or they may have met someone during their escape that offered them beer. Either way, the fact that they took the time to drink it attests to the relaxed nature of their escape once they descended into McElmo Canyon.

2. Police hypothesized that the suspects didn't intend to split up; rather the person riding in the bed of the truck was thrown from the

vehicle when it sped around the corner from Hovenweep Road onto Cross Canyon Road. It was a notion with no evidentiary basis. In fact, it ran counter to more reasonable extrapolations from known facts and evidence. It suggested that the fugitives in the flatbed were so hotly pursued that when they spilled a comrade from the vehicle, they didn't have time to stop and retrieve him. The fact is there were no patrol cars on their tail and had not been for the past half hour. In an unpressured escape, the fugitives stopped for cattle crossing the road, drank beer and appeared relaxed as they cruised past motorists. They were also extremely loyal to each other and it would have been out of character for them to leave a partner behind. Police also used the theory to explain why later in the manhunt they found Robert Mason and not the others—he was thrown from the truck, separated from his friends and alone. Witnesses earlier in the chase, however, positively identified Mason as the driver. Based on descriptions by motorists who saw the flatbed shortly before it would have turned onto Cross Canyon Road, McVean was the passenger and Pilon was in the bed of the truck. There was strong evidence that Mason (the driver) and Pilon (the fugitive in the bed of the truck) were together in the early days of the manhunt; that they were the ones who left the two sets of tracks heading away from the abandoned flatbed. McVean in the passenger side of the cab would have had to disembark purposely sometime before the truck was abandoned.

Police also used the "thrown from the truck" hypothesis to explain suspicious injuries found on Mason, or in another version in which Pilon was thrown, an injury to Pilon's ankle. Medical experts, however, concluded that Mason's injuries occurred at the time of his death. Pilon's injury was likely caused by force different than he would have suffered had he been thrown from the back of a truck.

Finally, a walkie-talkie radio discovered at one location where the fugitives stopped with the tanker before reaching Cortez suggests they had planned to separate. Found at the site were flashlight batteries and the CB radio. Whereas the batteries were tossed to the side as if they were being purposely discarded (the fugitives had used flashlights a few hours earlier and would have wanted to continue with fresh batteries), the radio unit was crushed in the tanker's tire track as if it had fallen unnoticed from the parked truck. The mate to the unit was found in the flatbed. If the radio was discarded purposely, both units would have been tossed. It is reasonable to assume the fugitives intended to take both units with them into the desert—equipment that would only make sense if they intended to split up.

CHAPTER 7. NAMES

1. Alan Pilon was an only child. Shawn was actually Alan's cousin and he had been killed in a car accident two years earlier. Identifying him as Alan's brother was a mistake the FBI made repeatedly in the course of the investigation.

CHAPTER 8. TANKER

1. The fact that no truck keys were found on Mason's body suggests that he gave them to someone else charged with retrieving his truck and their gear.

CHAPTER 9. JASON

1. The extent to which he used drugs other than marijuana has always been a matter of conjecture. Reports that he and Mason used methamphetamine in early high school seem true. As an adult his drug habits may have changed. During the investigation into Claxton's murder, a few people, most of whom didn't know him directly, made accusations that he was a crackhead and meth tweaker. The friends he socialized and partied with on a near-daily basis claimed he smoked pot frequently and peyote occasionally but they didn't know him to use other drugs. In a search of his trailer, police found those two drugs but no signs of other drug use. He was also a heavy beer drinker and his beverage of choice was Milwaukee's Best because it was "the best beer to drink warm in the desert."

2. As our computer-dependent society approached the millennium, there was widespread concern that a universal practice of programming dates using only the last two digits of the year—89, 90, 93, etc.—would lead to worldwide system failure when a two-digit designation for the year ceased to work—at midnight, New Year's Eve, 1999. Power plants would shut down, planes would fall from the sky, financial markets would implode, commerce and modern services would cease. Society would collapse.

CHAPTER 10. MANHUNT

1. Criminal Justice Professor William Gaut, Ph.D., noted that a drawn-out wilderness manhunt is a significant departure from the tactical experience of most police SWAT units, demanding differences in training, equipment, strategy and conditioning. Gaut is a former police commander, certified instructor at police academies and a nationally recognized expert on police training and procedures.

2. Los Angeles P.D. not only sent a SWAT team to help but, unable to imagine the manhunt terrain, it also volunteered its tank.

3. Dolores County Sheriff Jerry Martin is not related to Montezuma County Sheriff's Deputy Todd Martin.

4. One of the largest and best-trained police forces in the Southwest, the Navajo Nation Police operates seven districts across the 27,500 square-mile Navajo Reservation. (The reservation is larger than ten states.) The force has over 300 officers and 40 investigators supported by more than 250 civilian personel.

5. The Navajo Nation is a sovereign, semiautonomous Native American–governed territory whose reservation lies within the states of Arizona, New Mexico and Utah. The Utah section includes the southern half of San Juan County, of which Mike Lacy was sheriff. The rules regarding police juridiction on the reservation are complex but by and large authority for police actions falls to tribal police and federal law enforcement agencies.

6. Of the two hundred or more people present that day at Cross Canyon, Lacy later blamed the Navajo trackers as the officers who trampled the fugitives' tracks leading from the flatbed. His assessment of Navajo police capabilities was in stark contrast to observations by the FBI and CBI agents as well as other police in the canyons who were all more or less awed by the Native American officers' tracking, professionalism and stamina.

7. Although both Lacy's and Martin's departments were small and had limited special weapons and tactical (SWAT) experience compared to larger urban police agencies, their uncertainty as to how to proceed was not unique to them. The fact is, no domestic police agency had conducted or prepared plans for an extreme wilderness manhunt of the scale that quickly developed in response to the killing of Dale Claxton. Such a manhunt was unprecedented in modern history and few of the skills and tactics honed for urban SWAT response were transferable. Based on this incident, police agencies across the West have since planned and trained for wilderness manhunts.

CHAPTER 11. BOBBY

1. Ann Mason didn't like guns. She noted that her husband Gary and both their sons owned hunting rifles and sporting guns, but she didn't want them in the house.

CHAPTER 12. SWINGING BRIDGE

1. There is some unsubstantiated evidence that others may have met Mason that morning at Swinging Bridge. A witness looking at the river from a bridge several miles downstream from that location reported seeing two camouflage-dressed men in a flat-bottom boat float by. One of the men appeared distressed. There was also a positive sighting of the fugitives hauling a boat to Swinging Bridge a week before McElmo Bridge and police did find the drag marks from a boat being launched into the river. The timing of the sighting would have had the men leaving the Swinging Bridge area before shots were fired

at Wilcox, however. Wilcox could not positively identify the shooter but his general description fit Mason.

The socks found hanging from a branch were assumed to be Mason's even though he was later found wearing socks and had a dry pair in his pack. Typically a hiker would pack one extra pair of socks rather than two, but two extra pair would not be unheard of, especially if the hiker were anticipating a long trip with water crossings.

2. One officer present when the body was discovered stated that police turned the body in order to identify the victim by comparing his face to photos of the suspects. Others say that absolutely did not happen. An anonymous authority, reportedly with one of the manhunt police agencies, suggested the body was staged by others and left to be discovered or it may have been staged sometime afterward with crime scene photos in mind. Among other clues contradicting the official report listed by the anonymous letter-writer was the observation that the pipe bombs and pistol shown near Mason's body looked unnatural, as if they were all carefully arranged to fit neatly within the frame of the photo.

CHAPTER 13. UNCERTAIN DEATH

1. By that point, three patrol cars had arrived at the top of the bluff opposite Mason. The first vehicle parked nearest the edge of the bluff had been driven by San Juan County Deputy Kelly Bradford, who Mason shot. From his vantage point on the opposite side of the river and below the crest of the bluff, the windshield and roof of Kelly Bradford's car was visible. Parked behind that vehicle, farther from the edge of the bluff, were cars driven by Kelly's cousin; Blanding, Utah, police officer Mike Bradford; and his chief Mike Halliday. They were not visible from Mason's bunker. After getting the wounded deputy to the ambulance, Mike Bradford and Chief Halliday kept behind cover as they approached the edge of the bluff and took a position overseeing the valley. It is unknown if Mason knew the officers or their vehicles were there.

2. A kneepad is suggested because it would be a common piece of commando attire; it would be readily accessible; and it meets the other characteristics hinted at by autopsy findings, i.e., dense enough to loosen the bullet jacket and leave traces of a substance used for black dye or pigment, particularly of fabric. According to equipment specialists for Army Special Forces, there are several other items a well-equipped commando would typically have available that would serve the same purpose.

It was also possible that same evidence could be related to an assassin less expertly equipped. Ballistic expert Ron Scott noted it was possible a misaligned silencer on the end of the pistol could cause the bullet jacket to loosen before impact with a target. Misalignment would be unlikely with a manufactured model but may be more common with a homemade silencer. Homemade silencers often include a layer of fibrous sound-absorbent material that could account for the particles found in Mason's mouth.

CHAPTER 16. BLUFF

1. On hand were a hundred FBI agents from division offices in Denver, Salt Lake, Albuquerque and Phoenix, including an FBI SWAT team from the Denver division; nineteen CBI investigators; thirty officers for the Utah Highway Patrol; fourteen members of the New Mexico State Police tactical and bomb units; two hundred members of the Colorado National Guard, including flight crews and aircraft ground support for eight helicopters and eighty Special Forces troops from the Colorado 19th group (Colorado Governor Romer called for up to 350 Guard members); air elements of the Utah Army National Guard; US Customs Service aircraft and crew; BLM rangers; Navajo Nation Police SWAT teams and trackers; and an estimated two hundred officers from Four Corners police departments and sheriff's offices as well as volunteers from law enforcement agencies around the country.

2. The Navajo living in the area would have been hesitant to provide information to white officers but spoke freely to Navajo police who

relayed the information. Navajo police's close connections and trusted relationship with reservation residents reflects the importance of clans in tribal society, Butler explained. Emphasis is on a person's clan. (Butler, for example, is of the Deer Water clan. He would say, "I am Deer Water. I am *born* to Towering House"—his father's clan. His grandparents are of different clans.) The tribe is linked through the interweaving of clans, providing more intimate familial relationship between members. Butler might address his officers by their professional title—Sergeant, Lieutenant, etc.—but it would also be proper to address them (or others) as "little brother," "father," "uncle," "aunt" and so on. It is much more natural to share information and provide assistance to "relatives."

3. Cortez P.D. Detective Jim Shethar noted with some pride that the suspects' families were managed in a manner that they remained compliant and cooperative with authorities for about three weeks before turning angry, hostile and unhelpful; about three times longer than typical according to FBI statistics.

4. The exception might be love letters to a second girlfriend found in McVean's truck but not until more than two months after Claxton's murder. Also, police evidence gathering and analysis at one of the many crime scenes was less proficient.

5. A notable exception was San Juan County Sheriff Mike Lacy who in time refused requests from Cortez P.D. for permission to follow leads into Utah. CBI was also surprised when they weren't invited as a courtesy to observe the recoveries of Pilon's and McVean's remains in San Juan County.

CHAPTER 17. GRUBWORK

1. The legal implications of police working outside their areas of jurisdiction seemed to have been less of an issue of concern for Lacy in the early days of the manhunt when police from multiple states worked in both Colorado and Utah, ostensibly under his command.

He had also worked cooperatively with Colorado police agencies over the years, especially Sheriff Jerry Martin in neighboring Dolores County. He presumably could have overcome jurisdictional issues by assuming command of the operation in Utah and assigning a deputy to accompany officers and agents from outside agencies.

CHAPTER 18. PATRIOTS

1. The statistic applies to the states that in their entirety are west of the isohyetal line, a north-south climatological verge used to demarcate the American West: Arizona, California, Colorado, Idaho, Montana, New Mexico, Nevada, Oregon, Utah, Washington and Wyoming. Within the lower forty-eight states, the isohyetal line is roughly equivalent to the ninety-eighth meridian. West of the line annual rainfall drops below the twenty inches necessary to grow nonirrigated crops—at least the crops prevalent during the late nineteenth and early twentieth century before more drought-resistant hybrids. Geographers, demographers and sociologists have long used the isohyetal line to give boundaries to a region that is more concept than a specific patch of earth. It is the line of semiaridity that wrought the way of life, values and attitudes of those who ventured beyond it.

2. The head of the 4 P.M. Four Corners Patriot Militia told the police none of the suspects were members although they may have attended meetings and training sessions. Joining the group is a formal process complete with an organization chart, equipment requirement (sunscreen, toilet paper, four rifle magazines with pouches or bandolier, flashlight, sidearm holster, extra socks and underwear, night-vision goggles, nylon stockings, sniper veils . . .), a skills self-evaluation form (rate your experience/proficiency on a scale of 1 to 5 in the following skills: administrative/finance, demolitions, artillery, public relations . . .) and an application. The organization's charter and membership papers were found among Pilon's effects.

3. There were any number of extremist storylines cited to justify militia organization and activities. Within the extremist fringe, however,

there was enough similarity between the various theories that shared paranoia fed off the multiple permutations. The adherents were all brothers in the revolution. Even the environmental movement that in the mainstream aligned with liberal politics rather than antiregulatory conservatism found a footing within the militia-minded, focusing on a common enemy with a shared resolve to violent resistance.

The oppressed who, according to extremist rhetoric, were systematically being flayed of their rights, were usually white salt-of-the-earth Americans. The enemy was always the U.S. government, often all government and police authority, and in some sects—minorities, immigrants and liberals as well. The ominous conspirators were usually shadowy behind-the-scenes power brokers. Their agendas were secret plots of domination. Elected leaders were their puppets.

The common belief among extremists was that plans by an international financial cartel to establish a New World Order were by that time in advanced stages. Government actions had already usurped many of our individual rights and compromised the inherent power of the people. UN troops (the UN was an arm of the New World Order) and black helicopters were poised offshore for the final invasion of US territory. The only obstacle to the plans was a well-armed citizenry (gun rights). And even that may not forestall the final onerous government acts that could end only in police-state enslavement or bloody revolution. At Ruby Ridge, Idaho, and again at Waco, Texas, the government had already demonstrated its willingness to ruthlessly suppress those who proclaimed their liberty and urged resistance.

CHAPTER 20. FINAL BONES

1. Police claimed that bruises found on Manson's thighs were evidence he'd been thrown from the truck as it turned into Cross Canyon. Mason's bruises were on the inside of his thighs, not a body part that gets banged when thrown to the ground from the back of a truck.

2. This statement is qualified. The author had access to and reviewed hundreds of police reports from this period from the files of the Colo-

rado Bureau of Investigation and the FBI. The CBI files particularly are a cumulative record including reports from multiple police agencies. Within those files viewed, there was no report of a gunshot. It cannot be claimed that the review was exhaustive or that some records from that period hadn't already been destroyed or were otherwise unavailable.

3. Used for oil-field work, water tankers were relatively easy to steal unobserved. Driving them from isolated parking areas after workers had left for the day was a common crime of opportunity in the Southwest. Deputy Bradford was investigating the theft of a tanker by an escaped convict when he was called to check out a reported shooting at Swinging Bridge and ended up being shot himself. The two attempts to steal tankers referenced here, however, would not have been motivated by McVean's need for easy transportation but rather because he specifically wanted a tank truck.

4. According to police interviews of his acquaintances, Mason found that line of dialogue from *Star Trek II: The Wrath of Khan* particularly moving and personal. He quoted it often.

EPILOGUE: LOBO 11

1. Gilman, who specializes in trauma treatment for first responders, was a practitioner of Eye Movement Desensitization and Reprocessing (EMDR). Relatively new at the time, the therapy technique was not a mainstream approach for treating post-traumatic stress disorder but has since become more widely accepted.